Covenants Affecting Land

A Practical Guide

Andrew Olins

Acknowledgment

Crown copyright material is reproduced with the permission of the Controller of HMSO and the Queen's Printer for Scotland.

Published by the Royal Institution of Chartered Surveyors (RICS)

Surveyor Court

Westwood Business Park

Coventry CV4 8JE, UK

www.ricsbooks.com

No responsibility for loss or damage caused to any person acting or refraining from action as a result of the material included in this publication can be accepted by the author or RICS.

ISBN 978 1 84219 409 6

Typeset in Great Britain by Columns Design Ltd, Reading, Berks

Printed in Great Britain by Page Bros, Milecross Lane, Norwich

Printed on Greencoat Paper – Greencoat is produced using 80% recycled fibre and 20% virgin TCF pulp from sustainable forests.

Contents

About the author

Andrew Olins (andrew.olins@ibblaw) is a solicitor in private practice and a partner in IBB, West London's leading commercial law firm. Andrew specialises in real estate litigation and resolves disputes in relation to the buying and selling of development sites where overage provisions, covenants and easements are in issue. He has published various articles in legal journals and is a Professor Associate of Land Law at Brunel University where he tutors part-time. Andrew is an ADR Group approved mediator and is also a member of the Property Litigation Association and the RICS Dilapidations Forum.

Acknowledgments

Andrew would like to thank his colleagues at IBB, and especially Jon Mowbray and Ralph Bankes, for their support and encouragement in producing this book.

To Nonic and Chop Chop: put away your Harry Potter novels, here's a real roller coaster of a read!

List of Acts, Statutory Instruments and abbreviations

The following Acts and Statutory Instruments are referred to in this publication. Where an Act or Statutory Instrument is mentioned frequently, it is referred to by the abbreviation in brackets that follows.

Details on how to access the legislation online are provided in appendix D on pp. 224–225.

Chancery Amendment Act 1858
Commonhold and Leasehold Reform Act 2002
Compulsory Purchase Act 1965
Contracts (Rights of Third Parties) Act 1999
Conveyancing Act 1881
Conveyancing and Law of Property Act 1881
Housing Act 1971
Housing Act 1985
Housing, Town Planning, etc. Act 1919
Land Charges Act 1925
Land Charges Act 1972
Land Drainage Act 1930
Land Registration Act 1925
Lands Tribunal Act 1949
Law of Property Act 1925
Law of Property (Miscellaneous Provisions) Act 1994
Leasehold Reform Act 1967
Local Government (Miscellaneous Provisions) Act 1982
Local Land Charges Act 1975
London Building Act 1894

National Health Service and Community Care Act 1990
Negative Covenants (Discharge and Modification) Act 1960
Rentcharges Act 1977
Supreme Court Act 1981
Town and Country Planning Act 1971
Town and Country Planning Act 1990

Civil Procedure Rules (CPR) Part 35
Civil Procedure Rules Practice Direction 35
Civil Procedure Rules Pre-Action Protocol
Lands Tribunal Rules (LTR)

Table of cases

Case summaries for some of the cases are provided in appendix B on pp. 98–199.

Superscript numbers below indicate the cross-references in the text to reference details on pp. 242–246.

1

Introduction

Prior to the Second World War, central and local government tended to take little, if any, interest in the non-strategic development and use of land. It was left, therefore, to private landowners to endeavour to regulate the use of land within their locality. As the courts had historically enforced contracts made between parties, the use of the covenant – itself a form of contract – became the chosen mechanism by which landowners sought to regulate the development and use of land.

Landowners have made use of covenants to regulate the development and use of land since the 18th century. Despite the growth of public planning law in recent years, covenants still play a very important role in the development and use of land. Indeed, it is frequently the case that private law covenants are better able than public law planning controls to regulate the development and use of land. For example, covenants can be particularly effective in regulating the density, pattern, and design of any future development whether residential, commercial or industrial.

Further, the use of private law covenants is increasingly seen by local residents and conservationists as the only true protector of environmental amenity. The policy of central government to significantly increase the nation's housing stock to meet current social needs, and the pressure that this, in turn, places on local government to 'free up' land for development, is making it more and more difficult for local planning authorities, through the planning process, to adequately safeguard environmental amenity. At one time, the power of the Lands Tribunal to discharge or modify negative (or restrictive) covenants was viewed predominantly as a necessary weapon against small-minded landowners who, quite unreasonably, sought to put their own private interests ahead of the wider

1

community. Nowadays, however, against the background of planning permission (arguably) becoming easier to obtain, the Lands Tribunal is seen as the forum where proposals for development can be properly scrutinised and their impact on local neighbourhoods fully assessed. There are countless instances where planning permission has been granted to the fury of local residents, only for the Lands Tribunal to come to their rescue by dismissing an application to discharge or modify negative covenants because the proposed development, if implemented, would cause the local residents to suffer an unacceptable loss of amenity (see, for example, *Re Snaith and Dolding's Application* in appendix B).

Of course, developers view the situation very differently. They tend to look at matters from an economic perspective and argue that the development of land is hugely important to the well-being of the nation. In their opinion, the exploitation of land should not be criticised but rather encouraged as it increases prosperity. Indeed, it is undoubtedly true that central government is reliant on developers to help relieve poverty and the nation's other social ills through, inter alia, the building of affordable housing for the low paid and the construction of industrial sites that give rise to employment opportunities.

Developers also argue that, all too often, they face a stark truth. They may find a site with development potential and spend significant management time and professional fees seeking planning permission; yet, if covenants exist that adjoining or neighbouring landowners are threatening to enforce, their planning permission may be worthless.

When faced with a site that is burdened by covenants, developers will invariably have to consider the following two questions:

- Are the covenants enforceable?
- If so, is there a way of getting rid of them?

This book is intended primarily to enable the surveyors acting for developers to answer these two questions. Surveyors acting for local residents who wish to oppose an application to the Lands Tribunal to discharge or modify negative covenants that burden a developer's site will also find this book valuable. It is designed to be a readable and user-friendly practical guide and, as such, lawyers whose caseload periodically brings them into contact with covenants may also find this book a worthwhile alternative to an academic tome.

2

What is a covenant?

A covenant is an important device for exerting external control over the use and development of land. It can best be described as a promise (usually) contained in a deed whereby one party (the 'covenantor') promises another party (the 'covenantee') that it will or will not carry out a particular activity on its land for the benefit and protection of adjoining or neighbouring land owned by the covenantee.

Lawyers call the covenantor's land 'servient land' and the covenantee's adjoining or neighbouring land 'dominant land'. The terms servient land and dominant land will be used, where appropriate, throughout this book.

No formal wording is necessary to make a covenant. If it is apparent from the wording of the covenant that the covenantor and covenantee intended to make an agreement obliging the covenantor to do or to refrain from doing a particular activity on its servient land, a binding covenant will have been created.

It is important, however, that the wording of a covenant should be precise. If the wording of a covenant is too vague, it can be void for uncertainty[1]. Accordingly, a covenant that imposed an obligation on the covenantor not to erect a 'building of an unseemly description' has been held to be void for uncertainty. So, too, was a covenant that the National Trust sought to impose that stated that 'no act or thing shall be done or placed or permitted to remain on the land which shall injure prejudice effect or destroy the natural aspect and condition of the land'[2].

3

What types of covenant are there?

3.1 Private law covenants

There are two types of private law covenants:

- positive covenants; and
- negative (or restrictive) covenants.

As we shall see later, it is important to be able to differentiate between positive and negative covenants. Generally speaking, if it is necessary to incur expenditure to comply with a covenant, the covenant will be a positive covenant. Accordingly, a covenant that obliges the covenantor 'to put its hand into its pocket' will almost certainly be a positive covenant[3].

Examples of positive covenants include a promise by a covenantor:
- to build a house;
- to fence off a plot of land;
- to contribute towards the cost of making or maintaining in repair a road or sewer;
- to keep the flood banks of a river in repair[4]; or
- to restore a quarry to agriculture use[5].

In contrast, a negative covenant tends to prohibit a covenantor carrying out a particular activity on its land for the benefit and protection of adjoining or neighbouring land owned by the covenantee.

Examples of negative covenants include a promise by a covenantor:
- not to build on its land[6];
- not to use any buildings on its land for any purpose other than private dwellings[7];
- not to carry on any trade or business from its land[8]; and
- not to carry on any activity on its land that constitutes a nuisance, or is offensive or dangerous[9].

It is sometimes necessary to look to the substance of a covenant rather than its actual wording to ascertain whether it is a positive or negative covenant[10]. The actual wording can, on occasion, give a false impression. For example, a covenant to use land for agriculture only, while seemingly positive in its wording, is in substance a covenant not to use the land for any other purpose and thus a negative covenant[11]. Likewise, a covenant not to let a building fall into disrepair is, despite its negative wording, in truth a positive covenant because it can only be complied with by the covenantor incurring expense in carrying out repairs.

3.2 Statutory covenants and obligations

Parliament has given various statutory bodies power to make agreements with landowners imposing covenants and other obligations and to enforce such covenants and obligations as if they were private law covenants. Importantly, this power is not dependent on the statutory body owning any adjoining or neighbouring dominant land. So, for example, a local planning authority has power under section 106 of the *Town and Country Planning Act* 1990 to make the grant of planning permission conditional on the landowner entering into an agreement containing enforceable planning obligations. This type of agreement is commonly known as a 'section 106 agreement'. Where the landowner is a developer, a local planning authority will often seek to impose planning obligations that oblige the developer to:

- pay for improvements to nearby (off-site) road junctions to accommodate the flow of traffic that will be generated by the proposed development;
- pay for new sewers which will be needed to service the proposed development;
- demolish any existing buildings on the site after the replacement buildings authorised by the planning permission have been constructed;

- 'tie' the occupation or use of proposed buildings to an existing commercial or agricultural business operated at the site; or
- transfer to the local planning authority land for use as 'open space'.

Other statutory bodies that have the power to impose covenants include local housing authorities, the Forestry Commissioners, the Nature Conservancy Council and the Countryside Commission.

3.3 Particular covenants

3.3.1 Covenants against buildings, etc.

A covenant may prohibit any building on the covenantor's servient land. Although there is no precise definition of what a 'building' is, two features can be drawn from the decided cases:

- a building (properly so-called) will tend to be solid and enclose air space[12]; and
- it can include extensions or alterations to an existing structure[13].

3.3.2 Covenants not to build without submitting plans

A covenant to submit plans and drawings of any proposed building before starting construction works is treated as a negative covenant not to start works until the plans and drawings have been approved by the covenantee. If the covenantor fails to comply with the covenant but the covenantee would have approved the plans and drawings if the covenantor had submitted the plans and drawings before starting construction works, it is likely that the covenantee will only be entitled to recover nominal damages for the breach of covenant. However, the position may be far more serious for the covenantor if the covenantee would have objected to the proposed design or position of the building. In these circumstances, the covenantor risks the imposition of a 'mandatory' injunction forcing it to pull down the building.

There is no general principle that where the covenantor is obliged to submit plans and drawings before starting construction works, there is a corresponding (implied) obligation on the covenantee not to unreasonably withhold its approval. However, such a corresponding obligation will be implied if the context in which the covenant was imposed demands it. For example, if the covenantee knew at the time the covenant was imposed that the covenantor was intending to develop the servient land, it is probable that a corresponding obligation will be implied to give business efficacy to the covenant[14].

If the covenantee refuses to approve plans and drawings submitted by the covenantor, and a dispute follows, the onus will usually be on the covenantor to show that the covenantee has unreasonably withheld its consent. Further, the covenantee is not under any obligation to give reasons for refusing to approve the covenantor's plans and drawings. However, if it refuses to give reasons, this may give rise to an inference that it had no good reason to withhold its approval[15]. To prevent such an adverse inference arising, when notifying the covenantor of its decision not to approve the plans and drawings, the covenantee should always give reasons for its decision.

There are, in effect, only two 'good' reasons for refusing to approve a covenantor's plans and drawings; namely:

- that the proposed building will be detrimental or injurious to the covenantee's use and enjoyment of its adjoining or neighbouring dominant land; or
- that the proposed building will adversely affect the value of the dominant land[16].

Any other reason for refusing to approve plans and drawings is likely to be found to be unreasonable because it lacks a 'proprietary' connection with the covenant.

Where it is customary to do so, the covenantee is entitled to ask the covenantor to meet its costs (including the costs of its surveyors and lawyers) in considering the plans and drawings that have been submitted[17].

3.3.3 Covenants affecting houses and dwellings

A covenant may restrict the number, size, type, position and use of houses or dwellings to be built on the covenantor's servient land. A 'house' connotes a building that is intended for human habitation. A 'dwelling', in contrast. may be a house or part of a house.

A covenant that obliges the covenantor only to build dwellings will be breached if the covenantor puts up buildings that are not generally perceived as intended for habitation, such as a school or place of worship. A covenant only to build dwellings may also be effective in preventing a subsequent conversion of a dwelling for a non-habitable purpose, e.g. where a covenantor proposes converting a dwelling into a public house[18].

A covenant which states that a house or dwelling must be used as a 'private' residence emphasises the domestic nature of the user and, as such, is particularly restrictive. For example, it prohibits the use of a house or dwelling as a hotel, guesthouse, boarding school or an NHS 'care in the community' home[19]. Such a covenant would not, however, ordinarily prohibit the use of part of the house or dwelling as an office or medical consulting room.

A covenant that prohibits the use of a house or dwelling except as a 'single' residence will obviously be breached if it is converted into flats. It will also be breached if individual rooms are let out because the house or dwelling would then fall into multi-occupation.

3.3.4 Covenants against trade or business

Covenants prohibiting the carrying on of any trade or business are quite prevalent in residential areas. Frequently, an exception is made for a practice carried on by a doctor, lawyer, accountant or other professional.

Occasionally, a covenant will prohibit only trades or businesses that are offensive, noxious, dangerous or the like. When judging whether any particular trade or business is likely to fall foul of the covenant, it is necessary to consider carefully the dominant land that the covenant is intended to benefit. Although a particular trade or business may not be inherently offensive, it may be considered offensive if carried on at an inappropriate location.

Example:
A fish and chip shop could in no sense be described as inherently offensive but, nevertheless, it could be viewed as an offensive trade or business if located next to residential houses[20].

Again, a covenant may prohibit only a particular trade or business. Generally, when such a covenant is imposed, it is intended to stop the covenantor carrying out a trade or business in competition with a similar one carried on by the covenantee. It is always a question of fact and degree whether the covenantor's trade or business is so similar to the covenantee's trade or business so as to fall within the ambit of the covenant.

> **Examples:**
> A covenant prohibiting the use of the servient land as a 'motor garage' is not breached by the covenantor carrying on the business of a 'motor showroom'[21].
> Conversely, a covenant prohibiting the use of the servient land as a 'public garage' is breached by the covenantor operating a filling station[22].

Moreover, it is not generally possible for a covenantor to seek to excuse itself by arguing that the prohibited trade or business is only ancillary to another trade or business.

> **Example:**
> A newsagent that sells wine, spirits or beer, would breach a covenant that prohibited the business of an off-licence.

3.3.5 Covenants against nuisance and annoyance

Where a covenantee is conscious to ensure that the use and enjoyment of its own adjoining or neighbouring dominant land is not adversely affected by any activity carried on by the covenantor, it will doubtless seek to impose a covenant prohibiting the covenantor carrying out any activity on the servient land that will cause a nuisance, annoyance or injury.

'Nuisance' , 'annoyance' and 'injury' are construed quite widely. As a rule of thumb, any activity that, when viewed objectively, is likely to trouble a covenantee who possesses a reasonably robust disposition, will probably constitute a nuisance or annoyance. It is not necessary that the activity causes physical discomfort; it is sufficient if the activity plays on the covenantee's mind[23].

If carried out in a residential area, those activities that have regularly offended against a negative covenant not to cause a nuisance or annoyance include:

- operating a hospital or school;
- operating a 'take-away', e.g. a fish and chip shop; and
- erecting advertising hoardings.

3.3.6 Covenants not to permit or suffer

Where a covenant simply prohibits a particular activity, a covenantor will only commit a breach of covenant if it or its agents carry out that prohibited activity. A breach of covenant will not be committed if, for example, the prohibited activity is carried out on the servient land by a third party such as an independent contractor. However, to close this 'loophole', it has become practice nowadays to impose a separate covenant on the covenantor not to 'permit or suffer' any person who enters or occupies the servient land to carry out the prohibited activity. Such a covenant can be quite onerous and financially burdensome in practice. If the covenantor does not take all reasonable steps to stop the prohibited activity when it is in its power to do so, the covenantor may find itself in breach of covenant[24]. The 'reasonable' steps that a covenantor can be expected to take include pursuing court proceedings against the third party, particularly if the covenantor has a contractual relationship with that third party. A covenantor would have a contractual relationship with the third party if, for example, the third party was an independent contractor that the covenantor had engaged or a tenant or licensee whom the covenantor had let into occupation[25].

4

Who can claim the benefit of a covenant?

Historically, the common law has restricted the ability of a non-party to a deed, such as a successor in title of the covenantee's dominant land, to enforce covenants imposed by the deed. During the 19th and 20th centuries however, both equity and Parliament intervened to ameliorate the difficulties that this common law restriction caused the covenantee's successors in title. Accordingly, the benefit of a covenant can now be claimed through:

- common law;
- statute; and
- (in the case of negative covenants) equity.

4.1 At common law

A covenant created by deed takes effect as an enforceable contract and, as parties to the contract, the covenantor and covenantee are always bound by it under the common law 'privity of contract' rule. Indeed, it remains the case that a covenantee may bring a claim for breach of covenant even if the breach occurs after it has transferred its dominant land. In that instance, of course, the covenantee is unlikely to suffer any real loss and, therefore, will be entitled to recover only nominal damages[26]; the real loss, if there is one, will be suffered by the covenantee's successor in title.

4.1.1 The four-part test

The common law has a four-part test to determine whether the benefit of a positive or negative covenant may pass 'at law' to the covenantee's successors in title[27]:

- The deed creating the covenant must describe the dominant land and servient land so as to make each ascertainable with reasonable accuracy, if necessary, with the assistance of extrinsic evidence.
- There must be an intention at the time the covenant was created that the burden of the covenant should 'run with the [servient] land'[28]. This means that the covenantor and covenantee must have intended at the time the covenant was imposed that the burden of the covenant would attach permanently to the servient land, and be enforceable by all future owners of the dominant land. If necessary, an intention that a covenant should run with the land can be inferred from its purpose. For example, a covenant whose purpose is to improve the drainage of dominant land that is susceptible to flooding, and to prevent future flooding is, self-evidently, intended to benefit the covenantee's successors in title.
- The covenantee must own a legal (as opposed to equitable) estate in the dominant land. The person named in the title deeds (in the case of unregistered land) as owner, or the person named at the Land Registry (in the case of registered land) as registered proprietor will be the owner of the legal estate. Furthermore, the covenantee's successors in title must also own a legal estate in the dominant land to be able to enforce the covenant, although it need not be the same legal estate. So, for example, where the covenantee owns a freehold estate, and later grants a lease of the dominant land, the tenant who has a leasehold estate will be entitled to enforce the covenant burdening the (freehold) servient land[29].
- The covenant must 'touch and concern' the dominant land. In other words, the covenant must have been created for the (permanent) benefit and protection of the covenantee's neighbouring or adjoining land and not merely for the covenantee's own personal benefit. Accordingly, if a covenant is not intended to benefit the covenantee's successors in title, it cannot touch and concern the dominant land. A covenant will tend to touch and concern the dominant land if its breach adversely affects the value of the land.

As will be discussed in section 6.1, where the four-part test is met, the benefit of the covenant attaches to each and every part of the dominant land. Accordingly, if the dominant land is later fragmented, the future owners of each part are entitled to claim the benefit of the covenant[30].

4.2 Through statute

The common law rules for passing the benefit of a covenant are supplemented by several statutory provisions that are designed to ensure that persons, other than the covenantee, become entitled to enforce a covenant. These persons will usually be the covenantee's successors in title. Each one of the statutory provisions is discussed, in turn, below.

4.2.1 Section 136 of the Law of Property Act 1925

As a general rule, the benefit of a covenant can be assigned in writing by the covenantee to another person. To take legal effect:

- the assignment should be stated to be made pursuant to section 136 of the *Law of Property Act* 1925; and
- notice of the assignment should be given to the covenantor.

There is one exception to the general rule: a covenant that is created for the exclusive personal benefit of the covenantee cannot be assigned.

4.2.2 Section 56 of the Law of Property Act 1925

The common law 'privity of contract' rule that no person can pursue a claim founded on a deed unless it is a party to the making of the deed was modified by section 56(1) of the *Law of Property Act* 1925. Since the Act came into force on 1 January 1926, a person may seek to enforce a covenant if the deed creating the covenant states that it is to have the benefit of the covenant. Often, the benefit of a covenant is conferred on a person who is not a party to the deed by the use of a 'generic description'.

> **Example:**
> If a covenant is stated to be created not only for the benefit of the covenantee but, also, for 'the owners for the time being of the adjoining and neighbouring land known as the Blackacre estate', future owners of the Blackacre estate will be entitled, like the covenantee, to enforce the covenant[31].

However, it is important to appreciate that even if a person falls within the generic description, that person will only be able to make use of section 56(1) to claim the benefit of the covenant if, at that time the covenant was created, one or more persons falling within the generic description were in existence and identifiable. Accordingly, section 56(1) does not permit the benefit of a covenant to be conferred directly upon future plot purchasers although they may be able to obtain the benefit of the covenant as assignees of the seller[32].

4.2.3 Section 78(1) of the Law of Property Act 1925

Section 78(1) of the *Law of Property Act* 1925 provides that a covenant relating to land belonging to the covenantee is presumed to be 'made with the covenantee and his successors in title and the persons deriving title under him or them'. The words 'successors in title' include the owners and occupiers for the time being of the covenantee's dominant land. For the purposes of section 78(1), a covenant relates to land if it 'touches and concerns' the covenantee's dominant land and the covenant was created on or after 1 January 1926[33]. A covenant will tend to touch and concern the dominant land if its breach adversely affects the value of the land.

4.2.4 Contracts (Rights of Third Parties) Act 1999

The *Contracts (Rights of Third Parties) Act* 1999 came into force on 11 March 2000. The Act has the effect of enabling a person who is not a party to a deed that creates a covenant to enforce the covenant 'in its own right' if:

- the deed expressly states that it may do so; or
- the covenant is purportedly made for its benefit.

Such a person must be expressly identified in the deed by name or fall within a generic description. Unlike section 56(1) of the *Law of Property Act* 1925, for the purposes of the *Contracts*

(Rights of Third Parties) Act, persons falling within the generic description do not need to be in existence at the date the deed was executed[34].

However, the Act does not apply to a deed if it is apparent from the wording of the deed that the covenantor and covenantee did not intend that a non-party should be able to enforce the covenant[35]. Again, the Act only applies to deeds made after the Act came into force.

Interestingly, the *Contracts (Rights of Third Parties) Act* 1999 seemingly permits the benefit of a covenant to pass to a non-party even if the covenant does not relate to or 'touch and concern' the dominant land. Furthermore, it appears that the Act allows a non-party to seek to enforce a covenant even if it does not own or have any interest in the dominant land. A non-party who neither owns nor has an interest in the adjoining or neighbouring dominant land is unlikely however to suffer any real loss from a breach of covenant. Accordingly, it must be doubtful as to whether such a non-party would be entitled to recover anything other than nominal damages.

4.2.5 Commonhold and Leasehold Reform Act 2002

The *Commonhold and Leasehold Reform Act* 2002 created a new form of freehold land called 'commonhold land'. All owners of commonhold units that comprise the commonhold land are bound by a 'commonhold community statement'. The obligations contained in the commonhold community statement automatically pass to a new owner of a commonhold unit on taking a transfer of the unit. Invariably, the commonhold community statement will include obligations to observe positive and negative covenants. Accordingly, where commonhold land applies, it has the effect of making positive covenants enforceable against successors in title of this form of freehold land.

4.2.6 Section 7 of the Law of Property (Miscellaneous Provisions) Act 1994

Where dominant land is transferred, covenants benefiting the dominant land are 'impliedly' transferred too.

Prior to 1 July 1995 (the date the 1994 Act came into force), this implied transfer occurred pursuant to section 76 of the *Law of*

Property Act 1925. After 1 July 1995, the implied transfer occurs pursuant to section 7 of the 1994 Act.

4.3 In equity (in the case of negative covenants only)

If the benefit of a negative covenant is to pass in equity to a successor in title of the covenantee, it must be shown that the benefit of the covenant:

- has been 'annexed' to the covenantee's land;
- has been 'assigned' by the covenantee to its successor in title; or
- forms part of a building scheme or scheme of development.

Each of these alternatives is discussed at length in chapter 6.

5

Who is burdened by a positive covenant?

As a covenant created by deed takes effect as an enforceable contract, the covenantor, as a party to the contract, is always bound by the covenant (whether positive or negative) under the common law 'privity of contract' rule.

There is, however, no simple method for passing the burden of a positive covenant to a successor of the covenantor's servient land. The reason for this is that, historically, whilst the common law has permitted the benefit of a covenant to run with the dominant land[36], it has not permitted the burden of a covenant to run with the servient land.

5.1 The six devices

To circumvent the common law, a number of devices are used as an indirect means of passing the burden of positive covenants to successors in title of the servient land. The six devices that are most effective are considered below.

5.1.1 *Compulsory deed on transfer*

The first device is the 'compulsory deed on transfer'. This device imposes an obligation on the covenantor, as owner of the servient land, not to transfer or otherwise dispose of the servient land unless its transferee enters into a new deed direct with the (then) owner of the dominant land. The new deed repeats the positive covenants and obliges the transferee, in turn, not to transfer the servient land unless its transferee executes a similar deed direct with the owner of the dominant land. This device ensures that the owner of the dominant land has the benefit of a binding contract with the owner from time to time of the servient land which it can enforce under the common law privity of contract rule if the positive covenants are breached.

5.1.2 Use of leasehold land

The second device is the use of leasehold land. It has long been the case that the burden of positive and negative covenants runs with leasehold land. Accordingly, on taking a transfer of a lease, the new tenant becomes bound by the positive covenants contained in the lease. The freehold owner, as landlord, can enforce the positive and negative covenants, against the new tenant because, as between them, there is said to exist 'privity of estate'. In practice, a lease granted for, say, 150 years or more can make leasehold land virtually identical to freehold land. Accordingly it is often just as marketable, particularly when it is appreciated that the enforcement of positive covenants presents no difficulty.

5.1.3 Enlargement

The third device is the enlargement of leasehold land into freehold land. There are statutory provisions, such as section 153 of the *Law of Property Act* 1925 and section 8(3) of the *Leasehold Reform Act* 1967, that permit long leases to be converted or 'enlarged' into freehold land. On conversion, the positive and negative covenants contained in the long lease attach to the freehold land.

5.1.4 Commonhold scheme

The fourth device is the use of commonhold land (a form of freehold land) introduced by the *Commonhold and Leasehold Reform Act* 2002. A registered commonhold scheme and its participating unit holders are governed by a 'commonhold community statement'. When a unit holder transfers or otherwise disposes of its unit, any obligations set out in the commonhold community statement that affect the unit holder will automatically pass to the transferee. The unit holder who is transferring its unit remains liable for any breaches of the commonhold community statement committed prior to the transfer, but it has no responsibility for any breaches committed thereafter.

The use of commonhold land offers an attractive framework for a development that envisages multi-occupation: it enables unit holders to enforce covenants (whether positive or negative) against each other without difficulty. Developers have, however, since the passing of the *Commonhold and Leasehold Reform Act* 2002, been slow to make use of registered commonhold schemes. Indeed, up to December 2007, only 14 such schemes have been registered at the Land Registry.

5.1.5 Estate rentcharge

The fifth device is the use of an 'estate rentcharge' (see glossary) with a right of entry attached. The right of entry is usually framed so that it becomes exercisable when the covenantor breaches its covenants (whether positive or negative)[37]. Section 2(4) of the *Rentcharges Act* 1977 states explicitly that an estate rentcharge may be used to ensure that the covenantor contributes towards the cost of providing services or carrying out maintenance and repairs. As the right of entry is a legal interest in land, it can therefore run with the covenantor's servient land and, thus, bind its successors in title, forcing them to comply with the covenants or risk the covenantee 'forfeiting' their freehold estate.

5.1.6 Doctrine of mutual benefit and burden

Occasionally, the burden of a freehold covenant may pass to the covenantor's successors in title under the doctrine of 'mutual benefit and burden'. This doctrine states that 'he who takes the benefit [of a covenant] must bear the burden'[38].

> Example:
> Where a person purchases a new house on a recently built residential estate and, in consideration of covenanting to contribute towards the cost of maintaining the estate roads and sewers, is granted a right to use those roads and sewers, its successors in title will not be permitted to use the roads and sewers unless they too comply with the covenant and contribute towards the cost of maintenance[39].

The doctrine is intended to stop future owners of the servient land 'having their cake and eating it'; the doctrine therefore promotes common sense and fairness.

There are, however, two preconditions to the application of the doctrine of mutual benefit and burden.

- First, the burden imposed by the covenant (such as the payment of money for the maintenance of estate roads and sewers) must be relevant to the rights that benefit the covenantor's land (i.e. the use of those roads and sewers)[40]. In other words, there must be a direct link between the burden and the benefit.
- Second, the covenantor's successors in title must each have the opportunity to decide whether to take or reject the benefit, and, thus if they so desire, to avoid the burden of the covenant. In reality, where the benefit of a covenant is the use of infrastructure, successors in title are most unlikely to reject the benefit of the covenant so as to avoid its burden. Only where, for example, a plot of land can be accessed via a public highway (maintainable at public expense) and, separately, via a private road (the maintenance of which is to be met by the owners of all properties that abut the road), might a successor in title give serious consideration to relinquishing the right to use the private road so as to avoid contributing towards the cost of its maintenance.

6

Who can claim the benefit of a negative covenant?

The common law's historic refusal to permit covenants, even relatively simple ones, to be enforced against a covenantor's successors in title caused much frustration on the part of covenantees and their successors in title. Equity, however, responded to this frustration in the 19th century and intervened by exercising its jurisdiction to supplement the common law. Equity's intervention, although welcome, was rather modest. It enabled the benefit and burden of negative covenants (but not positive covenants) to be passed to successors in title if the following two preconditions were met:

- first, the covenant was, in character, one that could 'touch and concern' (see glossary) or otherwise 'benefit' adjoining or neighbouring dominant land; and
- second, one of several prescribed methods of passing the benefit of the covenant was used.

Today, if the benefit of a negative covenant is to pass in equity to a successor in title of the covenantee, it must be shown that the benefit of the covenant:

- has been 'annexed' to the covenantee's land;
- has been 'assigned' by the covenantee to its successor in title; or
- forms part of a building scheme or scheme of development.

6.1 Annexation

Annexation is the means by which the benefit of a negative covenant is attached to the dominant land belonging to the covenantee, in such a way that, when the covenantee transfers the dominant land, its successor in title also obtains the benefit of the covenant. It is important to understand that annexation is dependent on the covenantor and covenantee evincing an intention at the time the negative covenant was imposed that the benefit of the covenant should run with the dominant land and be enforceable, not just by the covenantee, but by its successors in title too. Usually, this intention of annexation is expressed in the deed creating the negative covenant.

Once a negative covenant becomes attached to the covenantee's dominant land, the benefit of the covenant passes automatically to the covenantee's successors in title. There is no need for any specific assignment in favour of the successors in title; nor do the successors need to have actual knowledge of the negative covenant prior to taking a transfer of the dominant land to claim the benefit of the covenant[41].

Annexation to the covenantee's dominant land can take place:

- expressly;
- impliedly; or
- by statute.

Each of these three alternatives is discussed in turn below.

6.1.1 Express Annexation

Express annexation is the preferred method of annexation. Express annexation occurs where the deed creating a negative covenant states explicitly that both the covenantor and covenantee intend the benefit of the covenant to run with the covenantee's dominant land.

It is always a matter of construction as to whether the benefit of any negative covenant is intended to be annexed to and, thus, run with the covenantee's dominant land. As annexation is the attaching of the benefit of a covenant upon land, not upon persons, it is, therefore, essential that the deed creating the negative covenant should refer to the covenantee's dominant land. Lawyers have developed 'magic' wording to express an intention of annexation in a deed. Phrases expressing that the negative covenant has been imposed, such as:

- 'for the benefit of the seller's retained land';
- 'for the benefit of X in its capacity as owner of Y property'[42]; or
- so 'that the covenant may enure for the benefit of the vendors, their successors and assigns and others claiming under them to all or any of their lands adjoining'[43];

have all been held to be effective to manifest the intention to annex and, thus, attach a negative covenant to the covenantee's dominant land. Ultimately, whatever wording is used in a deed, it must make plain that the negative covenant is not for the personal benefit of the covenantee, but, rather, for the benefit of its future successors in title too. A deed imposing a negative covenant that merely states that it is made with the vendors, 'their heirs, executors, administrators, and assigns'[44] fails to manifest the necessary intention to annex because it lacks any reference to the dominant land[45].

If the deed creating a negative covenant contains wording that establishes that the covenantor and covenantee intended the covenant to be annexed to the covenantee's dominant land, then, prima facie, the covenant will be attached to every part of the dominant land[46]. This means that if the dominant land fragments, each owner of part will be entitled to seek to enforce the negative covenant.

6.1.2 Implied annexation

If there are no 'magic words' in a deed expressly annexing a negative covenant to the covenantee's dominant land, annexation may, nevertheless, be implied if it is obvious that the covenantor and covenantee intended this[47]. To determine whether the covenantor and covenantee had such an intention, it is necessary to consider the circumstances surrounding the deed, its terms and any implications that can be drawn from those terms[48]. Ordinarily, if an intention to annex is to be found, the deed must:

- refer to the dominant land belonging to the covenantee; and
- indicate that the covenantor and covenantee intended for the benefit of the negative covenant to be attached to the covenantee's dominant land rather than to the covenantee personally[49].

Example:
A covenantee owns two adjoining retail shops in a high street. From one shop it operates the business of a dry cleaners called 'Lilywhites' and from the other shop it operates the business of a fishmongers. Assume that the covenantee sells the shop operating as a fishmongers subject to a non-competition covenant on the part of the purchaser (as covenantor) not to carry on the business of a dry cleaners. If there are no 'magic words' in the deed expressly annexing the negative covenant to the covenantee's dominant land (i.e. Lilywhites) but the covenantee's address in the transfer is given as Lilywhites, it may be possible to argue that the surrounding circumstances demand that annexation be implied. Therefore, should the covenantee sell the shop operating as Lilywhites, a successor in title to the dominant land might well be able to enforce the non-competition covenant.

6.1.3 Statutory annexation

Section 78(1) of the *Law of Property Act* 1925 has the effect of annexing a negative covenant to the covenantee's land if:

- the covenant was created on or after the Act came into force, i.e. 1 January 1926;
- the covenantee owned the dominant land at the time the covenant was created;
- the covenant 'touches and concerns' the dominant land, i.e. it genuinely relates to the land;
- the dominant land is relatively easy to identify from the wording of the deed creating the covenant (or any necessary implication from that wording)[50]; and
- there is no contrary intention expressed in the deed[51].

The meaning of the expression 'touches and concerns the dominant land' needs to be explained. A covenant touches and concerns the dominant land if its breach adversely affects the nature, quality, mode of use or value of the dominant land[52]. Generally speaking, if, on selling part of its land, the covenantee saw fit to impose a covenant for the purpose of benefiting or protecting its retained land, there will be a (rebuttable) presumption that the covenant touches and concerns that retained land[53]. If there is a dispute as to whether a covenant touches and concerns the dominant land because (for instance) the issue turns on a matter of opinion as to whether the covenant, if breached, will have an adverse affect on the dominant land, the issue can be resolved, if necessary, by the court after hearing expert evidence. Such expert evidence will, in all likelihood, be given by the parties' planning consultants and valuers.

If the deed creating the covenant identifies the dominant land by use of an expression such as 'the Blackacre Estate', extrinsic evidence is admissible to ascertain the boundaries of the dominant land. Often, such extrinsic evidence includes historic maps of the locality.

For section 78(1) to be engaged, the deed creating a covenant does not need to state expressly that the covenantor and covenantee intend that the covenant should be annexed to the dominant land. Rather, it seems that an intention to annex will be readily inferred in the absence of any contrary wording in the deed[54].

If a covenant is annexed to dominant land pursuant to section 78(1), prima facie it is annexed to each and every part thereof unless the deed creating the covenant states otherwise. Accordingly, if, after the covenant is created, the dominant land is fragmented, each owner of part will be entitled to seek to enforce the covenant. Of course, if any particular owner of part of the dominant land does not derive a practical benefit from the covenant, (for example, its part may be some distance away from the servient land), it is unlikely that a court will grant an injunction or make an award of damages if that owner of part seeks to enforce the covenant.

Pre-1926 negative covenants

As the *Law of Property Act* 1925 came into force on 1 January 1926, section 78(1) of the Act does not apply to negative covenants made before 1926. Pre-1926 negative covenants are governed by section 58 of the *Conveyancing Act* 1881. Under the 1881 Act, statutory annexation is more restrictive. As discussed in section 6.1.1 and 6.1.2, it only occurs if an intention to benefit identifiable land belonging to the covenantee can be found in (or implied from) the express wording of the deed creating the covenant[55].

6.2 Assignment

An express assignment can be an effective method to pass the benefit of a negative covenant. Accordingly, a successor in title to the dominant land may be able to enforce a negative covenant even if the covenant is not annexed to the dominant land, by establishing that it has taken an assignment of the benefit of the covenant.

There are important differences between annexation and assignment. First, annexation involves attaching the benefit of the negative covenant to the dominant land, whereas assignment involves conferring the benefit of the covenant upon a person (usually the covenantee's successor in title). Second, annexation takes place at the time the negative covenant is created, whereas assignment takes place as and when the covenantee transfers the dominant land.

6.2.1 Pre-conditions of assignment

An assignment of a negative covenant is usually included in the document of transfer executed by the covenantee (or, alternatively, executed by a successor in title who, itself, has previously taken an assignment of the covenant). To be effective, an assignment must meet the following four conditions:

- First, the assignment must state that the benefit of the negative covenant is to pass to the successor in title.
- Second, the dominant land that has the benefit of the negative covenant must be identifiable from the face of the deed creating the covenant with reasonable certainty (if necessary, by the use of extrinsic evidence)[56]. If the deed creating the covenant identifies the dominant land by use of an expression such as 'the Du Cane family estates at Streatham'[57] or 'the Wrotham Park Estate in its broad and popular sense'[58], extrinsic evidence is admissible to ascertain the boundaries of the dominant land. Often, such extrinsic evidence includes historic maps of the locality.
- Third, the successor in title must be able to establish that the negative covenant was created with the intention of protecting the covenantee's dominant land. Occasionally, this intention can be inferred from the terms of the covenant itself. An example of such a covenant is one that prohibits the covenantor from carrying on a business in direct competition with a similar business carried on by the covenantee on its neighbouring land[59].
- Fourth, the successor in title must show that it took an assignment of the benefit of the negative covenant at the same time as taking the transfer of the dominant land[60]. If the benefit of the covenant and the dominant land become 'separated', the covenant ceases to be enforceable[61].

6.3 Scheme of development

A scheme of development (also known as a 'building scheme') is another method of passing the benefit of negative covenants. A scheme of development envisages a developer developing a site and selling it off in plots to individual purchasers. A residential development is an obvious example.

6.3.1 Problems of timing

The burden of the negative covenants given by each original purchaser of the individual plots will pass to their respective successors in title if, as invariably happens, the developer registers the covenants for the benefit of its site. However, the developer's ability to pass the benefit of the negative covenants it has obtained can be rather problematic.

The benefit that the developer derives from the negative covenants given by each purchaser attaches to the developer's 'retained' land. Naturally, the retained land will reduce in size every time an individual plot is sold off. This, in turn, means that later purchasers of individual plots can benefit from the negative covenants given by earlier purchasers but not vice versa. Self-evidently, the retained land belonging to the developer cannot include the individual plots that already have been sold off. As the developer is not able to confer the benefit of negative covenants given by later purchasers to earlier purchasers, there can be no reciprocity of enforcement between individual plot owners without the imposition of a mechanism that passes the benefit of all negative covenants (whenever given) to all individual plot purchasers and their successors in title.

6.3.2 Solution

In the case of schemes of development, equity has evolved special rules for enabling reciprocity in the enforcement of negative covenants. If such a scheme exists, equity takes the view that the negative covenants given by each individual plot purchaser are attached to the entirety of the land covered by the scheme and, subject to their registration, enforceable by all owners (for the time being) of any part of the land covered by the scheme.

Accordingly, if a scheme of development exists, it has the following practical effect:

- It makes no difference if a person wishing to enforce a negative covenant is a covenantee (i.e. an original plot purchaser) or a successor in title to such a purchaser[62].
- Equally, it makes no difference when the negative covenants were given in terms of timing; earlier purchasers have the benefit of negative covenants entered into by later purchasers[63].

In short, equity imposes reciprocity of enforcement between the owners of any part of the land comprising the scheme of development.

6.3.3 Pre-conditions for a scheme of development

There are two conditions that must be met if a scheme of development is to exist[64].

First, the scheme of development must be a scheme of development 'properly so-called'. In other words, the land comprising the scheme must be identifiable and known to each purchaser of a plot so that all such purchasers are aware from the outset of the extent of the reciprocal benefits and burdens that the scheme imposes[65]. This can be ensured by clearly identifying the land that is to have the benefit of the 'reciprocal' negative covenants in the document of transfer giving effect to each sale to a purchaser of a plot.

Second, as a scheme of development rests on the principle of 'reciprocity', each purchaser of a plot must appreciate that, not only will the developer benefit from the negative covenants that it gives, but the developer's other purchasers will also have the benefit of those covenants; likewise, it will in turn enjoy the benefit of their negative covenants. In short, it must be apparent that all the developer's purchasers bought their respective plots on a 'common understanding' that they would be mutually bound by and mutually entitled to enforce specified negative covenants.

The existence of this necessary common understanding may be found in the terms of the documents of transfer to the individual plot purchasers. For example, it is often the case that the documents of transfer give expression to the common understanding by stating, explicitly, an intention to create a scheme of development.

Where the necessary common understanding is not expressed on the face of the documents of transfer, it may still be possible to establish its existence through the use of extrinsic evidence. Extrinsic evidence could include:

- advertisements placed by the developer;
- marketing material produced by the developer;
- statements made by the developer or its lawyers to purchasers of plots;
- auction particulars[66]; and
- information passing between purchasers of plots[67].

Factors that would, however, militate against the existence of a common intention to establish a scheme of development would include:

- the developer's failure to produce or disclose an estate plan for the benefit of purchasers[68];
- the developer's failure to inform purchasers that it was intending to impose similar covenants on the purchasers of other plots;
- the imposition on purchasers of different covenants that were inconsistent with each other; and
- the imposition on purchasers of different covenants which, although consistent with each other, were nevertheless substantially more onerous on some purchasers than others[69].

6.3.4 Subscheme

Occasionally, within an area covered by a scheme of development, there may exist a subscheme[70]. A subscheme arises where the owners of two or more plots agree that their plots shall be released from the covenants imposed by the scheme of development or, alternatively, be burdened by different covenants to those imposed by the scheme of development. In this situation, the owners of plots who participate in the subscheme can only enforce amongst themselves the covenants that comprise the subscheme. The owners of plots who do not participate in the subscheme are entitled to enforce the covenants imposed by the scheme of development on those owners who do participate in the subscheme and vice versa.

6.3.5 Registration of the scheme

As a scheme of development operates in equity (as opposed to the common law), it is unenforceable against a purchaser who pays money for a plot unless it has 'notice' of the scheme. If the scheme was created after 1925 and affects unregistered land, a purchaser of a plot is only deemed to have notice of the scheme and thereby is bound by it, if the scheme is registered as a land charge before the purchaser completes its purchase. Likewise, if the scheme affects registered land, the purchaser of a plot will only be taken to have notice of the scheme if the scheme has been noted in the registered title to the plot.

6.4 Unity of dominant and servient land

After a negative covenant is created, there will be occasions when the dominant land (or part of it) and the servient land fall into common ownership. As a person cannot sue himself, the dominant land (or that part of it that has fallen into common ownership with the servient land) ceases to have the benefit of the negative covenant or, to put it the other way around, the servient land ceases to be burdened by the covenant.

If, after falling into common ownership, the dominant land and servient land are later separated, any negative covenants that previously burdened the servient land will not be revived. The common owner, on disposing of part, must impose new covenants if it wishes to secure a benefit or otherwise protect the land that it will be retaining. There is, however, one exception. Where a scheme of development exists and one or more plots are in common ownership, there is a presumption that, on separation, the negative covenants will revive so that all future owners of the plots will be bound by the scheme.

7

Who is burdened by a negative covenant?

The notion that the burden of a negative covenant may be enforced against any person other than the covenantor is a concept alien to the common law. However, as explained in chapter 6, equity started to intervene in the mid-19th century to soften the harshness of the common law by permitting negative covenants (but not positive covenants) to be enforced against a covenantor's successors in title[71]. Equity's strongest intervention came in 1848 when the case of *Tulk v Moxhay* came before the courts on appeal. The Court laid down the principle that when a negative covenant is imposed, the owner of the servient land loses certain rights to enjoy and make use of the servient land entirely as it pleases. Accordingly, successors in title of the servient land who, at the time they acquired the land, had 'notice' of the negative covenant, are bound by the covenant because they are not entitled to exercise rights that they did not acquire.

7.1 Pre-1926 covenants

The burden of a freehold negative covenant created before the *Law of Property Act* 1925 came into force on 1 January 1926 passes to a covenantor's successors in title by the equitable doctrine of notice. Under this equitable doctrine, a negative covenant made prior to 1926 binds all future owners of the covenantor's servient land except a purchaser who brought the land for value and without notice of the covenant[72].

Notice of the negative covenant can be 'actual', 'imputed' or 'constructive'. A purchaser will have 'actual' notice of a covenant if, during the pre-contract negotiations, it becomes aware of the covenant's existence. Further, as a purchaser is 'imputed' with the knowledge of its lawyers, if its lawyers become aware of the existence of the covenant whilst carrying out the usual pre-contract searches and enquiries, their knowledge will be imputed to the purchaser. Again, a purchaser will have 'constructive' notice of a negative covenant if its existence would have been discovered had it (or its lawyers) made the usual pre-contract searches and enquiries. Constructive notice is intended to prevent a purchaser taking free of a negative covenant by deliberately failing to carry out a reasonable investigation of the seller's title.

The equitable doctrine of notice is not particularly robust. For example, once the servient land comes into the ownership of a purchaser who purchased the land for value and without notice of the covenant, the 'chain' between successive owners breaks down and the negative covenant ceases to be enforceable; it cannot not be revived even if, for example, a later owner purchases the servient land with prior knowledge of the covenant.

Persons such as licensees and those who acquire ownership of the servient land through adverse possession, remain bound by a negative covenant created prior to 1926 even if they entered occupation of the land without knowledge of the covenant. This is because they are not 'purchasers' of the servient land.

Finally, it is important to appreciate that the equitable doctrine of notice continues to govern the passing of the burden of freehold negative covenants created before 1926. The equitable doctrine also applies to any post-1925 restrictive covenants contained in a lease that relates to unregistered land not demised by the lease.

7.2 Post-1925 covenants

The *Law of Property Act* 1925, the *Land Registration Act* 1925 and the *Land Charges Act* 1925 introduced a more robust 'mechanism' for passing the burden of a negative covenant to the covenantor's successors in title. The Acts, however, only apply to negative covenants created on or after 1 January 1926.

The Acts replaced the equitable doctrine of notice with 'statutory notification'. Under the Acts (and the later amending and consolidating legislation), the burden of a negative covenant passes to the covenantor's successors in title if, and only if, the covenant is 'registered'. The mode of registration depends on whether the covenantor's servient land is registered or unregistered.

7.2.1 Registered land

If the covenantor's servient land is registered at the Land Registry, a freehold negative covenant burdening the servient land created after 1925 will bind future owners of the land if the covenantee registers the covenant at the Land Registry. Registration is by the entry of a notice at the Land Registry in the Charges Register of the title to the servient land.

7.2.2 Unregistered land

If, however, the covenantor's servient land is unregistered, a restrictive covenant made after 1925 is registerable in the Register of Land Charges under the *Land Charges Acts* of 1925 and 1972. Registration is by entry in the Register of Land Charges of a D(ii) land charge against the name of the covenantor.

7.2.3 Non registration

There are many instances where a negative covenant has failed to be registered at the Land Registry or in the Register of Land Charges. More often than not, the failure to register a negative covenant is simply an oversight on the part of the covenantee's lawyers. In one case of particular note, a negative covenant had been correctly entered in the Register of Land Charges while the servient land was unregistered, but upon registration of the title, it was not registered at the Land Registry in the Charges Register to the title. This omission meant that the subsequent purchaser of the registered title to the servient land took free of the negative covenant[73].

It may be said, of course, that where there has been a failure to correctly register a negative covenant, the covenantee only has itself to blame if it loses the protection that the covenant was intended to confer. However, where the negative covenant forms part of the scheme of development, a serious problem can arise if one or more owners of plots are not bound by the scheme because of (inadvertent) non-registration. In circumstances such as this, the very cornerstone of a scheme of development – the principle of reciprocity – is undermined.

7.3 Local land charges

Particular types of covenant imposed by central or local government are registerable as land charges under the *Local Land Charges Act* 1975. If the covenant was made after 1 August 1977, any failure to register the covenant in the register of local land charges will not render the covenant unenforceable. Instead, any person who takes a transfer of the land burdened by the covenant will be entitled to claim statutory compensation if it can show that it suffered prejudice by reason of the non-registration.

8

What planning obligations can a local planning authority impose?

Since 25 October 1991, local planning authorities have had the statutory power to impose planning obligations to restrict or regulate the development of land within their area. This statutory power is conferred by section 106 of the *Town and Country Planning Act* 1990. Where a developer seeks planning permission to carry out a significant development, a local planning authority will often make use of its statutory power by making the grant of planning permission conditional on the developer entering into a 'section 106 agreement'.

The section 106 agreement will contain the planning obligations that the local planning authority wishes to impose on the developer. Those planning obligations will be designed to extract some public benefit which may or may not (directly) relate to the proposed development. Section 106 enables a local planning authority to require particular operations or activities to be carried out on the developer's land or a sum or sums of money to be paid to the authority.

Typically, a local planning authority will seek to impose planning obligations to get a developer to:

- contribute towards the provision of infrastructure such as improvements to nearby (off-site) road junctions to accommodate the flows of traffic that will be generated by the proposed development;

- pay for new sewers that the proposed development will necessitate;
- demolish any existing buildings on the site after the replacement buildings authorised by the planning permission have been put up;
- 'tie' the occupation or use of proposed buildings to an existing commercial or agricultural business operated at the site; or
- transfer to the local planning authority land for use as 'open space'.

It will be apparent from these typical planning obligations that a section 106 agreement is designed to enable a local planning authority, in consultation with a developer, to overcome legitimate planning objections to the developer's proposed development.

The planning obligations contained in a section 106 agreement may be positive or negative in nature and, unlike private law covenants, their enforceability is not dependent on the local planning authority owning any neighbouring or adjoining land. Further, a section 106 agreement 'runs with the (servient) land' and, as such, may be enforced not only against the landowner entering into the agreement but also its successors in title.

To be valid and enforceable, a section 106 agreement must comply with certain formalities. These formalities state that the section 106 agreement must:

- be executed as a deed;
- identify the planning obligations that the local planning authority wishes to impose;
- identify the (servient) land that is to be burdened by the planning obligations; and
- identify the parties to the agreement, i.e. the owner of the (servient) land and the local planning authority that will be entitled to enforce the planning obligations.

9

What remedies are available for breach of a restrictive covenant?

9.1 Injunction and award of damages

To obtain any remedy when a breach of a covenant is threatened or has actually occurred, a claim must be issued at court. Where the claim is likely to involve complex issues or the value of the dispute is substantial, the claim ought to be brought in the Chancery Division of the High Court. The judges of the Chancery Division have particular expertise in handling disputes relating to land. Where, however, the claim is likely to be relatively straightforward and the value of the dispute is modest, it may be appropriate to issue the claim in a local County Court.

The covenantee (or a successor in title to the dominant land) will usually be the claimant; likewise, the covenantor (or a successor in title to the servient land) will usually be the defendant.

A covenantee will only be entitled to one of the available remedies if, and only if, it can establish that:

- it has benefit of the covenant;
- the covenantor is burdened by the covenant; and
- the covenantor has breached or is threatening to breach the covenant.

The remedies available to a successful covenantee are an award of damages and the grant of an injunction. An award of damages is a common law remedy intended to compensate the covenantee financially for the covenantor's wrongdoing; the grant of an injunction is an equitable remedy intended to make the covenantor comply with its obligations. The jurisdiction of the court to grant an injunction is contained in section 37(1) of the *Supreme Court Act* 1981. The two remedies of injunction and an award of damages are not mutually exclusive.

9.1.1 The general rule

Where a covenantee has issued a claim at court, one of the issues, if not the most important issue, that the court must determine at trial is often whether:

- (simply) to make an award of damages to the covenantee; or
- to exercise its discretion to grant an injunction compelling the covenantor either to restrain from breaching the covenant ('a prohibitory injunction'), or demolish any building and construction that it has erected ('a mandatory injunction').

In determining this issue, the court has to decide whether the covenantor should be made to comply with its obligations (i.e. the terms of the covenant) or be permitted to buy its way out of the covenant. As a general rule, the court prefers to grant an injunction rather than make an award of damages[74]. There are two main reasons for this:

- Quantifying in money terms how much the covenantee should be awarded in damages for the loss of the benefit and protection that a negative covenant confers on the dominant land is an inherently difficult task.
- The court does not wish to, nor be seen to, condone the conduct of a covenantor who has blatantly and calculatedly breached a covenant[75].

There are many reported cases where the court has imposed a mandatory injunction on a covenantor forcing it to demolish a construction that has been erected in breach of a covenant[76].

Example:
One case, in particular, that came before the Court of Appeal in 1981 is worthy of note because of the trenchant comments made by the Court. The covenantor had erected a building which obscured the covenantee's scenic view of the sea and beach in breach of a negative covenant that was imposed in 1930[77]. Part of the judgment of the Court reads as follows:

> 'Here is a man [the Claimant] who has been living in his house for 33 years with a view of the sea protected by a restrictive covenant. The Defendant purchased the land subject to the restriction with the knowledge of it at the time of the purchase. He did not make any enquiry of [the Claimant] either directly or indirectly, he did not inform his architect of the restriction, he took no notice of his builder telling him of [the Claimant's] objection and he put the roof trusses up in spite of letters from [the Claimant's] solicitor. A more flagrant disregard of [the Claimant's] rights it is difficult to imagine. As I have already indicated, the judge concluded that there was a serious interference with [the Claimant's] legal right to view the sea. I find it difficult to say that where one has a view protected by covenant the denial of that view is capable of being estimated in money terms and therefore it seems to me it cannot be adequately compensated by a small money payment. It no doubt will be oppressive to the Defendant if a mandatory injunction is granted against him, but it is entirely his own fault for proceeding with the construction in breach of the covenant after warning.'

The court will, however, depart from the general rule to grant an injunction if there are good reasons for doing so. Where such reasons exist, the court has jurisdiction to award damages in lieu of injunction pursuant to section 50 of the *Supreme Court Act* 1981.

The court might decide against imposing an injunction if, for example, the covenantee's loss is small and can be compensated by the payment of a modest sum of money, and the effect of an injunction would be disproportionately oppressive to the covenantor[78]. Unfortunately, there is no hard and fast rule as to what a 'modest sum of money' is.

Example:
In a case that came before the courts in 2001, a covenantee was awarded damages of £375,000 in lieu of an injunction where a hotel had been built four metres over a building line in breach of a negative covenant[79].

Another reason for departing from the general rule might be where the court is, in effect, left with a fait accompli, i.e. the covenantor's breach is irreversible. For example, if houses are built by a developer in breach of a negative covenant and sold off to individual purchasers who are already in occupation, it would be impractical and nonsensical for the court to order the houses to be demolished. Instead, the court may content itself by making an award of damages (in lieu of an injunction) equal to the sum that the covenantee could have reasonably negotiated in return for granting a release or modification of the covenant. An award on this basis can be substantial. In 1974, the court set a precedent for quantifying the sum that the covenantee could have negotiated by reference to a percentage of the developer's anticipated profit from the development[80]. In cases that have come before the court since 1974, there has been a tendency for the covenantee to be awarded between 5 per cent and 33 per cent of the developer's anticipated profit depending on the particular facts of the case. An award of 20 per cent or more of the developer's anticipated profit is likely to be warranted where, for example, the breach of covenant is particularly serious and the terms of the covenant are such that the covenantee would have had a strong bargaining position in any negotiation with the developer[81].

Again, a covenantee can expect the court to depart from the general rule where the covenantee knew that it had the benefit of a covenant but, nevertheless, stood by whilst a 'permanent or substantial structure' was erected on the servient land in breach of the covenant[82]. This does not mean however that, in order to preserve its ability to seek an injunction, a covenantee must always 'rush off to court' as soon as it becomes aware that a breach of the covenant is threatened. In many cases, if the covenantee puts the covenantor on notice of its potential claim, advises the covenantor that if it puts up any construction it does so entirely at its own risk, and issues a claim at court within a reasonable period, the covenantee's ability to obtain a permanent injunction from the court at trial is unlikely to be jeopardised[83].

9.1.2 No remedy

The court has been known to refuse the covenantee a remedy even though it has succeeded in establishing a breach of covenant on the part of the covenantor. Such a refusal is rare and it tends to arise in two instances.

First, where there has been such a (dramatic) change in the character of the neighbourhood that the purpose for which the negative covenant was imposed has come to an end. The court would, however, have to be satisfied that the negative covenant had become valueless to the covenantee thereby implying that the covenantee has an (improper) ulterior motive for seeking to enforce the covenant[84]. An example of such a motive would be where a covenantee, knowing that the negative covenant does not afford its dominant land any practical benefit, nevertheless seeks to enforce the covenant with the sole or primary intention of trying to extort a sum of money from the covenantor.

Second, the entitlement to a remedy may be lost where the covenantee has been guilty of 'acquiescence'. Acquiescence occurs where there has been an overt and continuous breach of covenant for a significant period and, in all the circumstances, to let the covenantee enforce the covenant after such a passage of time would be unconscionable[85]. It may be, for instance, that the covenantee for a significant period had actual knowledge of the particular breach of covenant complained of and had not sought to stop it or, alternatively, previously had not sought to prevent similar infringements. Conduct on the part of a covenantee giving rise to acquiescence may equally amount to a waiver of the breach or a release of the covenant[86].

9.1.3 *Statutory bodies*

Where Parliament has entrusted a statutory body to carry out functions in the public interest, such as the delivery of education or health care services, a negative covenant burdening land that the statutory body acquires to perform its functions may become unenforceable. Where such a situation arises, the owner of the dominant land who enjoys the benefit of the negative covenant is normally entitled to statutory compensation for the loss of protection that the covenant affords.[87]

9.2 Interim injunction

Quite often, it is desirable for the covenantee to consider whether it ought to apply to the court for an interim injunction restraining the covenantor from committing a breach of covenant that is in progress or is threatened. For example, a developer may be threatening to 'send in the bulldozers'. An application for an interim injunction to restrain a breach of covenant tends to be made by the covenantee at the same time as it issues a substantive claim at court. Assuming that the covenantee can show that it enjoys the benefit of the covenant and the covenantor's proposed development breaches the covenant, then, prima facie, the covenantee will be entitled to an interim injunction. It will be for the covenantor to show that an injunction should not be granted. In other words, the onus will lie with the covenantor to show a good reason as to why an interim injunction should not be granted. This will usually entail the covenantor satisfying the court that the grant of an injunction will be unnecessarily oppressive. Moreover, even if the covenantor is able to demonstrate that the injury to the covenantee is small (in the sense that the extent to which the covenantee's dominant land is devalued in monetary terms is small or non-existent), the covenantor will still have to show why it is that the covenantee should not be entitled to the relief that, prima facie, equity entitles it to. This can be a difficult hurdle for the covenantor to jump. For example, if the covenant has 'ransom' value, the court may be reluctant to deprive the covenantee of this benefit even if the breach or threatened breach of covenant would not devalue the dominant land.

Applying for an interim injunction is not without its risks. To obtain an interim injunction, the covenantee will invariably be asked by the court to give a 'cross undertaking in damages'. By giving this undertaking, the covenantee promises that if, at trial, its claim is unsuccessful, it will pay the covenantor damages to compensate it for any loss suffered by reason of the imposition of the interim injunction. If the covenantee's claim is ultimately unsuccessful, then, in hindsight, it ought not to have been granted an interim injunction; hence the need to compensate the covenantor for being unable to carry out a lawful activity whilst the interim injunction was in place. The amount of compensation payable to the covenantor can be very substantial and for the covenantee (depending on its means) financially crippling. Where, for example, the covenantor is a developer who is contractually committed to building contractors and others but is unable to proceed with its proposed development because the covenantee has obtained an interim injunction, compensation payable under the cross undertaking in damages has the potential to be enormous. For this reason, no decision should ever be made by a covenantee to apply to the court for an interim injunction unless it has first given very careful consideration to the financial consequences that it may face if, at trial, it is unable to make good its claim against the covenantor for breach of covenant.

To apply for an interim injunction, the covenantee does not have to persuade the court that its claim against the covenantor for breach of covenant has good prospects of success. It is sufficient for the covenantee to establish that there is a serious issue to be tried[88]. Once the covenantee jumps this hurdle, the court will decide whether or not to grant an interim injunction by weighing up where the 'balance of convenience' between the parties lies. The court will weigh the consequences for the covenantee in not granting an interim injunction against the consequences for the covenantor in granting an injunction. If the consequences to the covenantee outweigh the consequences to the covenantor, the court will grant an interim injunction (see specimen form 3 in appendix C); if the consequences to the covenantor outweigh the consequences to the covenantee, an interim injunction will be refused.

From a tactical perspective, it is, in practice, usually easier to obtain a permanent injunction at trial prohibiting the construction of a building or buildings, rather than a mandatory order for buildings to be pulled down. Accordingly, if between the start of proceedings and the trial, an interim injunction is not sought, and a substantial development is completed, the court will inevitably be more reluctant to grant a permanent injunction requiring the buildings to be pulled down. That said, it is important to emphasise that each case will be decided on its own facts. Certainly in recent cases, it is possible to detect a trend for the court to pay small heed to the fact that the covenantee has not sought an interim injunction, provided it has always made clear to the covenantor that it intends to seek a permanent injunction at trial[89].

9.3 Stay of claim

Where a covenantor faces a claim brought by a covenantee seeking to enforce a negative covenant, the covenantor is entitled to ask the court to stay the claim whilst it pursues its own application in the Lands Tribunal for a discharge or modification of the covenant (see chapter 12). The covenantor's application for a stay will be made pursuant to section 84(9) of the *Law of Property Act* 1925. A covenantor should consider making an application for a stay where, for example, it has been granted planning permission for its proposed development and believes that it has good prospects of obtaining a discharge or modification of the restrictive covenant on the ground that the covenant (wrongly) impedes a reasonable user of the servient land. If the court considers that the covenantor's application to the Lands Tribunal has reasonable prospect of success, it is unlikely to refuse a stay[90]. Further, if the covenantor's application to the Lands Tribunal proves to be successful, the claim before the court brought by the covenantee will fall away.

Section 84(9) may not be invoked by a covenantor where the covenantee is seeking to enforce a positive covenant, as the Lands Tribunal has no jurisdiction to discharge or modify positive covenants.

9.4 Declaration

Section 84(2) of the *Law of Property Act* 1925 enables a covenantee or covenantor (or any other person interested in the dominant or servient land) to apply to the Chancery Division of the High Court for a declaration as to:

- whether a negative covenant is enforceable and, if so, by whom; and
- the true meaning and effect of a negative covenant.

An application for a declaration can be particularly useful for a developer who has recently exchanged contracts for or completed the purchase of the servient land that is ripe for development. Such a developer may be anxious to know whether its proposed development might breach a negative covenant burdening the servient land. Equally, the developer may wish to resolve any potential dispute with its neighbours concerning the covenant before starting the development. The advantage to the developer of making an application to the Court under section 84(2) in these circumstances is that, if it obtains the declaration sought, the negative covenant will be cleared from the title to the servient land.

Generally speaking, a claim for a declaration under section 84(2) tends to be made only where the covenantor is able to make good a legal (as opposed to factual) argument to the effect that the covenantee is not entitled to enforce the negative covenant. The reason for this is that a claim under section 84(2) is determined 'on paper' without oral evidence from witnesses of fact. Accordingly, a covenantor should consider pursuing a claim for a declaration under section 84(2) if it:

- disputes that a scheme of development has been validly created;
- disputes that each and every part of the servient land is burdened by a negative covenant;
- disputes that a negative covenant is enforceable because the dominant land cannot be ascertained;
- disputes the covenantee's interpretation of particular words or phrases in a negative covenant such as 'building' or 'private dwelling house'; or
- disputes that a particular activity is caught by a negative covenant.

A claim under section 84(2) would not be appropriate, however, where, for example, a covenantor wishes to argue that the covenantee should not be entitled to enforce a negative covenant because there has been either delay or acquiescence on the covenantee's part or, alternatively, a change in the nature of the neighbourhood. The outcome of this type of dispute usually turns on the oral evidence of witnesses of fact and, as such, cannot be determined 'on paper'.

Although a large majority of the claims that come before the Court pursuant to section 84(2) relate to negative covenants that burden freehold land, the Court does have jurisdiction to entertain claims where the negative covenant burdens leasehold land providing the term of the lease is more than 40 years of which not less than 25 years have expired.

9.5 Planning covenants and obligations

Like private law covenants, the remedies available to a local planning authority for breach of a planning covenant or planning obligation imposed pursuant to section 106 of the *Town and Country Planning Act* 1990 are contractual. Under section 106(5), a local planning authority may apply to the court for an injunction to restrain a breach of a planning obligation. Importantly, a planning obligation is enforceable against the covenantor (as the original contracting party) and, if the servient land has passed into new ownership, the present landowner too. Moreover, a local planning authority is entitled under section 106(6) to enter the servient land on 21 days' notice and carry out operations to remedy any breach of a planning obligation and to recover the cost of carrying out those operations from the landowner.

10

What is the procedure for progressing a claim in the High Court or County Court?

10.1 Appropriate forum

The Chancery Division of the High Court or County Court is the appropriate forum for determining a claim by a covenantee (or a successor in title) for an injunction to enforce a covenant or, alternatively, an award of damages for the loss suffered by reason of its breach. Where the claim is likely to involve complex issues of law or fact, or the amount at stake in the dispute is substantial, the litigation should be started in the High Court rather than the County Court.

Further, the Chancery Division of the High Court is the appropriate forum for adjudicating a claim by a covenantee or covenantor (or any other person interested in the dominant land or servient land) under section 84(2) of the *Law of Property Act* 1925 for a declaration as to:

- whether a covenant is enforceable and, if so, by whom; or
- the 'true' meaning and effect of a covenant.

10.2 Civil Procedure Rules

There is one set of rules, known as the *Civil Procedure Rules* (CPR), which applies to any claim started in the High Court or County Court. The CPR governs the procedure for progressing a claim.

10.3 Claim for an injunction or damages

Each of the stages in the procedure for claiming an injunction for breach of covenant or an award of damages is explained below (see also flow chart 2 in appendix A). To make the stages easier to understand, a hypothetical claim will be used. The claimant will be a covenantee who is seeking to enforce a covenant against a defendant who, as owner of adjoining land burdened by the covenant, is the covenantor.

10.3.1 Pre-action period

Before a claimant issues a claim against a defendant at court, it is necessary for the claimant and the defendant to comply with the *CPR Pre-Action Protocol*. The Protocol is intended to encourage the parties, through an early exchange of information and documentation, to settle their dispute without the need to litigate. If either the claimant or the defendant, without good excuse, fails to comply with the Protocol, there is every likelihood that it will be penalised on costs in any subsequent litigation.

The *Pre-Action Protocol* sets out the steps that the claimant must take before it issues any claim at court. The Protocol states that the claimant should write to the defendant:

* stating the nature of its claim, i.e. a claim for breach of covenant;
* stating what remedy it is seeking, i.e. an injunction and/or an award of damages;
* enclosing the important documents that support the claim, e.g. the title deeds establishing that it has the benefit of the covenant; and
* stating whether it wishes to enter into mediation or another form of alternative dispute resolution (ADR).

The defendant must be given a reasonable period of time to consider the claim and give its response. An appropriate period for responding to the claim can be anywhere between 14 days and 3 months depending upon the complexity of the issues that the claim raises. The defendant's response should:

* explain why it intends to defend the claim;
* (if appropriate) put forward any proposals to settle the claim; and

- indicate whether it is willing to participate in mediation or another form of ADR.

Inevitably, the defendant's response may lead to a further period of correspondence between the parties. This correspondence will be aimed at promoting a settlement of the dispute or narrowing the issues in dispute.

This pre-action period can last weeks, if not months, particularly if the claimant believes that litigation can be avoided because the defendant is co-operating and responding constructively to the claim. There are no guidelines as to how long the pre-action period should be permitted to continue. It will, however, normally become apparent to the claimant when an impasse has been reached, making any further pre-action dialogue with the defendant futile.

10.3.2 Starting a claim

A claim is started by the claimant issuing a 'claim form' at court which is later served on the defendant. The claim form sets out the nature of the claim in brief. A fee is payable to the court on the issuing of the claim form and the sum payable depends on the value of the claim and the type of remedy sought, i.e. an award of damages or an injunction.

Normally, the claim form is supported by 'particulars of claim' (see specimen form 1 in appendix C) which will disclose the nature of the claim in greater detail and set out the essential facts that the claimant intends to rely upon at trial to establish its claim.

After the defendant has been served with the claim form, it has 14 days to file an 'acknowledgment of service' with the court stating whether or not it intends to defend the claim.

(If the defendant fails to file an acknowledgement of service, the claimant can apply to court to enter judgment.)

10.3.3 Defence

If the defendant files an acknowledgment of service indicating an intention to defend the claim, it then has a further 14 days to serve a 'defence' (see specimen form 2 in appendix C). The parties may, by agreement, extend the period for the service of the defence by a further 28 days (making 56 days in total). Any extension beyond this period will need the court's approval. Unless a claim is quite straightforward, it is usual for the defendant to ask for (and be given) an extension.

(If the defendant fails to serve a defence, the claimant can apply to court to enter judgment.)

The defendant must explain in its defence why it disputes the claim. This will include disclosing the essential facts that the defendant proposes to rely upon to dispute the claim at trial. For example, a defendant who believes that the claimant is unable to enforce a covenant because it no longer confers any practical benefit on the claimant's dominant land, will have to explain in its defence why a breach of the covenant will not cause the claimant's dominant land to suffer a diminution in value or loss of amenity.

10.3.4 Counterclaim

When serving its defence, it may also be appropriate for the defendant to issue a 'counterclaim' against the claimant. For example, the defendant may wish to argue that the claimant is not entitled to pursue a claim against it for breach of covenant because the claimant's land does not enjoy the benefit of the covenant; in other words, it is not dominant land. In this situation, it would be entirely appropriate for the defendant to serve a counterclaim asking the court to make a declaration to this effect.

Any counterclaim will proceed in parallel with the claimant's claim and, usually, they will be dealt with together. The claimant will have a further 14 days (or such longer period as the parties may agree) to file a 'defence to counterclaim'.

10.3.5 Third Party claims

A defendant may also bring a claim against any person, whether or not already a party, for a contribution or indemnity against the claim brought against it by the claimant.

> Example:
> Where a covenant not to build within ten feet of a boundary has been breached because, contrary to their instructions, the defendant's contractors have laid foundations five feet from the boundary, the defendant may wish to pursue a third party claim against the contractors.

10.3.6 Reply

Following receipt of the defence, the claimant may, if it wishes
to, serve a reply. The reply affords the claimant an opportunity
to respond to any allegations contained in the defence.

10.3.7 Further information

The particulars of claim, the defence, the counterclaim and the
reply are all known as 'statements of case'. Quite often, a
party's statement of case may contain insufficient information
to enable the opponent to understand fully the arguments that
the statement of case seeks to advance. Where this occurs, the
party serving the statement of case can be asked to clarify it or
provide further information. For example, if a claimant asserts
that it is entitled to enforce a negative covenant in equity
because a scheme of development exists, the defendant may
wish the claimant to clarify whether the (alleged) scheme was
created expressly or impliedly and, if the latter, the facts relied
upon. If a request for further information is ignored, or not
answered properly, the opponent may make an application to
the court for an order compelling compliance.

10.3.8 Directions

Following the service of the defence (and any reply), the court
will send each party an 'allocation questionnaire' to complete.
The questionnaire is intended to solicit information from the
parties to enable the court to properly supervise the conduct of
the litigation. The questionnaire asks for information such as:

- the number of witnesses that will be called by each party to
  give oral evidence at trial;
- what experts (if any) each party proposes to call to give
  evidence at trial; and
- when the parties are likely to be ready for trial.

At this stage in the litigation, the court will expect the parties
to consider using some form of ADR to try to settle the dispute.
If either party considers that the claim is unsuitable for ADR, it
must be willing to explain its decision to the court. A party who
(wrongly) refuses to participate in ADR can be penalised by the
court in costs.

Further, the court encourages the parties to agree directions for
taking the claim through to trial (see specimen form 4 in

appendix C). If, however, directions cannot be agreed, the court will hold a case management conference (CMC) and decide what directions should be made.

The directions agreed between the parties or made by the court at the CMC will include a timetable for completing each of the remaining stages in the litigation. The timetable will also give a 'window' within which the trial will take place. The parties must comply with the timetable and, if a party fails to comply, the opposing party may apply to court for an order compelling compliance.

10.3.9 Disclosure

Disclosure normally occurs about 28 days after the directions timetable is put in place.

Disclosure obliges each party to make a list of all documents that it has (or has had) in its possession, custody or control relating to the dispute, which either advance its own case and on which it relies or, alternatively, which may be detrimental to its own case and support its opponent's case.

The parties must exchange lists. Following this, each one can request copies of any documents mentioned in the other's list, except those documents that are privileged from production, e.g. written advices that the party has obtained from its own lawyers.

The obligation to make disclosure continues until the trial. Accordingly, if, after a party has served its list, further disclosable documents come into its possession, it must serve the opponent with a supplemental list.

Each party will consider very carefully the list of documents served by its opponent. If a party believes that the opponent has failed to disclose potentially important documents, that party may make an application to the court for an order compelling the opponent to disclose the 'missing' documents. For example, if a claimant withholds its title deeds so that the defendant cannot satisfy itself that the claimant has the benefit of a covenant, the defendant would be acting quite properly in making an application to the court.

Disclosure is a vitally important stage of the litigation. Many cases settle following disclosure because the weaknesses of a party's case often become evident from the documents that both sides disclose.

10.3.10 Witness statements

Exchange of witness statements is the next stage in the litigation. The parties usually exchange witness statements about four to six weeks after disclosure has taken place.

Each party will prepare a witness statement for each witness that it intends to call at trial. The witness statements will set out the evidence that the witnesses will give at trial. The statements should contain the factual background to the dispute. So, for example, the claimant's witness statements should explain how the dominant land came into its ownership, and why the defendant is (allegedly) in breach of covenant. It is important that witness statements are both full and accurate as witnesses may not be able to elaborate on their statements in the witness box.

10.3.11 Expert evidence

It may be necessary for the parties to adduce expert evidence at trial. For example, if a claimant is contending that a covenant, which a developer is threatening to breach, protects its dominant land, expert evidence will usually be needed to evaluate the likely extent of any loss of amenity, and to assess whether the dominant land will suffer a diminution in value. In this example, expert evidence would be given by a planning consultant and a valuer. The planning consultant would give a qualitative evaluation as to the (social or environmental) impact of the loss of amenity that would flow from a breach of covenant; the valuer would, in turn, give an opinion as to whether the loss of amenity identified by the planning consultant would adversely affect the value or marketability of the dominant land and, if so, by how much.

The parties are asked in the allocation questionnaire what expert evidence they wish to adduce at trial. In a relatively straightforward claim, the parties are discouraged by the court from instructing their own experts; instead, and in the interest of preserving costs, the court prefers the parties to jointly instruct a single expert.

All experts who are instructed to give evidence at trial owe an overriding duty to the court to offer impartial and objective opinions. The experts will each set out their opinions in a report. This will usually be exchanged six to eight weeks after the exchange of witness statements. Following exchange, the experts are encouraged to meet to see if they can agree, or at least narrow, the issues in dispute that fall within their professional discipline.

10.3.12 Trial and preparation for trial

The parties will then each be asked by the court to complete and return a 'pre-trial checklist' confirming that they are ready to proceed to trial. If either party is in default of the directions timetable (e.g. they have failed to exchange witness statements or expert reports by the due date etc.), the court may hold a 'pre-trial review' to decide what further directions should be made to put the litigation back on track.

About 14 days before the date fixed for the trial, the claimant will, in consultation with the defendant, prepare a paginated trial bundle containing all documents that will be used at trial. Again, about two days before the start of the trial, the parties will exchange 'skeleton arguments' that will set out in a concise form the issues of fact and law that each party believes the trial judge needs to decide.

The trial will then take place before a single judge; there is no jury. After hearing all the evidence and any legal submissions, the judge will decide where the merits of the case lie and give judgment accordingly. The judge will also decide which party or parties should bear the costs of the litigation.

Following judgment either party may consider an appeal if there is reason to believe that the trial judge misunderstood the law that applies to the dispute or, alternatively, made a finding of fact that, in all the circumstances, was unreasonable to make. Appealing against a finding of fact can be particularly difficult as the Court of Appeal, to whom any appeal is made, needs a lot of persuading before it will interfere with a trial judge's assessment of the witnesses and their evidence.

Most claims take 9 to 12 months to come to trial once a claim form is issued.

10.4   Claim under section 84(2)

A different procedure applies to claims for a declaration under section 84(2) of the *Law of Property Act* 1925 (see flow chart 3 in appendix A). Such claims are determined 'on paper' without witnesses of fact giving oral evidence.

Further, as a declaration is binding on everyone who is entitled to the benefit of the negative covenant, the Court take steps to ensure that adjoining or neighbouring landowners that potentially enjoy the benefit of the covenant are given the opportunity to contest the claim. Usually, after the claim form is issued, the covenantor is directed by the Court to circulate a letter giving notice of the claim to anyone who seemingly has the benefit of the negative covenant. Any recipient of the circular can then decide, if it so wishes, to defend the claim by becoming a party to the litigation. Any recipient who decides to defend the claim, will be ordered to serve a defence. Broadly speaking, the parties will, thereafter, follow the procedure that applies to a claim for an injunction or damages for breach of covenant.

(The stage allowing for exchange of statements for factual witnesses will be omitted.)

10.5   After trial

If the claim under section 84(2) asks the Court to determine whether a negative covenant is enforceable and, at trial, the judge determines that it is not, the Court will issue an order containing a formal declaration to this effect. The covenantor will place the order with its title deeds (in the case of unregistered land) or register it at the Land Registry (in the case of registered land) against the title to its servient land.

10.6   Settlement

At every stage of litigation the parties should actively consider whether the claim can be settled. There are various forms of ADR that the parties can use to help promote a settlement. These include:

- mediation, i.e. without prejudice negotiations facilitated by a trained mediator; or

- early case evaluation by an independent person, e.g. a lawyer or other professional who has expertise in handling similar claims.

All forms of ADR have a common theme: they aim to encourage a constructive dialogue between the parties so as to enable them to settle the claim. It is important to appreciate that ADR may be used at any time during a dispute. Often, it is most effective before litigation has actually started when the parties' positions may not yet have become entrenched.

11

What are the costs rules in the High Court and County Court?

11.1 Claim for an injunction or damages

The Chancery Division of the High Court or County Court is the appropriate forum for determining the following claims: a claim by a covenantee (or a successor in title) who seeks an injunction to enforce a covenant or, alternatively, compensation (an award of damages) for the loss suffered from its breach.

Once a claim is issued, the court (whether it be the High Court or the County Court) has a wide discretion to decide whether any party to the dispute should pay all or any part of the costs that another party to the dispute has incurred.

The court can assess the amount of costs that one party ('the paying party') must pay the other ('the receiving party'), decide when the paying party must pay the receiving party and order the paying party to pay an amount paid on account pending assessment of the receiving party's costs. The court can order that the paying party pay the receiving party:

- costs from or until a certain date only;
- costs incurred before the start of the litigation process;
- costs relating to particular steps taken in the litigation process;
- costs relating only to a distinct part of the dispute; and
- interest on any such costs from or until a certain date, including a date before judgment is given by the court.

11.2 The general rule

The general rule is that the costs of a claim usually 'follow the event'. This means that the party who is successful overall in the dispute is entitled to an order that the other party pay its costs of the dispute. However, the court, in the exercise of its wide discretion, can and does make different orders. The court may depart from the general rule where, for example, a party has:

- conducted itself unreasonably either before or after the start of the litigation process;
- unreasonably pursued a particular aspect of the dispute;
- exaggerated its loss or damage; or
- failed to make any serious attempt either before or after the start of the litigation process to try and resolve the dispute.

Where a party obtains an order for 'costs', this does not mean that the paying party will have to pay all the money that the receiving party has expended in relation to the costs covered by the order. When the court comes to assess a receiving party's 'recoverable' costs it usually only orders the paying party to pay between 75–85 per cent of the money that the receiving party has actually expended.

At the conclusion of an interim hearing (or a trial lasting not more than two days), the court usually carries out a summary assessment of the receiving party's costs, and orders the paying party to pay the assessed amount within a specified period, normally 14 days.

If the paying party fails to make the payment within the specified time, the court may prevent the paying party from prosecuting or, as the case may be, defending the dispute until the payment is made. Alternatively, the court may order that final judgment be entered against the paying party.

At the conclusion of a trial lasting more than two days, the court will generally order that there be a detailed assessment of the receiving party's costs. The court may, pending the detailed assessment, order the paying party to pay the receiving party a sum on account of its 'recoverable' costs.

The lawyers acting for the receiving party will endeavour to ensure that the receiving party's recoverable costs are as much as possible. The receiving party should, however, always bear in mind that it remains responsible for paying any bill that its own lawyers render even though it may have the benefit of a costs order entitling it to be reimbursed with all or part of the fees and disbursements covered by the bill.

Before a claim is issued, each party to the dispute should appreciate that:

- even if it is successful in due course in obtaining a costs order from the court, the opponent (as the paying party) may not have the financial means to pay the recoverable costs;
- where the opponent is legally-aided, it is most unlikely that it will recover any of its costs, even if it is successful; and
- if it is unsuccessful in the dispute and is ordered to pay the opponent's costs, it will be obliged to pay its opponent's recoverable costs plus the fees and disbursements that it incurs with its own lawyers.

11.2.1 Interest on costs

A receiving party is entitled to interest on its recoverable costs from the date that the costs became payable (usually the date upon which the court hands down judgment following a trial, or, in the case of an interim application, 14 days thereafter) until the date of payment at the judgment rate. The judgment rate is presently eight per cent.

11.3 Offers

Whilst there is no prohibition against the parties making an offer to settle in any way it chooses, there can be costs, interest and tactical advantages in making an offer to settle which complies with the rules of court. Such an offer is known as a 'Part 36 offer'. A Part 36 offer is intended to promote a settlement of a dispute. Where one party makes a sensible Part 36 offer, that offer tends to focus the opponent's mind and, even if the offer is rejected, it may nevertheless have the effect of encouraging a dialogue that in due course may lead to a settlement of the claim. Making a Part 36 offer should not be regarded as a sign of weakness, but, rather, an appropriate way of putting pressure on an opponent to settle the dispute. Pressure is felt because a Part 36 offer has cost consequences for a party who refuses to accept a reasonable offer to settle. A Part 36 offer can be made in respect of the whole or any part of a claim, including discrete issues that the claim raises. Part 36 offers to settle can be made by either a covenantee or covenantor at any stage in the dispute. Indeed, Part 36 offers are frequently made before a claim is issued at court.

11.3.1 Formalities

To be a valid Part 36 offer, the offer must be a genuine offer to settle the dispute. Further, a Part 36 offer is made 'without prejudice save as to costs'; it cannot be produced in evidence until the claim (or the part of the claim covered by the offer) has been determined by the court.

A party wishing to make a Part 36 offer must ensure that the offer is in writing. Further, the Part 36 offer must:

- state that it is made pursuant to Part 36 of the *Civil Procedure Rules*;
- state the period for accepting the offer, which must not be less than 21 days;
- state whether the offer relates to the whole of the claim or part of it and, if only part of it, which part;
- state whether the offer takes into account any counterclaim that the opponent is pursuing;
- contain sufficient information to enable the opponent to assess the reasonableness of the offer; and
- (in the case of a covenantor making an offer) state that any offer to pay a sum of money (as compensation for the breach of covenant) will be paid by a single payment within 14 days of the acceptance of the offer.

An offer to make a payment in settlement of a claim is treated as inclusive of all interest unless the offer states otherwise.

11.3.2 Clarification

It is often the case that the information contained within a Part 36 offer is insufficient to enable the opponent to assess the reasonableness of the offer. Where this occurs, the opponent is entitled to ask the party making the Part 36 offer to clarify it so that it may be better understood. Such a request for clarification must be made within 7 days of receipt of the offer.

11.3.3 Acceptance

If a party wishes to accept a Part 36 offer, it must do so in writing. The court's permission to accept a Part 36 offer is not needed unless the trial of the claim has already started or is listed to start within 21 days. If a Part 36 offer is accepted that offers a sum of money in settlement of the dispute, that sum of money must be paid within 14 days otherwise the party who has accepted the offer may enter judgment for the unpaid sum.

Generally speaking, if a Part 36 offer made by a covenantor is accepted by the covenantee within the period of acceptance (usually 21 days):

- the covenantee is entitled to its costs of the claim up to the date of acceptance on the standard basis; and
- the claim is stayed upon the terms of the Part 36 offer.

If, however, a Part 36 offer is accepted by the covenantee after the expiry of the period of acceptance, the parties must try to agree between themselves who should bear the costs of the claim and, if they are unable to reach agreement, the court will decide the matter for them. As a rule of thumb, the covenantee will be entitled to its costs of the claim on a standard basis up to the date of expiry of the period of acceptance, and from thereafter, the covenantor will be entitled to its costs to the date of acceptance. Again, where a Part 36 offer is accepted 'out of time', the claim is stayed upon the terms of the offer.

A covenantee's costs will usually include any costs incurred in defending a counterclaim if the Part 36 offer states that it takes the counterclaim into account.

Further, if a covenantee makes an offer to settle which includes its costs, such an offer will not be strictly in accordance with Part 36. In these circumstances, the court will have a discretion as to whether any of the costs or interest advantages that Part 36 confers should be given to the covenantee. Where an offer, albeit one that does not comply strictly with Part 36, is unreasonably rejected by a covenantor, it is likely that the court will give the covenantee some or all of the advantages that Part 36 confers.

11.3.4 Worked examples

The consequences of a covenant not accepting a covenantee's Part 36 offer can be illustrated by the following examples:

Example 1:
A covenantee is claiming an award of damages of £400,000 in compensation for the breach of a covenant and makes a Part 36 offer for £200,000 plus its costs.

Decision at trial	Consequence of the covenantor not accepting the covenantee's Part 36 offer
Covenantee awarded £400,000 at trial	The covenantee has clearly won. Usually, where a covenantee 'wins', the covenantor will be ordered to pay the covenantee's costs on the standard basis, and to have to bear its own costs. However, as the covenantee has beaten its own Part 36 offer, the court may order that the covenantee should also be entitled to: • interest on the award of damages of £400,000 at a rate not exceeding 10% above base rate, for some or all of the period starting with the date upon which the period of acceptance expired; • costs on an indemnity basis from the date that the period of acceptance expired; and • interest on those costs at a rate not exceeding 10% above base rate.
Covenantee awarded £200,000 at trial	The covenantee has equalled its Part 36 offer. The cost consequences set out above will usually apply as the covenantee has obtained an award of damages as advantageous as the terms of its own offer.
Covenantee awarded £175,000 at trial	A covenantee has not beaten its Part 36 offer. The offer will, therefore, normally be ignored and the covenantor will pay the covenantee's costs on the standard basis, and have to bear its own costs.
Covenantee's claim is dismissed at trial	The covenantor has won. The covenantee's Part 36 offer will be ignored. The covenantee will usually be ordered to pay all the covenantor's costs on the standard basis and have to bear its own costs.

Example 2:
A covenantee is claiming an award of damages of £400,000 in compensation for breach of a covenant and the covenantor makes a Part 36 offer to pay the covenantee £200,000 plus costs.

Decision at trial	Consequence of the covenantee not accepting the covenantor's Part 36 offer
Covenantee awarded £400,000 at trial	The covenantee has beaten the covenantor's Part 36 offer. The offer has no effect. The covenantor will normally be ordered to pay the covenantee's costs on the standard basis and have to bear its own costs.
Covenantee awarded £200,000 at trial	Although the covenantee has won at trial, it has equalled, but not beaten, the covenantor's Part 36 offer. Normally, the covenantor will be ordered to pay the covenantee's costs on the standard basis up to the expiry of the period of acceptance and bear its own costs up to that date. However, from the period starting after the expiry of the period of acceptance, the covenantee can expect to be ordered to pay the covenantor's costs on the standard basis and have to bear its own costs.
Covenantee awarded £175,000 at trial	Although the covenantee has won at trial, it has failed to beat the covenantor's Part 36 offer. Usually, the covenantor will be ordered to pay the covenantee's costs and bear its own costs up to the expiry of the date of acceptance. However, from the period starting with the expiry of the period of acceptance, the covenantee can be expected to be ordered to pay the covenantor's costs on the standard basis and to have to bear its own costs.
Covenantee's claim is dismissed at trial.	The covenantor has won. The covenantee will usually be ordered to pay all the covenantor's costs on the standard basis and have to bear its own costs.

It is important to appreciate that the examples given above are intended to give general guidance only as to the cost consequences of rejecting a Part 36 offer. The examples do not address all the various cost scenarios and potential orders that the court can make as to costs at the end of a trial.

Although the examples above concentrate on claims for an award of damages, a Part 36 offer can contain non-monetary proposals. For example, a developer facing a claim for breach of a covenant may offer to revise its proposed development so as to reduce its adverse impact on adjoining or neighbouring land owned by the covenantee. Where a Part 36 offer contains a non-monetary proposal, it can be considerably harder for the court to decide after the trial whether a non-monetary proposal has been unreasonably rejected.

11.4   Claim for a declaration

The Chancery Division of the High Court is the appropriate forum for determining a claim by a covenantor or covenantee (or any other person interested in the dominant land or servient land) under section 84(2) of the *Law of Property Act 1925* seeking a declaration as to:

- whether a negative covenant is enforceable and, if so, by whom; or
- the 'true' meaning and effect of a covenant.

There is, in effect, only one significant difference between the costs rules that apply to a claim for a declaration under section 84(2) and a claim for an injunction or damages for breach of covenant.

Before the coming into force of the *Civil Procedure Rules*, a covenantor seeking a declaration could be expected to bear its own costs of the whole proceedings and the costs of those persons whom the Court had directed should be notified of the claim up to, and including, the stage that such persons had had a proper opportunity of considering the claim. Thereafter, if any such person became a party to the litigation and served a defence, the worst costs order that it was likely to face, even if its defence was unsuccessful at trial, was an order that it should bear its own costs[91]. It was unlikely that such a person would be ordered to pay the covenantor's costs of the litigation. However, since the introduction of the *Civil Procedure Rules*, the Court has been encouraged to make costs orders at trial that emphasise the need for parties to act reasonably in pursuing any particular aspect of the claim or defence. Accordingly, there is now more likelihood of a successful covenantor obtaining an order that an unsuccessful defendant pay all or part of its costs, especially where the defendant has run (plainly) bad points in contesting the claim for a declaration.

12

Can negative covenants be discharged or modified against the wishes of the covenantee?

A negative covenant, by its very nature, is intended to restrict the long-term use of the servient land. There will undoubtedly be cases, however, where it would be quite inappropriate for a negative covenant to continue indefinitely. The circumstances that existed at the time the negative covenant was imposed may have altered greatly over the years making the 'protection' that the dominant land once warranted no longer necessary. An obvious example would be where the character of a neighbourhood has changed dramatically since a negative covenant was imposed making the covenant (in reality) worthless or redundant. It is not difficult to conceive, therefore, that the continued imposition of a negative covenant can start to work against the interests of the wider community, if, for example, there was a particular need for new key worker or other social housing in the neighbourhood.

The problem of the worthless or redundant restrictive covenant is tackled by section 84 of the *Law of Property Act* 1925. Section 84 gives the Lands Tribunal the power to discharge or modify a negative covenant on specified grounds. If the Lands Tribunal decides to discharge or modify a negative covenant, it may also award, in an appropriate case, compensation to those persons affected, i.e. the owners of the dominant land.

In recent years, section 84 has become a fierce battleground pitching developers against local residents. Developers wish to exploit for financial gain land which they perceive has development potential; whereas local residents feel that their neighbourhood is under threat from overdevelopment. These competing interests have equal legitimacy and it falls, therefore, to the Lands Tribunal to adjudicate between the two sides in any particular case.

12.1 Section 84(1) of the Law of Property Act 1925

The Lands Tribunal has jurisdiction under section 84 to discharge or modify negative covenants that restrict the user of land. Importantly, the Lands Tribunal has no jurisdiction to discharge or modify positive covenants[92].

Further, the Lands Tribunal has no jurisdiction to interfere with a negative covenant that has been imposed for the sole personal benefit of the covenantee[93]. Most applications issued in the Lands Tribunal pursuant to section 84 relate to negative covenants burdening freehold land. The Lands Tribunal is, however, able to entertain applications that relate to negative covenants burdening leasehold land where the term granted by the lease is more than 40 years of which not less than 25 years has expired[94].

The Lands Tribunal's jurisdiction to discharge or modify restrictive covenants is not limited to 'private law' covenants. The Lands Tribunal has jurisdiction to modify or discharge negative covenants contained in an agreement made under section 106 of the *Town and Country Planning Act* 1990 (and its predecessor, section 52 of the *Town and Country Planning Act* 1971) providing the covenant was created prior to 25 October 1991. Where, however, the covenant was created on or after 25 October 1991, it can only be modified or discharged against the wishes of the local planning authority that imposed it by an appeal to the Secretary of State (see section 13.1).

The Lands Tribunal also has jurisdiction to discharge or modify covenants imposed by section 609 of the *Housing Act* 1985 and section 19 of the *Leasehold Reform Act* 1967. There is one minor exception to the jurisdiction that the Lands Tribunal has to discharge or modify negative covenants. The Lands Tribunal is not permitted to entertain an application where the negative covenant was imposed gratuitously, or for nominal consideration, or for public purposes. Nor is the Lands Tribunal able to modify or 'lift' a negative covenant for a limited period of time.

It is unlikely that any agreement between a covenantee and covenantor that seeks to oust the jurisdiction of the Lands Tribunal by forbidding the covenantor (or its successors in title) from making an application under section 84 will survive a judicial challenge. Such an agreement is likely to be viewed as a restriction on user and, therefore, is itself susceptible to discharge or modification under section 84.

An application under section 84 can be made by any person who has an interest in the servient land burdened by the negative covenant. The persons who may pursue an application in the Lands Tribunal therefore include:

- the present owners of the servient land;
- a person (such as a developer) who has exchanged contracts to purchase the servient land with completion conditional on obtaining an order from the Lands Tribunal discharging or modifying a negative covenant; and
- any person (such as a developer) who has an option to purchase the servient land.

Likewise, only a person who is 'entitled to the benefit' of a negative covenant is able to object to an application seeking its discharge or modification[95]. Persons who may object therefore include:

- the owners of the dominant land;
- a local planning authority if the covenant was imposed pursuant to an agreement made under section 52 of the *Town and Country Planning Act* 1971 or section 106 of the *Town and Country Planning Act* 1990; and
- other certain statutory bodies such as the Forestry Commissioners, the Nature Conservancy Council, the Countryside Commission and the National Trust where the servient land burdened by the covenant falls within their 'patch'.

It will be noted that persons who are 'merely' local residents may not object to an application seeking a discharge or modification of a negative covenant however violently they oppose the proposed development. The position is, of course, rather different in the planning context where any person is entitled to make representations to a local planning authority opposing the grant of planning permission.

If there is any doubt as to whether a person is entitled to object to an application seeking a discharge or modification of a negative covenant, the Lands Tribunal will usually determine the issue at an early stage at an interim hearing. The Lands Tribunal has power under section 84(3A) to strike out a 'notice of objection' lodged by any objector whom it judges does not have the benefit of the negative covenant.

12.2   Grounds of discharge or modification

Discretionary power

The Lands Tribunal's power to discharge or modify a negative covenant is discretionary and the power is never exercised lightly. The Lands Tribunal is always conscious that, if it exercises its discretionary power, it is, in effect, taking away property rights belonging to the owners of the dominant land (invariably) for the benefit of someone seeking to exploit the servient land for financial gain[96]. As the power is discretionary, even if an applicant succeeds at trial in establishing one of the grounds in section 84 for claiming a discharge or modification, it is not entitled 'as of right' to an order relaxing the negative covenant. When deciding how to exercise its discretion in any particular case, the Lands Tribunal must act judiciously; its decision must be founded on relevant factors and not irrelevant ones[97]. The Lands Tribunal cannot therefore dismiss an application simply because of the applicant's past behaviour or its desire to profit financially from the discharge or modification sought. The factors that the Lands Tribunal can take into account must relate to the property and its history.

When determining any application under section 84, the Lands Tribunal is obliged to consider the local planning authority's 'development plan and any declared or ascertainable pattern for the grant or refusal of planning permissions' within the neighbourhood[98]. This obligation on the Lands Tribunal to consider the local development plan and local planning decisions implies that, in exercising its discretion whether to discharge or modify a negative covenant, the Lands Tribunal must take into account not only the competing interests of the owners of the dominant land and servient land but also the interests of the wider community. So, where the applicant proposes to build several new houses (for which it has

previously obtained planning permission) in a neighbourhood
that has a desperate housing shortage, this might well weigh in
the mind of the Lands Tribunal when it comes to exercise its
discretion.

It is often the case that objectors to an application made under
section 84 contend that, if the application is successful, it will
be 'the thin end of the wedge'. In advancing this argument, the
objectors are not, necessarily, saying that the applicant's
proposed development is itself harmful; rather it is the actual
making of an order by the Lands Tribunal that is harmful. For
example, it is not unusual that, in objecting to an application,
the owners of a residential estate find it difficult to point to
anything specific in the proposed development that is likely to
be harmful or cause a loss of amenity. However, they are able –
and sometimes with considerable force – to point to the fact
that, if an order is made permitting the proposed development,
this will only encourage other similar applications that, if
allowed, will over time have a serious impact on the character
of the estate. With the 'thin end of the wedge' argument in
mind, the Lands Tribunal might well refuse to exercise its
discretion where, for example, one resident of a residential
estate seeks a modification of a negative covenant so as to
permit a second house to be built on a plot, and is met by
objections from other residents worried about the future
density of housing within the estate[99].

Although an application under section 84(1) to discharge or
modify a negative covenant burdening freehold land can be
made at any time, even immediately after the covenant has
been imposed, common sense dictates that recently imposed
covenants will be harder to dislodge. Likewise, a covenantor
who is seeking to discharge or modify a leasehold covenant is
likely to find it more difficult to persuade the Lands Tribunal to
exercise its discretion than in a freehold case. The reason is as
follows. Where a covenant burdens freehold land, the Lands
Tribunal has to consider whether to relax restrictions that the
covenantor entered into for the benefit of adjoining or
neighbouring land. However, where the covenant burdens
leasehold land, the Lands Tribunal must decide whether the
covenantor should be permitted to change the character of the
covenantee's reversion.

There are four grounds set out in section 84(1) for applying for
a discharge or modification of a negative covenant, namely:

- the covenant ought to be deemed obsolete (section 84(1)(a));
- the covenant impedes a reasonable user of the servient land without securing a substantial benefit to the persons entitled to the benefit of the covenant (sections 84(1)(aa) and (1A));
- the persons entitled to the benefit of the covenant consent to its discharge or modification (section 84(1)(b)); and
- the proposed discharge or modification of the covenant will not cause injury to the persons entitled to the benefit of the covenant (section 84(1)(c)).

Although each of the four grounds stands alone, there is overlap. More often than not, applications issued in the Lands Tribunal seek the discharge or modification of a negative covenant on more than one ground. Each of the four grounds will now be discussed in turn below.

12.2.1 Obsolescence

The Lands Tribunal has power under section 84(1)(a) to discharge or modify a restrictive covenant where:

> ' ... by reason of changes in the character of the property or the neighbourhood or other circumstances of the case which may deem material, the restriction ought to be deemed obsolete ... .'

In deciding whether a negative covenant should be deemed obsolete, the Lands Tribunal will consider whether there has been a change in the character of the servient land or the neighbourhood (peculiar to the particular locality) or other material circumstances exist.

Applications that seek to establish obsolescence by virtue of a change in the character of the servient land are quite rare. This, no doubt, is reflected in the fact that it is not easy to conceive of a change in the character of the servient land that might warrant a negative covenant to be deemed obsolete.

> **Example:**
> Where a retail shop has a restricted user (e.g. it can only operate a haberdasher) but, owing to social trends, that user is no longer viable, thus forcing the retailer to close the shop and cease trading, it may be possible to establish obsolescence.

When the Lands Tribunal considers applications asserting obsolescence by reason of changes in the neighbourhood, an obvious question arises in every case: what area should be treated as the 'neighbourhood'? In each case, the Lands Tribunal will hear evidence, carry out a site inspection, and then seek to identify an area that is sufficiently distinctive to constitute a neighbourhood of its own[100]. In the residential context, the distinctiveness of an area will usually be marked out by the style, arrangement, and appearance of the houses within it. A neighbourhood can be fairly modest in size. Indeed, it can be as small as four residential roads[101].

The test for establishing obsolescence, whether in reliance of a change in the character of the servient land or the neighbourhood or the existence of other material circumstances, is a stiff one. The applicant has to show that:

- the original purpose for which the negative covenant was imposed can no longer be fulfilled; and
- in consequence, the covenant does not afford any practical benefit or protection to the owners of the dominant land.

Applications that meet the stiff test tend to be ones where the applicant has been able to demonstrate that the character of the neighbourhood has undergone a (dramatic) transformation over a number of years.

> Example:
> A residential estate was laid out 100 years ago and gradually, over a period of time, the purpose for which the negative covenant was imposed can no longer be achieved because what once was a residential neighbourhood has become, through the express or tacit waiver of the covenant, substantially a commercial area[102].

12.2.2 Reasonable use of land impeded

The Lands Tribunal has power to discharge or modify a negative covenant if:

- its continued existence impedes some reasonable user of the land for public or private purposes;
- the covenant no longer confers on the owners of the dominant land practical benefits of substantial value or advantage, or is otherwise contrary to the public interest; and

- a sum of money would be adequate compensation for any loss that the owners of the dominant land will suffer from the discharge or modification.

Practical benefits

The Lands Tribunal adopts a broad approach when considering whether a negative covenant affords the dominant landowner a practical benefit of substantial value or advantage.

Accordingly, a practical benefit of substantial value or advantage has been held to exist where, if discharged or modified, the negative covenant would cause:

- an increase in traffic flows[103];
- a loss of privacy and seclusion[104];
- a loss of peace and quiet[105]; and
- an increase in housing density within a residential estate thereby undermining the integrity of a scheme of development[106].

Although the practical benefit that a negative covenant can confer is construed widely, it does not, however, include the ability of the owner of the dominant land to extract a ransom sum. Accordingly, an objector is not entitled to complain that, if the covenant is discharged or modified, it would lose its bargaining power to negotiate a payment for permitting the owner of the servient land to carry out its proposed development.[107]

Most, if not all, applications that seek a discharge or modification of a negative covenant on the ground that a reasonable use of the servient land is impeded, are pursued once the applicant has obtained planning permission for its proposed development. The grant of planning permission, in effect, gives rise to a 'presumption' that the negative covenant impedes a reasonable user of the servient land. Moreover, in appropriate cases, the Lands Tribunal may be greatly influenced by the fact that planning permission has been obtained when it comes to decide whether it should exercise its discretionary power to grant the discharge or modification that the applicant seeks.

However, an applicant should never assume that because it has obtained planning permission from the local planning authority, the Lands Tribunal will, in turn, 'rubber stamp' its section 84 application. The reason for this is simple. The criteria that a local planning authority applies when determining applications for planning permission are rather different to the criteria that the Lands Tribunal applies when deciding section 84 applications.

Contrary to public interest

The Lands Tribunal will need some persuasion before concluding that the continued enforcement of a negative covenant is against the public interest. Accordingly, a mere shortage of land within a neighbourhood for residential or commercial development does not, of itself, make a negative covenant prohibiting development contrary to the public interest[108]. However, if the prohibition on development adversely affects the implementation of local or central government policy, the Lands Tribunal will be amenable to weighing the competing interests of protecting the benefit that the negative covenant confers on the owners of the dominant land with the wider benefits that would accrue to the local community from a much needed development. Accordingly, in one case, the Lands Tribunal has modified a negative covenant so as to permit a psychiatric care facility to be built in a locality where no such facility previously existed. Without such a facility, central government's 'care in the community policy' could not have been implemented in that locality[109].

12.2.3 Consent

If the owners of the dominant land have agreed expressly or impliedly to a discharge or modification of a negative covenant, the Lands Tribunal has power to make an order giving effect to the agreement.

12.2.4 Non-injurious discharge or modification

The Lands Tribunal has power to discharge or modify a negative covenant if the applicant's proposed development will not cause injury to the owners of the dominant land. The term 'injury' has a broad meaning. Accordingly, if a proposed development does not itself give rise to a loss of amenity, but is likely to fuel similar applications to the Lands Tribunal that, if granted, would have an adverse effect by, for example, undermining the integrity of a scheme of development governing a residential estate, a discharge or modification of the covenant would be injurious.

The Lands Tribunal has shown a tendency to reserve this particular ground for discharging or modifying a negative covenant as a 'longstop against vexatious objections' filed by those entitled to the benefit of the covenant[110].

12.2.5 Conversion of a dwelling house

The County Court has jurisdiction under the *Housing Act* 1985 to entertain an application seeking a variation of a covenant that prohibits the conversion of a dwelling house into two or more flats. The applicant must show that the covenant has the effect of impeding a letting of the dwelling house for residential use.

12.3 New restrictions

If the Lands Tribunal decides, in principle, that a covenantor has established one of the grounds for modifying a negative covenant burdening its servient land, the Lands Tribunal will then go on to consider whether the modification should be conditional on the covenantor accepting new restrictions. Any new restrictions that the Lands Tribunal is minded to impose will be designed to give comfort and protection to the owners of the dominant land.

> Example:
> If, despite objections from adjoining or neighbouring landowners, a covenantor persuades the Lands Tribunal that a negative covenant prohibiting the use of the servient land as a nightclub should be modified, the Lands Tribunal may wish to make the modification conditional on the covenantor accepting opening hours that restrict the operation of a nightclub to, say, 12 midnight on weekdays and 1am on the weekends.

Alternatively, the Lands Tribunal may wish to make the modification of a negative covenant that prohibits any commercial development conditional on the covenantor accepting new restrictions designed to safeguard the privacy and seclusion of neighbouring residential owners. In this scenario, new restrictions might include:

- an obligation to landscape and 'screen' by planting trees;
- an obligation not to build within, say, 150 feet of the boundary line; and
- an obligation not to put up any building of more than two storeys.

12.4 Compensation

If the Lands Tribunal decides to discharge or modify a negative
covenant, it has the power to award the owners of the dominant
land compensation under section 84(1). There are two heads of
compensation, which are mutually exclusive.

- Under the first head, the Lands Tribunal can award the
  owners of the dominant land a sum equal to the loss or
  disadvantage suffered by reason of the discharge or
  modification. Interestingly, there is no prescribed method in
  section 84(1) for assessing 'loss or advantage'[111].
- Under the second head, the Lands Tribunal can award the
  owners of the dominant land a sum equal to the diminution
  in value that the servient land suffered (at the time the
  negative covenant was imposed) by reason of its imposition.

Although theoretically possible, it is hard to comprehend the
Lands Tribunal awarding compensation where the covenantor
establishes that the negative covenant is obsolete, or contrary
to the public interest, or its discharge or modification will not
cause injury, or the owners of the dominant land consent to the
discharge or modification. In practice, therefore, the Lands
Tribunal only makes an award of compensation where the
covenantor establishes that the negative covenant impedes a
reasonable user and it does not secure to the owners of the
dominant land a substantial benefit or advantage. It is
self-evident that any award of compensation will be relatively
modest as it is only intended to recompense the loss of an
'insubstantial' benefit or advantage.

The award of compensation is discretionary and, therefore, the
Lands Tribunal is not obliged to make an award even if a
discharge or modification causes the owners of the dominant
land to suffer loss or injury. However, the exercise of discretion
is not unfettered and, therefore, the Lands Tribunal would need
to have strong reasons for not making an award of
compensation where loss or injury will be suffered. Strong
reasons for denying compensation would exist if, for example, a
relaxation of the negative covenant were to cause loss or
damage that the covenant was not (at the time that it was
imposed) intended to prevent[112]. This situation would arise
where the dominant land has undergone a change in character
since the negative covenant was imposed.

Example:
Dominant land and servient land were both single private dwellings at the time that the negative covenant was imposed. The covenantor is seeking a modification of the covenant so as to enable it to demolish the existing house on the servient land and in its place put up a block of flats. If, in the intervening years, the dominant land has itself been redeveloped for use as a local GP medical centre, it could be argued that the covenant no longer secures for the dominant land the benefit that it was (originally) intended to confer, i.e. the protection of a residential dwelling against loss of amenity.

12.4.1 First head

An award under the first head of compensation is intended to recompense the owners of the dominant land for any 'actual' loss or disadvantage that they suffer in consequence of the discharge or modification. In other words, the loss or disadvantage to be compensated must arise as a direct result of the Lands Tribunal making an order discharging or modifying the negative covenant. Accordingly, an award under this head tends to compensate the owners of the dominant land for loss of amenity. Loss of amenity in this context includes any disturbance that the owners of the dominant land suffer whilst building operations are carried out to the servient land.

Although the making of an order discharging or modifying a negative covenant deprives the owners of the dominant land of their bargaining power to negotiate the payment of a sum of money in return for granting a relaxation of the covenant, this loss of bargaining power is not compensatable[113].

Quantifying loss of amenity is an art and not an exact science. Traditionally, loss of amenity has been quantified by assessing the diminution in the value of the dominant land. However, in recent times, the Lands Tribunal has shown a willingness to take a broader view of loss of amenity so as to bring the compensation payable under section 84(1) more into line with damages awarded for breach of covenant. Accordingly, the Lands Tribunal has been known to award the owners of the dominant land compensation equal to half the 'realisable development value of the servient land', i.e. half the difference in the development value of the servient land with and without the negative covenant[114].

Can negative covenants be discharged or modified against the wishes
of the covenantee?

12.4.2 *Second head*

Conceptually, it is difficult to fathom why the owners of the
dominant land should be paid compensation assessed by
reference to the adverse impact that the negative covenant has
on the value of the servient land. Be that as it may, an award of
compensation under this head tends to be made only where
ownership of the dominant land has not changed during the
intervening years.

13

Can planning covenants and obligations be discharged or modified?

13.1 Post-25 October 1991

Since 25 October 1991, local planning authorities have had the statutory power to impose planning obligations to restrict or regulate the development of land within their area. This statutory power is conferred by section 106 of the *Town and Country Planning Act* 1990. Where a developer seeks planning permission to carry out a significant development, a local authority will often make use of its statutory power by making the grant of planning permission conditional on the developer entering into a 'section 106 agreement'.

If a landowner wishes to apply for a discharge or modification of a positive or negative planning obligation burdening its land imposed by a section 106 agreement, the application must be made to the local planning authority with the statutory power to enforce the obligation. Unless the section 106 agreement states otherwise, an application to the local planning authority cannot be made until five years have elapsed since the making of the section 106 agreement. Where an application is made, the local planning authority, pursuant to section 106A(3), may decide:

- that the planning obligation should continue unmodified;
- that the planning obligation no longer serves a useful purpose and should be discharged; or
- that the planning obligation continues to serve a useful purpose, but would serve that purpose equally well if it was subject to specified modifications and should therefore be modified in accordance with those modifications.

The principal issue to be determined therefore on any application to discharge or modify a planning obligation is the extent to which (if at all) it continues to serve a useful purpose 'in land use planning terms'. If the planning obligation is found by the local planning authority to no longer serve a useful purpose, then the authority must discharge it. If, however, the authority believes that the planning obligation continues to serve a useful purpose, then it must consider whether it would serve that purpose equally well if it were subject to any modifications proposed by the landowner. If so, the authority must give effect to the proposed modifications.

Curiously, section 106A(3) does not appear to give the local planning authority power to modify the planning obligation in terms different to those proposed by the landowner. If the landowner believes that the local planning authority has wrongly decided its application, section 106B gives the landowner a right of appeal to the Secretary of State.

13.2 Pre-25 October 1991

Prior to 25 October 1991, agreements under section 106 contained 'planning covenants' that were enforceable by the local planning authority as if it owned adjoining or neighbouring land. As with planning obligations today, local planning authorities imposed planning covenants to extract some public benefit in return for granting planning permission. Accordingly, planning covenants that obliged a developer to meet the cost of off-site infrastructure were commonly imposed.

The discharge or modification of planning covenants (to the extent that they are negative in nature) fall within the jurisdiction of the Lands Tribunal. To obtain a discharge or modification of a planning covenant, the landowner must:

- establish one of the four grounds set out in section 84(1) of the *Law of Property Act* 1925; and
- persuade the Lands Tribunal that the discretionary power that it has to relax a planning covenant should be exercised.

If a local planning authority decides to object to an application for a discharge or modification of a planning covenant, it will be treated by the Lands Tribunal as acting in the capacity of 'custodian of the public interest'[115].

14

What is the procedure for progressing a claim in the Lands Tribunal?

The Lands Tribunal is the appropriate forum for determining applications under section 84(1) of the *Law of Property Act* 1925 for a discharge or modification of a negative covenant.

14.1   Lands Tribunal Rules

There is one set of rules, known as the *Lands Tribunal Rules* (LTR), which applies to any claim started in the Lands Tribunal. The LTR is supplemented by Practice Directions and the two govern the procedure for progressing an application under section 84(1). Each of the stages in the procedure is explained below (see also flow chart 4 in appendix A). To make the stages easier to follow, a hypothetical application will be used. The applicant will be a successor in title of the covenantor who is seeking to discharge or modify a negative covenant burdening its servient land. The opponents, who are called 'objectors', will be the owners of the dominant land that has the benefit of the negative covenant.

14.2   The stages of the application

14.2.1   Pre-application period

Before an applicant issues an application in the Lands Tribunal it is desirable for the applicant to try and identify who is entitled to object to its application. If the applicant is able to identify who the potential objectors are, it should endeavour to enter into a dialogue with them to see whether they are willing to agree voluntarily to a modification or discharge of the negative covenant and thus obviate the need for litigation.

The applicant should open the dialogue by writing to the potential objectors. The letter to the potential objectors should:

- state the nature of the intended application, i.e. a discharge or modification of the negative covenant;
- state the grounds within section 84(1) for making the intended application, i.e. obsolescence, reasonable user impeded, consent or no injury;
- (in the case of modification) state the actual modification sought;
- (in the case of modification) state the 'replacement' restrictions (if any) that the applicant is willing to accept;
- enclose a copy of the deed creating the negative covenant or, if appropriate, a copy of the official entries to the registered title of the servient land; and
- propose that the parties enter into a deed of release or variation on terms to be negotiated.

If the potential objectors are unwilling to countenance a discharge or a modification of the negative covenant, or, if the applicant is unable to identify who has the benefit of the negative covenant, the applicant will generally have no alternative but to issue an application in the Lands Tribunal.

14.2.2 Starting an application

An application is started by the applicant issuing an application at the Lands Tribunal. There is a prescribed form that the applicant must use (see specimen form 5 in appendix C) and a fee is payable on issuing the application. The application will set out the essential facts, including:

- the particulars of the deed that imposes the negative covenant;
- the location of the servient land burdened by the negative covenant;
- the location of the dominant land that has the benefit of the negative covenant;
- the identities of the persons who enjoy the benefit of the negative covenant (if known);
- the wording of the negative covenant;

- whether a discharge or modification of the negative covenant is sought and, if modification, the proposed wording;
- whether the applicant is willing to accept replacement restrictions and, if so, what those restrictions are; and
- the grounds within section 84(1) upon which the application is made.

Quite often, an applicant will lodge with the Lands Tribunal a bundle of supporting documents at the same time as issuing its application. The bundle will usually include a copy of the deed creating the negative covenant and any planning permission that the applicant has obtained for developing the servient land.

14.2.3 Publicity notice

The next stage is the publication of the application. The Lands Tribunal will send the applicant a publicity notice (a prescribed form) to complete and return for approval (see specimen form 6 in appendix C). The publicity notice, as its name infers, is intended to publicise the application to all persons who enjoy the benefit of the negative covenant and inform them of their right to lodge an objection opposing it. The Lands Tribunal will give directions as to how the publicity notice should be publicised. Where the potential objectors are known, the Lands Tribunal may simply direct that a copy of the publicity notice be sent to each potential objector. However, where there is doubt as to who is entitled to object to the application, the Lands Tribunal can be expected to direct that the publicity notice be advertised in a local newspaper. In every case, it is normal for the Lands Tribunal to direct that the publicity notice be placed in a prominent position on the servient land where it can be seen by passers-by.

The publicity notice will state the period within which objectors must lodge their objections at the Lands Tribunal. Usually, the period will be 28 days from the date that the publicity notice is dispatched through the post to those persons known to be entitled to the benefit of the covenant, or from the date that the publicity notice appears in the local newspaper.

Once the applicant has complied with the directions for publicising the application, it must lodge a certificate to this effect with the Lands Tribunal.

14.2.4 No objections filed

If no objections are filed with the Lands Tribunal in response to the publicity notice, the applicant may ask the Lands Tribunal to determine its application for a discharge or modification of the negative covenant without a hearing. In an ordinary case, the Lands Tribunal will send the applicant a final order granting the discharge or modification sought. A fee is payable on the Lands Tribunal issuing the final order.

The applicant will place the final order with its title deeds (in the case of unregistered land) or register it at the Land Registry (in the case of registered land) against the title to its servient land.

14.2.5 Objections filed

If a person entitled to the benefit of the negative covenant wishes to object to the application for a discharge or modification, it should complete and file with the Lands Tribunal a 'notice of objection'. The notice of objection is a prescribed form (see specimen form 7 in appendix C).

On receipt of a notice of objection, the Lands Tribunal will ask the applicant if it admits that the objector is entitled to the benefit of the negative covenant. If the applicant does admit this, the Lands Tribunal will give directions for taking the application through to trial.

If the applicant disputes that the objector is entitled to the benefit of the negative covenant, the objector will be directed to file copies of the deeds and other documents that it believes prove its entitlement to the benefit of the negative covenant. If, after considering the objector's deeds and documents, the applicant still disputes that the objector is entitled to the benefit of the negative covenant, the Lands Tribunal will fix a preliminary hearing under section 84(3A) to determine the issue. If the Lands Tribunal decides that the objector is not entitled to the benefit of the negative covenant, its notice of objection will be struck out and it will no longer participate in the litigation. If, however, the Lands Tribunal finds in the objector's favour, it will proceed to give directions for taking the application through to trial.

If, at the preliminary hearing, the Lands Tribunal strikes out all the notices of objection that have been filed, so that there are no objectors 'left standing', the applicant may ask the Lands Tribunal to issue a final order (see specimen form 9 in appendix C) granting the relaxation of the negative covenant that it seeks.

Where the issue as to whether an objector enjoys the benefit of a negative covenant is particularly complex so that, in fairness to the parties, it ought to be decided by a judge of the Chancery Division of the High Court, either the objector or the applicant can invite the Lands Tribunal to stay the litigation whilst the issue is referred to the High Court for determination under section 84(2) (see section 9.4).

14.2.6 Directions

The directions that the Lands Tribunal make to bring the application to trial will include a timetable for the exchange of statements of any witnesses of fact and reports of any experts that either party intends to rely on at trial. If either the applicant or the objector fails to comply with the timetable, the other may ask the Lands Tribunal to order compliance.

14.2.7 Witness statements

The applicant and the objectors will each prepare statements for each witness that they intend to call at trial. The statements should set out the evidence that the witnesses will give at trial. It is important that the statements should contain the factual background to the dispute. So, for example, if the applicant is a developer seeking a modification or discharge on the ground that the negative covenant unreasonably impedes a reasonable user of its servient land, it will describe its proposed development and the planning permission which it (presumably) has obtained from the local planning authority. In contrast, the objectors, in their witness statements, may well describe their fears for the neighbourhood and how they believe the proposed development will adversely affect the amenity that they presently enjoy if the Lands Tribunal gives it the 'go-ahead'.

14.2.8 Expert evidence

In any application for a discharge or modification of a negative covenant, it is likely that the parties will wish to adduce expert evidence. That evidence will be aimed at evaluating the practical benefit, if any, that the objectors derive from the negative covenant, and the adverse affect, if any, that they will suffer if the covenant is discharged or modified so as to enable the applicant to implement its proposed development.

The parties can be expected each to instruct a planning consultant and valuer to give expert evidence (see specimen form 8 in appendix C). When evaluating what practical benefit a negative covenant confers, and the extent to which that benefit would be eroded by the proposed development, the planning consultant tends to focus on 'amenity'. In other words, the planning consultant will consider whether the negative covenant protects the objectors from a loss of privacy, or preserves a scenic view, or staves off increases in noise, smells, vibration, traffic flows, etc. If so, the planning consultant will go on to consider whether the protection that the covenant affords will be materially undermined if the proposed development goes ahead. In a complex case, it is not uncommon for a planning consultant's evidence to be supplemented by evidence from an architect, surveyor, traffic and transport consultant, or civil engineer.

Assuming that the planning consultant has been able to identify a loss of amenity, the valuer will give an opinion as to whether this loss of amenity is likely to diminish the value of the objectors' properties, or their marketability, and if so, by how much.

All experts who are instructed to give evidence at trial owe an overriding duty to the Lands Tribunal to offer impartial and objective opinions. The experts will each set out their opinions in a report that will be exchanged in accordance with the directions timetable. Following exchange, experts of like discipline will be encouraged to meet to see if they can agree, or at least narrow, the issues between them that are in dispute.

14.2.9 Listing questionnaires

The Lands Tribunal will send the applicant and the objectors a listing questionnaire to complete. The listing questionnaire asks the parties to indicate their availability dates for a trial, estimate the length of the trial, and state their preferred venue. As the judge may need to carry out a careful inspection of the neighbourhood, it often makes sense for the trial to be held nearby.

Once the parties return the listing questionnaires to the Lands Tribunal, a date for the trial is fixed.

14.2.10 Trial and preparation for trial

Shortly before the date fixed for the trial, the applicant will, in consultation with the objectors, prepare a paginated trial bundle containing all documents that will be used at trial. The parties will also exchange 'skeleton arguments' that will set out in a concise form the issues of fact and law that each party believes the trial judge needs to decide.

The trial will then take place before a single judge; there is no jury. After hearing all the evidence and any legal submissions, and (usually) after carrying out a site inspection, the judge will decide where the merits of the case lie and give judgment accordingly. The judge will also decide the party or parties that should bear the costs of the litigation.

Following judgment, either party may consider an appeal if there is reason to believe that the trial judge misunderstood the law that applies to the application or, alternatively, made a finding of fact that, in all the circumstances, was unreasonable to make. Appealing against a finding of fact can be particularly difficult as the Court of Appeal, to whom any appeal is made, needs a lot of persuading before it will interfere with the judge's assessment of the witnesses and their evidence.

Most claims take 9 to 12 months to come to trial once an application has been issued.

14.2.11 After trial

If the trial judge finds in the applicant's favour, the Lands Tribunal will issue a final order (see specimen form 9 in appendix C) formally discharging or modifying the negative covenant (as the case may be). The applicant will place the final order with its title deeds (in the case of unregistered land) or register it at the Land Registry (in the case of registered land) against the title to its servient land.

14.2.12 Settlement

At every stage in the litigation, the applicant and the objectors should actively consider whether the application can be settled.

What is the procedure for progressing a claim in the Lands Tribunal?

There are various forms of ADR that the parties can use to help promote a settlement. These include:

- mediation, i.e. without prejudice negotiations facilitated by a trained mediator; or
- early case evaluation by an independent person, e.g. a lawyer or other professional who has expertise in handling similar claims.

All forms of ADR have a common theme: they aim to encourage a constructive dialogue between the applicant and the objectors so as to enable them to settle the application. It is important to appreciate that ADR may be used at any time during a dispute. Often, it is most effective before litigation has actually started when the parties' positions may not yet have become entrenched.

15

What are the costs rules in the Lands Tribunal?

15.1 The general rule

Under section 3(5) of the *Lands Tribunal Act* 1949, the Lands Tribunal may order that:

> ' ... the costs of any proceedings before it incurred by any party shall be paid by any other party ... .'

The Lands Tribunal, therefore, has a wide discretion to decide whether any party to the litigation should pay all or any part of the costs that another party to the litigation has incurred. This discretion will usually be exercised in accordance with the principles applied in the High Court and the County Court (see chapter 11).

However, there is one important difference. The general rule that costs usually 'follow the event' does not apply to an application for a discharge or modification of a negative covenant burdening land pursuant to section 84 of the *Law of Property Act* 1925. The nature of an application under section 84 is that the applicant is seeking to have removed from an objector particular property rights that the objector owns. In view of this (and subject to any offer to settle that either the applicant or objector has made), an unsuccessful objector who had the benefit of the negative covenant that has been discharged or modified will not normally have to pay any part of the applicant's costs unless it has acted unreasonably; a successful objector will normally get all its costs paid by the applicant (to be assessed, if not agreed) unless it has in some respect been unreasonable. The costs rules peculiar to section 84 applications are given effect by paragraph 22.4 of the Lands Tribunal Practice Directions dated May 2006.

15.2 Unreasonable conduct

The Lands Tribunal is conscious that an objector may be tempted to make use of the 'protection' that the cost rules peculiar to section 84 applications confer in order to exploit the situation. Accordingly, the Lands Tribunal has made clear that it is willing to order the objector to pay all or part of the applicant's costs where the objector has behaved unreasonably either before or during the litigation. The following are examples of unreasonable conduct that might well warrant an order that the objector pays the applicant's costs.

- The applicant has attempted to resolve the dispute amicably with the objector on several occasions and the modifications to the negative covenant sought are of negligible impact on anyone in the surrounding area.
- The objector does not accept an offer of compensation made by the applicant before the start of the litigation and, at trial, the objector recovers no compensation or significantly less compensation than the sum that the applicant had offered.
- The objector has an agenda not to use the benefit of the negative covenant to safeguard the amenity of the neighbourhood but instead to use its right to enforce the covenant to ransom as much money as possible out of the applicant and others who wish to carry out developments in the area.

Example:
One case that came before the Lands Tribunal in 2007 is particularly worthy of note because of the strong criticism that was directed at the objector who happened to be a solicitor in private practice[116]. Part of the Lands Tribunal's judgment reads as follows:

'The question therefore is whether Mrs Stuart acted unreasonably in pursuing her objection. In light of the correspondence between the parties, I find as a fact that Mrs Stuart's predominant motive in lodging an objection to both applications was the extraction of a large sum of money from the applicants, even though she was scarcely affected by the developments to which the applications related. In each case, she claimed compensation of £50,000 and at no stage before her objections were withdrawn did she put forward any reasoned justification for that figure or anything approaching it, apart from the general reference to the need to preserve the high-class residential nature and ethos of the neighbourhood. In the case of The Lantern House, the offer of £10,000 made by Mr and Mrs Jones was accompanied by an offer to attend a without prejudice meeting with

Mrs Stuart if there was a prospect that the meeting could bridge the gap between the two parties, but no meeting took place because Mrs Stuart declined an invitation to state the sum she required in advance of the meeting. In the case of Merrifield, the only offer by either side was the £50,000 stated in Mrs Stuart's notice of objection and, again, she did not attempt to justify such an exorbitant figure or suggest that a significantly lower figure might be acceptable. These considerations alone would in my view justify an award of costs against Mrs Stuart. In addition, I consider that Mrs Stuart acted unreasonably in using threats that went well beyond fair bargaining ... . In view of what I regard as her unreasonable conduct, I determine that Mrs Stuart must pay the costs of Mr and Mrs Jones and Mr and Mrs Nester, incurred between the date of her objections and the date of their withdrawal.'

Every objector must therefore appreciate that, if its predominant motive in opposing an application for the discharge or modification of a negative covenant is the extraction of a large sum of money, even though it will be scarcely affected by the applicant's proposed development, it will be susceptible to an adverse order as to costs.

15.3 Assessment of costs

Where the Lands Tribunal has decided that one party should pay all or part of another party's costs, and there is a dispute as to the sum that the paying party should pay to the receiving party, the Lands Tribunal will resolve the dispute by carrying out a 'detailed assessment' of the costs to be paid.

16

Is there an alternative to litigation?

16.1 Developer's perspective

Every developer should consider whether there is an alternative to litigation. Pursuing a claim to 'clear off' negative covenants burdening the development site under section 84(2) or, alternatively, to discharge or modify those covenants under section 84(1), is never risk-free, whether done before or after construction work starts.

- Very few claims that come before the court or the Lands Tribunal are clear-cut, and seldom will a developer be advised that its prospects of success are better than 75 per cent.
- Litigation is a process that takes time to complete and most cases tend to take the best part of a year to reach trial.
- The general rule in litigation that 'costs follow the event' does not apply to claims for a discharge or modification of negative covenants.

So, whenever a developer contemplates litigation, it must appreciate that:

- it faces a (not insignificant) risk that the negative covenants may be upheld;
- until trial, it will have 'holding costs' to bear; and
- even if it is successful in the litigation, it may not be able to recover its costs from the owners of the dominant land.

A good lawyer – i.e. one who is focused on the developer's commercial objective of bringing the proposed development to fruition – ought, therefore, to advise the developer to 'buy certainty of outcome' wherever the circumstances permit.

In practice, a developer has two avenues to buying certainty of outcome. First, it can seek to negotiate with the owners of the dominant land. Invariably, the negotiations will involve the developer offering the owners of the dominant land a sum of money in return for the grant of a deed of discharge or modification. Such negotiations can be fraught with difficulties if, which is not unusual, the owners of the dominant land have unrealistic expectations or are a disparate group of individuals who lack an ability to act in unison. Second, the developer can approach an insurer for 'defective title insurance'. Such insurance tends not to be available unless the developer has already applied for and obtained planning permission for its proposed development, and the owners of the dominant land did not make representations to the local planning authority opposing the development. Where defective title insurance is available, the developer is able to insure against the risk of the owners of the dominant land successfully upholding the negative covenants. The developer will usually ask for a level of cover equal to the estimated built out value of the development. Although the premium payable by the developer will reflect the insurer's view of the 'risk', generally speaking, the premium tends to equate to between 0.05 per cent and 0.2 per cent of the estimated built out value of the development. Importantly, the benefit of the insurance can be passed to the future owners of the servient land (i.e. the developer's plot purchasers) and their mortgagees. This enables the developer to convey a 'good and marketable title' against which a bank or building society will be willing to advance a mortgage.

16.2 Objector's perspective

There will be occasions when the owners of the dominant land, faced with the prospect of a development on their doorstep, take the view that it is preferable to enter into negotiations with the developer rather than risk all in trying to enforce the negative covenants that the proposed development will, if implemented, breach. The 'bargaining chip' that the owners of the dominant land have in any negotiations with a developer is the (implicit) threat that, if the negotiations cannot be concluded to their reasonable satisfaction, a claim to enforce the negative covenants will be pursued.

There are two obvious benefits to the owners of the dominant land negotiating with the developer. First, they may be able to influence the developer's plans so as to minimise any loss of amenity that they would otherwise suffer. It may be, for instance, that the developer could be persuaded to re-site a building away from a particular boundary or to carry out landscaping to preserve privacy and seclusion. Second, the owners of the dominant land may be able to secure a sum of money significantly in excess of any sum in compensation that the Lands Tribunal might order the developer to pay them as a condition of granting a discharge or modification of the negative covenants burdening the developer's site.

Appendix A: Flow charts

1 Types of covenants

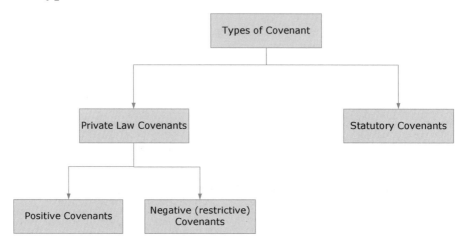

2 Claim for breach of covenant seeking an injunction or damages (see section 10.3 and specimen forms 1–4)

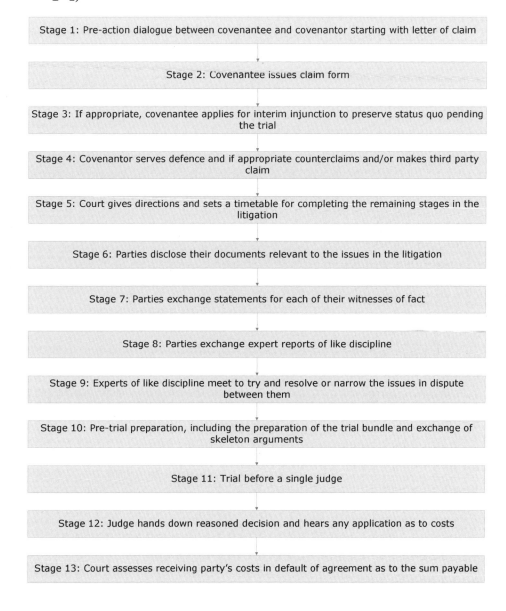

Stage 1: Pre-action dialogue between covenantee and covenantor starting with letter of claim

Stage 2: Covenantee issues claim form

Stage 3: If appropriate, covenantee applies for interim injunction to preserve status quo pending the trial

Stage 4: Covenantor serves defence and if appropriate counterclaims and/or makes third party claim

Stage 5: Court gives directions and sets a timetable for completing the remaining stages in the litigation

Stage 6: Parties disclose their documents relevant to the issues in the litigation

Stage 7: Parties exchange statements for each of their witnesses of fact

Stage 8: Parties exchange expert reports of like discipline

Stage 9: Experts of like discipline meet to try and resolve or narrow the issues in dispute between them

Stage 10: Pre-trial preparation, including the preparation of the trial bundle and exchange of skeleton arguments

Stage 11: Trial before a single judge

Stage 12: Judge hands down reasoned decision and hears any application as to costs

Stage 13: Court assesses receiving party's costs in default of agreement as to the sum payable

3 Claim for a declaration (see section 10.4)

Stage 1: Covenantor issues claim form

Stage 2: Covenantor publicises its claim form to persons who (potentially) enjoy the benefit of the covenant binding the covenantor's servient land

Stage 3: Any person who wishes to oppose the claim serves a defence and becomes a party to the litigation

Stage 4: Court gives directions and sets a timetable for completing the remaining stages in the litigation

Stage 5: Parties disclose their documents relevant to the issues in the litigation

Stage 6: Pre-trial preparation, including the preparation of the trial bundle and exchange of skeleton arguments

Stage 7: Trial before a single judge

Stage 8: Judge hands down reasoned decision and hears any application as to costs

Stage 9: Court assesses receiving party's costs in default of agreement as to the sum payable

Stage 10: If covenantor is successful, the declaration issued by the Court is lodged with the Land Registry or placed with the covenantor's title deeds

4 Claim for a discharge and/or modification of a negative covenant (see section 14.2 and specimen forms 5–9)

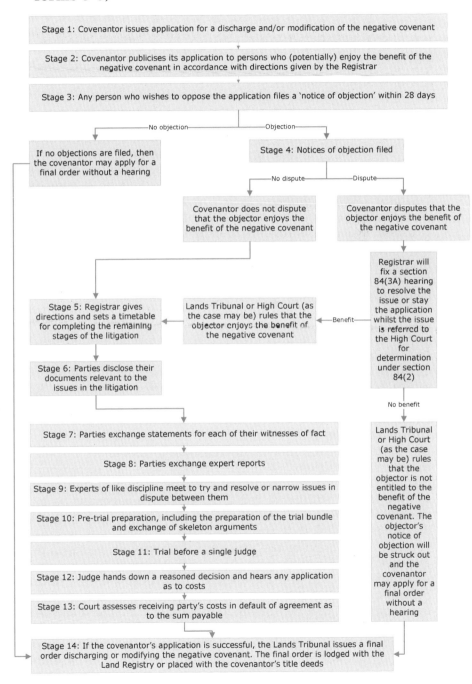

Stage 1: Covenantor issues application for a discharge and/or modification of the negative covenant

Stage 2: Covenantor publicises its application to persons who (potentially) enjoy the benefit of the negative covenant in accordance with directions given by the Registrar

Stage 3: Any person who wishes to oppose the application files a 'notice of objection' within 28 days

No objection — Objection

If no objections are filed, then the covenantor may apply for a final order without a hearing

Stage 4: Notices of objection filed

No dispute — Dispute

Covenantor does not dispute that the objector enjoys the benefit of the negative covenant

Covenantor disputes that the objector enjoys the benefit of the negative covenant

Registrar will fix a section 84(3A) hearing to resolve the issue or stay the application whilst the issue is referred to the High Court for determination under section 84(2)

Stage 5: Registrar gives directions and sets a timetable for completing the remaining stages of the litigation

Lands Tribunal or High Court (as the case may be) rules that the objector enjoys the benefit of the negative covenant

— Benefit —

No benefit

Stage 6: Parties disclose their documents relevant to the issues in the litigation

Stage 7: Parties exchange statements for each of their witnesses of fact

Stage 8: Parties exchange expert reports

Stage 9: Experts of like discipline meet to try and resolve or narrow issues in dispute between them

Stage 10: Pre-trial preparation, including the preparation of the trial bundle and exchange of skeleton arguments

Stage 11: Trial before a single judge

Stage 12: Judge hands down a reasoned decision and hears any application as to costs

Stage 13: Court assesses receiving party's costs in default of agreement as to the sum payable

Lands Tribunal or High Court (as the case may be) rules that the objector is not entitled to the benefit of the negative covenant. The objector's notice of objection will be struck out and the covenantor may apply for a final order without a hearing

Stage 14: If the covenantor's application is successful, the Lands Tribunal issues a final order discharging or modifying the negative covenant. The final order is lodged with the Land Registry or placed with the covenantor's title deeds

Appendix B: Case summaries

Amec Developments Ltd v Jury's Hotel Management (UK) Ltd (2001)

Facts

The Defendant was the owner of land (the servient land) burdened by a negative covenant imposed in 1989 in favour of the Claimant's adjoining land (the dominant land). The covenant stated that no buildings were to be constructed on the servient land in front of a line marked A–B on a plan (the building line). During 1998 and 1999, the Defendant constructed a hotel on the servient land, which, due to its cavalier attitude, extended four metres beyond the building line. Although the Claimant conceded that the Defendant's breach of covenant had not caused a diminution in the value of the dominant land, or otherwise adversely affected it, the Claimant nevertheless pursued a claim for damages.

Decision

In assessing the amount of damages to be awarded to the Claimant, the Court had to ascertain the sum of money that might reasonably have been demanded by the Claimant from the Defendant as a quid pro quo for permitting the encroachment. This necessitated considering objectively the sum that would have been arrived at in negotiations between the parties, if each had made reasonable use of its respective bargaining positions, without holding out for unreasonable amounts. It should be assumed that, in their negotiations, the Claimant was willing to relax the negative covenant so as to permit the Defendant to construct the hotel, but only at a proper price; and that the Defendant, in turn, was willing to obtain a relaxation of the covenant, but only at a proper price and not for a large ransom. Moreover, the negotiations would have proceeded in the knowledge that there was an obvious benefit to the Defendant in constructing the hotel beyond the building line and no (obvious) detriment to the Claimant's dominant land. Further, the parties should be taken to have concluded their negotiations before the Defendant started construction works. The value of the benefit to the Defendant would not have been readily apparent. Assessing the value to the Defendant of constructing its hotel beyond the building line was a complex task, necessitating an assessment of:

(i)   what size and design of hotel would have been possible and likely if it had been constructed within the building line; and

(ii)   the value of the extra benefit gained by building beyond the line.

The Court could take into account the various uncertainties that would be present in a negotiation centring on those factors; but also the actual events that had happened, and the actual benefits which had accrued as at the date of the trial.

The hotel as built had 265 rooms. If it had been constructed within the building line, it would have had between 240 and 260 rooms; exactly how many was not clear to the Court, and would not have been to the negotiating parties. The Defendant's gain was the additional profit available from operating up to 25 extra rooms, taking into account the extra costs of constructing and operating them, and capitalised appropriately. In their negotiations, the parties would have had genuine differences as to discount factors and yields. Whilst the additional area of land and building was significant (4 metres wide, and 11 per cent of the whole), the fact that the Defendant had paid £2.65m for the servient land put a common sense limit on the amount it would have been prepared to pay for the right to construct its hotel beyond the building line. In the final analysis, the sum which the Court thought would have been negotiated by the parties must feel right. On that basis, damages were assessed at £375,000.

Amsprop Trading Ltd v Harris Distribution Ltd (1997)

Facts

In 1975, USF Nominees Ltd (USF) granted G. J. Keddie & Sons (Keddie) a lease of a warehouse at Josselin Road, Basildon, Essex for 99 years from 1973. In 1987, USF sold its freehold reversion to Amsprop Ltd (Amsprop). On 21 December 1987, Keddie granted an underlease of the premises to the First Defendant, Harris Distribution Ltd (Harris). In the underlease, Harris covenanted with the landlord (which was defined to mean Keddie and its successors in title and assigns):

(i)   to keep the premises in repair and to deliver them up at the end of the term in good repair;

(ii)   to permit the superior landlord and the landlord to enter the premises in order to view the state of repair; and

(iii)   to remedy any disrepair within three months of being given notice thereof, and, in the event of the superior landlord or the landlord carrying out such works on its failing to do so, to pay their costs and expenses.

On 2 February 1993, Harris assigned the underlease to TDG Ltd (TDG), and on 7 May 1993, Amsprop Trading Ltd (ATL) purchased the freehold reversion from Amsprop Ltd. In February 1996, ATL served notice on TDG requiring it to carry out certain repairs within three months of service of that notice. However, one month later TDG vacated the premises and surrendered the underlease and soon afterwards ATL forfeited the head lease. Subsequently, ATL commenced proceedings against Harris and TDG seeking a declaration that they were liable to pay ATL the costs of remedying any disrepair in the premises, or alternatively, damages. A preliminary issue was ordered to be tried as to whether ATL was entitled to enforce the covenants directly against Harris and TDG. ATL contended that it was, on the ground that Amsprop could have done so by virtue of section 56(1) of the *Law of Property Act* 1925 since covenants (ii) and (iii) had been imposed for Amsprop's benefit and the right to enforce the covenants passed to ATL when ATL purchased the freehold reversion.

Decision

A non-party to a deed that imposed a covenant could only rely on section 56 to enforce the covenant if the covenant purported to be made with him; it was not enough for the non-party merely to show that the covenant was made for his benefit. The covenants contained in the underlease were made with Keddie and its successors in title and assigns – an expression which did not include Keddie's landlord, Amsprop Ltd. Accordingly, although covenants (ii) and (iii) expressly referred to the superior landlord, it would not have been open to Amsprop Ltd to enforce the covenants contained in the underlease directly against Harris or TDG. It followed that ATL could not do so either and the claim would therefore be dismissed.

Baxter v Four Oaks Properties (1965)

Facts

In 1891, Lord Clanrikarde owned an estate of some 288 acres at Sutton Coldfield known as the Four Oaks Estate (the estate). Over a period of ten years between 1891 and 1899, Lord Clanrikarde sold off the whole of the estate for development in plots of various sizes. The first plot to be sold off (plot 1) comprised part of the estate fronting Lichfield Road and Four Oaks Road. The purchaser of plot 1 was Samuel Hope. On 27 April 1891, Hope entered into a deed (the deed) with Lord Clanrikarde and 'all other persons whose names were or might thereafter be entered in the second column of the second schedule thereto' – who were intended to be purchasers of other plots. It was stated in the deed that:

(i)   Hope had covenanted in the conveyance to him to perform and observe the covenants in schedule 1 to the deed;

(ii)   subsequent purchasers of plots should give similar covenants; and

(iii)   all purchasers of plots, their heirs and assigns and all persons claiming under them should be entitled to take action to restrain any breach of covenant.

Schedule 1 to the deed contained the following negative covenant: 'No dwelling house or other building shall be used ... otherwise than as a private residence ... .'

There was no evidence that when Lord Clanrikarde sold off plot 1 to Hope, he had laid out the remaining part of the estate that fronted Lichfield Road and Four Oaks Road into plots. However, all the conveyances of plots contained covenants in substantially the same terms as those contained in the conveyance to Hope. The five Claimants were owners and occupiers of four houses in Lichfield Road. In October 1963, the Defendant bought a plot that had originally been sold off by Lord Clanrikarde on 14 December 1894. The Defendant had notice of the existence of the negative covenants when it bought. It was advised that the covenants did not preclude the erection of residential flats. It demolished the house on its plot and built in its place a three-storey building comprising nine self-contained flats. There was no covenant expressly prohibiting flats. The first and second Claimants derived title from persons to whom Lord Clanrikarde had sold plots before 14 December 1894. The third, fourth and fifth Claimants derived title from persons who bought plots from Lord Clanrikarde after 14 December 1894. The occupants of several flats were able to see into the first Claimant's garden. The Claimants brought a claim to enforce the covenants, seeking:

(i)   a declaration that the Defendant was bound by a scheme of development;

(ii) an injunction to stop the Defendant using its three-storey building as flats, or

(iii) damages in lieu of an injunction.

By the date of the trial, the first Claimant had contracted to sell off her house and the fourth and fifth Claimants had conceded that the three-storey building was too far from their houses for them to suffer a measurable loss.

Decision

As the execution of the deed was direct evidence that Lord Clanrikarde and the purchasers of plots from him intended a scheme of development, the Court was not precluded from giving effect to that intention by the fact that Lord Clanrikarde had not laid out all the land fronting Lichfield Road and Four Oaks Road into plots before starting to sell it off. A scheme of development had been created and the covenants it imposed were enforceable not only by those Claimants whose plots had been sold off by Lord Clanrikarde after 14 December 1894 but also by those Claimants whose plots had been sold off before that date.

An injunction would not be granted in the circumstances, but damages in lieu of an injunction would be awarded to the first, second and third Claimants. The fourth and fifth Claimants would be adequately safeguarded by a declaration to the effect that a scheme of development existed and the Defendant's use of its three-storey building as flats was a breach of covenant.

Bedwell Park Quarry Co v Hertfordshire County Council (1993)

Facts

Bedwell Park Quarry Company (Bedwell) and its local planning authority, Hertfordshire County Council (the Council), entered into an agreement pursuant to section 52 of the *Town and Country Planning Act* 1971 and section 33 of the *Local Government (Miscellaneous Provisions) Act* 1982. The agreement related to a quarry where Bedwell wished to extract chalk. Under the agreement, Bedwell covenanted, inter alia, to restore the quarry for agricultural use once extraction was complete. After the chalk had been extracted, Bedwell applied to the Lands Tribunal under section 84(1) of the *Law of Property Act* 1925 to modify the covenant so as to permit it to postpone the necessary restoration works. There was a dispute as to whether the Lands Tribunal could hear the application as its jurisdiction is limited to the discharge or modification of 'negative' covenants, and Bedwell's covenant to restore the quarry for agricultural use seemed 'positive' in nature.

Decision

In determining whether a covenant was positive or negative in nature, the substance rather than the wording of the covenant needed to be examined. On a plain reading of the covenant, it involved positive and extensive acts and duties, namely 'infilling and restoration of the quarry to agriculture' within a given time limit. The argument that the covenant was negative because it obliged Bedwell not to carry out its quarrying operations in such a way so as to prevent restoration by the specified date, had to be rejected. It was hard to think of a covenant which was more positive in substance as well as in form.

Berton v Alliance Economic Investment Co Ltd (1922)

Facts

Alliance Economic Investment Company Ltd (AEI) was the assignee of a lease dated 31 December 1907 of premises known as Tollgate House, College Road, Dulwich (the premises) which included a dwelling house and offices. The lease was for a term of eighty years from 25 March 1907. The lease contained the following two covenants on the part of the tenant:

(i) 'not without the landlord's previous licence in writing use the premises or any part thereof or permit the same to be used for any purpose whatsoever other than for the purpose of a private dwelling house wherein no business of any kind is carried on'; and

(ii) 'not without the landlord's previous licence in writing ... do or suffer to be done in or on the demised premises anything which may in the judgment of the lessors be or grow to the injury or annoyance of the lessors or any of their tenants or of any of the occupiers of any contiguous or adjoining premises or of the public or neighbourhood'.

AEI granted an underlease of the premises to MacIntosh for a term of seven years from 29 September 1919. In the underlease, Macintosh covenanted:

(i)   'not to do or permit to be done any act or thing upon the premises which may be or grow to the annoyance nuisance damage or disturbance of [AEI] or of the adjoining occupiers … ';

(ii)   not without the consent of AEI 'to … assign underlet or part with the possession of the premises or any part thereof but such consent shall not be unreasonably withheld if a respectable and responsible person be proposed as assignee or under lessee and such person enters into a covenant with [AEI] to pay the rent and observe and perform the covenants on the lessee's part herein contained'; and

(iii)   'not without [AEI's] consent to put up in upon or in front of the premises any bill or the like for the letting of lodgings or any notification of any trade business or profession but to use the said premises as a private dwelling house only'.

Without the consent of AEI, Macintosh sub-underlet various parts of the premises on weekly tenancies. AEI brought an action for possession against Macintosh and obtained judgment against him. However, AEI did not take proceedings against the persons who had been permitted by Macintosh to occupy parts of the premises on weekly tenancies, nor did AEI take any steps to evict them. Instead, they advised the occupants to apply to the superior landlord, Arthur Berton, for permission to remain in occupation and to take legal advice as to their rights. AEI so agreed with the occupants that their rent should be paid into a joint account in the names of one of the occupants and AEI's solicitor. AEI wrote to Berton stating that if the occupants were not permitted to remain at the premises, an application to the court will be made pursuant to section 27 of the *Housing, Town Planning, etc. Act* 1919, for permission to convert the premises for multiple occupation. AEI also wrote to the occupants informing them that Berton was threatening proceedings for vacant possession. Berton brought an action against AEI for a forfeiture of the lease dated 31 December 1907 for breach of covenant. Berton claimed that, in 'permitting' the premises to be used otherwise than as a private dwelling house and for 'suffering' to be done an act that caused him annoyance, AEI was in breach of covenant.

Decision

The covenants in the lease dated 31 December 1907 not to 'permit' an unauthorised use of the premises and not to 'suffer' unauthorised acts only obliged AEI to take reasonable steps to ensure that the premises were used in accordance with the covenants. AEI had not failed to take reasonable steps to ensure compliance with the covenants merely by refraining from taking proceedings to evict the occupants. In showing sympathy to the occupants, AEI was not breaching the covenants, and Berton's claim for forfeiture would be dismissed.

Brown v Heathlands Mental Health NHS Trust (1996)

Facts

The Defendant was a National Health Service trust established under section 5 of the *National Health Service and Community Care Act* 1990. It had responsibility for those suffering from mental health disability within its catchment area. The Defendant purchased a residential property (the servient land) which it proposed to use for the purpose of housing five adult patients. The servient land was burdened by a negative covenant imposed by a conveyance dated 25 October 1909 that stated:

> 'that no building to be erected ... shall be used otherwise than as a private dwelling house only or as a professional residence of a Medical Practitioner Dentist Solicitor or Architect'.

The Claimants were the owners of adjoining properties that had the benefit of the negative covenant burdening the servient land. The Claimants applied for an injunction to restrain the Defendant from using the servient land in any way other than as a private dwelling house. The Defendant conceded for the purposes of the application that it was bound by the covenant in equity but, nevertheless, contended that the Claimants were not entitled to an injunction or damages in lieu.

Decision

Where (as here) Parliament had:
(i)   entrusted a statutory body with functions to be discharged in the public interest;
(ii)   given that body power to acquire and hold land for the purpose of discharging that function; and

(iii) made provision for statutory compensation to be paid to those affected;

private rights such as negative covenants could not be enforced by injunction or damages as they could not be permitted to frustrate the statutory purpose for which the servient land had been acquired. Furthermore, the compensation payable to the Claimants extended to the adverse affect that resulted from the use of the servient land for the purpose for which it was acquired; and not merely to the adverse affect resulting from the building works necessary to adapt the servient land for its intended purpose.

Brunner v Greenslade (1971)

Facts

By a conveyance dated 5 September 1928, a residential builder bought a half-acre plot (the blue land), which formed part of the Bromley Palace Estate in Kent, for development. The builder intended to divide the blue land into subplots. In the 1928 conveyance, the builder covenanted with the Seller by way of indemnity to observe a covenant given by the Seller in an earlier conveyance that restricted the number of houses to be built on the blue land. The covenant in this earlier conveyance was expressed to be made 'to the intent that' it might enure for the benefit of owners of the land capable of deriving benefit from it. The builder also entered into a direct covenant with the Seller that no more than one house would be erected on each intended subplot. The covenant was expressed to be 'for the benefit and protection of' the Seller's estate and every part of it. The Seller reserved the right to alter the plotting or general scheme of development within its retained estate.

The builder divided the blue land into five subplots, built a house on each, and sold them off. The Claimant purchased one of the subplots subject to the negative covenant imposed by the 1928 conveyance, and he covenanted with the builder, by way of indemnity, to observe the covenant. The owner of a corner subplot adjoining the Claimant's subplot sold part of her garden to the Defendant who proposed to build a house there. The Claimant sought an interim injunction to restrain the Defendant from building the house. Although the Defendant admitted that he was subject to the burden of the negative covenant, he disputed that the Claimant had the benefit of the covenant.

Decision

Where a plot was bound by a scheme of development and had been divided into subplots, there would be a presumption that the negative covenants imposed by the scheme would be mutually enforceable by the buyers of each subplot, even though they had not covenanted to that effect. A scheme of development gave rise to an equity independent of contract requiring effect to be given to the original common intention that the covenants of the scheme should be observed.

There was sufficient evidence before the Court from which to infer that the blue land was part of an area covered by a scheme of development and, therefore, the purchasers of subplots from the builder were all bound inter se (amongst themselves) to observe the negative covenants imposed by the scheme. As the Claimant had established a prima facie case that he was entitled to enforce the negative covenants, and had satisfied the Court that the Defendant, unless restrained, was intending to breach the covenants, the interim injunction sought to restrain the Defendant from building the house would be granted.

C&G Homes Ltd v Secretary of State for Health (1991)

Facts

A district health authority, on behalf of the Secretary of State for Health, purchased two adjoining houses (the houses) on the Claimant's newly built residential estate. The district health authority intended to use the houses to provide supervised accommodation for a small number of former hospital patients (the residents) who had suffered from mental disability and who were to be returned to the community under the 'care in the community' policy.

The Secretary of State's purchase of the houses was subject to several negative covenants that restricted their use. The covenants were as follows:
(i)   not to cause or permit or suffer to be done in or on the property any act which might become 'a nuisance, annoyance, danger or detriment' to the Claimant or owners or occupiers for the time being of other parts of the estate; and
(ii)   not at any time within ten years of the date of transfer to carry on at or from the property any trade or business

and not to use the dwelling house 'for any ... purposes other than those incidental to the enjoyment of a private dwelling house'.

The residents were to be encouraged to treat the houses as their permanent home and were given, so far as practicable, responsibility for domestic duties and the right to determine the composition of their group. The Secretary of State, however, was to remain responsible for their care. In particular, he would make provision for a patient services manager and the attendance of staff during the day and at night. Further, the Secretary of State also would retain the power to terminate a resident's licence to occupy. The residents were not to be required to make any payment for their board and lodging since they were technically under NHS care and the district health authority was to make full financial provision for the running expenses of the houses.

When the Claimant became aware of the proposed use of the houses, it brought a claim against the Secretary of State for a declaration that the proposed use would breach the negative covenants burdening the houses. In particular, the intended use was not use as a 'private dwelling house' and that it would cause the Claimant to suffer a 'detriment' by adversely affecting the marketability of the other houses on the estate.

Decision

It was doubtful whether the Secretary of State was proposing to carry on a business on or from the houses. The small number of intended residents, the likely permanence of their occupation, the relationship between the residents and the absence of any payment for their board and lodging suggested that the 'arrangement' was not a business of a lodging house. However, the Secretary of State was proposing to use the houses for a purpose or purposes other than those of a private dwelling house. The expression 'use as or for the purposes of a private dwelling house' seemed to assume that there was at least one private individual who, whenever he chose, could occupy the house as his own, even though he might not be in actual occupation. In the present case, however much emphasis was placed on the residents' ability to treat the accommodation as their permanent home, or of the advanced degree of autonomy that was given to them in the running of it, this could not obscure the continuing responsibility of the Secretary of State for their care or the incidental powers vested in him – in particular, the power to determine a resident's licence to occupy

– and his responsibility to provide supervision and support for the residents. Moreover, with the responsibility being one of a minister of the Crown, the houses would, in that sense, be used for public and not for private purposes. A declaration would therefore be made to the effect that the proposed use would breach the negative covenant not to use the houses for any purpose other than a private dwelling house.

Further, there had been no breach of the negative covenant not to cause a nuisance, annoyance, danger or detriment. The wording of the covenant did not impose any restriction on the persons who might occupy the house but only restricted the acts or things the occupants might do. This accorded with the construction that most conveyancers would put on a covenant in this form. Again, the only detriment that could fall within the ambit of the covenant was one that affected the enjoyment of some part or parts of the estate. Any financial loss that the Claimant would suffer in seeking to exploit its retained land, but dissociated from the enjoyment of it, fell outside the covenant.

Cadogan v Royal Brompton Hospital NHS Trust (1996)

Facts

By a conveyance dated 24 December 1912, a plot of land (the servient land) was given by the Claimant's predecessor in title to the trustees of the Chelsea Hospital for Women. The 1912 conveyance imposed the following negative covenants on the servient land:
(i)   that the servient land could be used only for the purposes of the Chelsea Hospital for Women; and
(ii)   that the plans for the erection of any building had to be submitted to the surveyor to the Cadogan Estate.

The servient land passed into the ownership of the Defendant NHS Trust and the Claimant sought a declaration that the negative covenants imposed by the 1912 conveyance were enforceable against the Defendant.

Decision

The Defendant was a body created by statute and, as covenant (i) was contrary to that statutory intention, it was unenforceable. The Claimant had a right, however, to compensation under section 10 of the *Compulsory Purchase Act 1965*. Further, covenant (ii) could be enforced against the NHS

Trust to prevent the erection of a building without plans first being submitted. But covenant (ii) might not be sufficient to restrain the Defendant from constructing a building for a statutory purpose.

Chambers v Randall (1923)

Facts

In 1882, John Bullbrook purchased a large piece of land at Chatham. On part of this piece of land he built Cambridge Terrace, which was a cul-de-sac comprising 11 houses. Later, by a conveyance dated 15 March 1884, Bullbrook sold to Humphrey Wood a strip of land lying on the west side of Cambridge Terrace (the strip). The strip was immediately opposite numbers 8, 9 and 10 Cambridge Terrace. The conveyance dated 15 March 1884, contained negative covenants in the following terms:

> 'The said Humphrey Wood for himself his heirs executors and assigns hereby covenants with the said John Bullbrook his heirs executors and administrators that no dwelling house to be erected on the said piece of land hereby conveyed shall be used as a shop and every such dwelling house shall be of not less value than £300 ... and shall not nor will carry on or permit to be carried on in or upon the said piece of land or any messuage or other building to be erected thereon any trade or business of a noisome or offensive nature and will not do or permit to be done on the said premises any act matter or thing which may be or become a nuisance to the tenants or prejudicial to the value of the houses belonging to the said John Bullbrook in Cambridge Terrace adjacent to the said premises and that except and until the said piece of land is built upon either as hereinbefore provided for or by the erection thereon of a greenhouse the same shall be used as and for garden purposes only.'

By a deed of settlement dated 16 March 1889, Bullbrook conveyed numbers 8, 9 and 10 Cambridge Terrace to the Claimant upon trusts for the benefit of his son, his son's wife and their children. Bullbrook died on 28 November 1898, and by his will, he appointed the Claimant to be his executor. Before the date of his death, Bullbrook had parted with all his houses in Cambridge Terrace. Wood died too and by his will dated 11

December 1903, he left the strip to Harry Roberts who subsequently conveyed it in 1914 to the Defendant with notice of the covenant in the conveyance of 15 March 1884. In May 1922, the Defendant began to build four private lock-up motor garages on the strip. The Claimant issued a claim for an injunction to restrain the Defendant from breaching the covenant contained in the conveyance of 15 March 1884.

Decision

Where a negative covenant has been entered into by a purchaser of land (as covenantor) for the protection of the seller's retained land, but not so as to annex the benefit of the covenant to that retained land, the covenant could not be enforced by the seller (as covenantee) against the covenantor's assignee after he had parted with all his interest in the retained land. If Bullbrook, therefore, could not whilst he was alive enforce the covenant against the Defendant because he had parted with all his interest in the retained land, the Claimant, as Bullbrook's executor, was in no better position to do so. It made no difference that the Claimant was a person upon whom Bullbrook had, prior to his death, settled part of the retained land, as there had been no express assignment to him of the benefit of the covenant imposed by the conveyance of 15 March 1884.

Commercial General Administration v Thomsett (1979)

Facts

Sally Thomsett, a well known actress, had a tenancy of a flat. Her tenancy contained a covenant that she was:

> 'not to do or permit to be done on the premises anything which may be or become a nuisance or annoyance or be injurious or detrimental to the reputation of the premises.'

An overzealous fan caused annoyance to adjoining occupiers. He telephoned, rang the entry phone and shouted. Further, Thomsett held rowdy parties and gave interviews to newspapers, which the landlord thought 'lowered the tone' of the premises. The landlord decided to bring proceedings for possession.

Decision

The word 'permit' means:

'to give leave for an act which without that leave could not be legally done, or to abstain from taking reasonable steps to prevent the act where it is within a man's power to prevent it.'

Thomsett had installed an answerphone, disabled the entry phone, called the police to remove unwelcome partygoers and conducted interviews off the premises. There was no basis for suggesting that she was in breach of covenant and the claim for possession would be dismissed.

Crest Nicholson Residential (South) Ltd v McAllister (2004)

Facts

The Claimant had a conditional contract to purchase several residential properties at Claygate Common, Surrey (the blue land), which it proposed to redevelop. The Defendant owned an adjoining property (the red land). The blue land and the red land originally had been in common ownership of two brothers, Percy and Charles Mitchell, and their company, Mitchell Brothers (Builders) Ltd, but, between 1926 and 1936, they sold it off in seven plots. The red land formed part of the plot that the brothers had sold to Richard Wing by a conveyance dated 27 May 1936. The conveyance of each of the seven plots contained negative covenants including a restriction on building unless plans were approved by the brothers, and a user restriction limiting use to that of 'a private dwelling house'. The brothers had died by 1949 and their company had been dissolved in 1968. It was common ground that, as the Defendant derived her title from the conveyance dated 27 May 1936, she could not claim an entitlement to the benefit of covenants imposed by it. She claimed, however, to be entitled to enforce the negative covenants contained in the other six conveyances so as to prevent the Claimant's proposed redevelopment. In three of the six conveyances, the benefit of the covenants was expressly annexed to the 'property at Claygate belonging to the Vendors or the part thereof for the time being remaining unsold'. In the other conveyances, there were no express words annexing the benefit of the negative covenants. Two of these latter conveyances described the land conveyed as being on the Fee Farm Estate but no plans or descriptions indicating the extent of the estate accompanied them. The Claimant argued that, on a true construction of the six conveyances and having regard to section 78 of the *Law of Property Act* 1925, the negative covenants ceased to be annexed to any land belonging to the brothers or their company after it was sold off. This included the red land following the sale to Richard Wing on 27 May 1936.

Decision

A necessary condition for annexation is that the land which is intended to be benefited by a negative covenant must be so defined as to be easily ascertainable. Further, the provisions of section 78 could be excluded if an intention to that effect was manifested in the deed imposing the negative covenant. Applying these two principles, none of the negative covenants imposed by the six conveyances benefited the red land owned by the Defendant and, as such, she was not entitled to seek to enforce them. The six conveyances lacked either the express words necessary to annex the covenants to the land owned by the brothers and their company after it was sold off in plots, or a sufficient description of the land to be benefited by the covenants so as to make that land ascertainable.

Cryer v Scott Brothers (Sunbury) Ltd (1988)

Facts

By a transfer dated 29 September 1955 (the 1955 transfer), Ernest Scott, the owner of the Benwell Meadow Estate, Sunbury, Middlesex, transferred a part of his estate (the servient land) to Scott Bros (Sunbury) Ltd (the Company). In the transfer, the Company entered into covenants with Scott for the benefit of the remainder of Scott's unsold estate. One of these covenants (the building covenant) obliged the Company to submit to Scott for his approval all building or other plans before starting building operations. On 27 August 1956, the Company sold a house, 22 Pine Wood, which had been built on the servient land, to Cryer. The covenants imposed by the 1955 transfer, including the building covenant, were entered in the Charges Register of the registered title to 22 Pine Wood. On 14 October 1958, the Company took a transfer (the 1958 transfer) of the remainder of Scott's estate (the dominant land). Thus, the Company who was the original covenantor under the 1955 transfer became entitled, by virtue of the 1958 transfer, to the benefit of the covenants imposed by the 1955 transfer.

On 8 February 1982, Cryer wrote to the Company informing it that he wished to build an extra bedroom over his garage. The Company replied refusing to grant approval for the extension.

Cryer issued proceedings for a declaration that the Company's approval was not needed under the building covenant as the covenant only applied to the original construction of a house and did not apply to an extension of an existing house. Cryer also argued that if he was bound by the building covenant there was an implied term that the Company would not withhold its approval unreasonably. Cryer also contended that the Company did not own sufficient 'dominant' land and, the dominant land that it did own was incapable of benefiting from the building covenant.

Decision

On a true construction of the building covenant, the words 'building work', that necessitated the submission of plans for approval before building operations started, applied not only to the erection of a dwelling house, but also applied to later extensions to the structure of a dwelling house. The ordinary and natural meaning of the words was wide enough to cover extensions, and there was nothing in the 1955 transfer that warranted giving them a narrower meaning. The parties to the 1955 transfer cannot have intended that the covenantee should have control over the initial building of a dwelling house but should have no control over later extensions.

A term could be implied into a covenant obliging a covenantee not to withhold approval unreasonably where the covenantee's approval was needed before building operations could be started if, in accordance with the ordinary principles of the law of contract, such a term was necessary in order to give business efficacy to the contract. The intentions of the parties to the 1955 transfer were that the land would be developed by the Company. A covenant that enabled the covenantee to refuse approval arbitrarily and capriciously would be liable to defeat the purpose of the transfer. Accordingly, to give business efficacy to the building covenant, it was necessary to imply a term that the covenantee would not unreasonably withhold its approval to plans that have been submitted.

To enjoy the benefit of the building covenant the Company's dominant land had to be affected by its performance or breach. The onus was on Cryer, as covenantor, to establish that the dominant land that the Company owned could not reasonably be affected by a breach of the building covenant. It was necessary to consider not only the particular building operations that Cryer wished to undertake, but also whether the Company obtained any benefit in obliging Cryer to submit plans before any building operations could be started. Cryer had failed to produce any evidence to support his contention that the Company's dominant land would not be affected by a breach of the building covenant. The contention must, therefore, be rejected. Where a negative covenant was negotiated by parties and expressed to be for the benefit of an estate, the covenant should be upheld so long as the owner of the dominant land might reasonably take the view that the covenant remained of value.

In deciding whether approval could reasonably be refused for the proposed extension, the criteria to be applied was whether or not the extension would be detrimental or injurious to the dominant land that benefited from the building covenant. The Company was only entitled, therefore, to consider the effect of the extension on its dominant land. The evidence indicated that the Company had not acted solely on this criterion, but had taken into consideration whether or not Cryer's proposed extension would be desirable in the interests of the estate as a whole. Of particular concern to the Company had been the fact that if the extension was approved, a precedent would be set that might encourage applications from other owners of dwelling houses built on the servient land to the detriment of the estate as a whole. There was no evidence that the extension of 22 Pine Wood by the construction of an extra bedroom would affect the dominant land owned by the Company. The extension would not be visible from the Company's dominant land, nor would the value of the Company's dominant land be adversely affected. If Cryer's plans were approved, this would not make it more difficult for the Company to turn down other applications for approval. The Company could only consider the effect of any proposed building operations on the dominant land that it owned; it was not entitled to consider the effect that those building operations would have on the estate as a whole.

Cryer would be granted a declaration to the effect that the Company had acted in breach of the building covenant by unreasonably withholding its approval to the plans that he had submitted.

Elliott v Safeway Stores plc (1995)

Facts

In 1957, the first three Claimants sold a parcel of land in Bideford, Devonshire (the servient land) to a local authority.

The conveyance contained, for the benefit of land retained by those Claimants (the dominant land), a negative covenant, duly registered as a land charge, that the local authority and its successors in title would not at any time carry on or permit to be carried on upon the servient land any business comprising the sale and purchase of fuel and lubricants for mechanically propelled vehicles.

In March 1965, the local authority sold the servient land to a company which subsequently sold off a small triangular piece to the owners of adjoining land. Part of that adjoining land was bought by the Defendant to be developed as a supermarket. In 1992, the first three Claimants gave possession of part of the dominant land to the fourth Claimant for the purpose of a petrol filling station. In 1995, the Defendant entered into a contract to buy the remainder of the adjoining land, including the small triangular piece of land that comprised part of the servient land. The Defendant proposed to use the small triangular piece of land for access to the remainder of its adjoining land, which was not subject to the negative covenant, on which it intended to erect and operate a petrol filling station.

The Claimants applied for a declaration that the intended use of the small triangular piece of land for access to the Defendant's proposed petrol filling station would constitute a breach of the negative covenant.

Decision

Merely to use (part of) the servient land as part of an access route to facilitate business on land not subject to the negative covenant did not constitute the carrying on of business on (that part of) the servient land, and such use could not amount to a breach of covenant. The negative covenant was a restriction on the use of a specific piece of land in a particular way and its burden could not be extended to land not subject to it so as to prevent the Defendant's customers coming onto (part of) the servient land with the intention of trading on land not subject to the covenant. Accordingly, the Claimants' application for a declaration would be dismissed.

Emile Elias & Co Ltd v Pine Groves Ltd (1993)

Facts

In 1938, Maravel Lands Limited owned a 90-acre estate in Trinidad from which it operated St. Andrews Golf Club. The company decided to sell off part of its estate in five plots for development. Plots 4 and 5 were sold to the same purchaser. Plot 5 was shown on a plan attached to the conveyance of plot 4 but not on the plans attached to the conveyances of plots 1, 2 and 3. The purchaser of plot 1 and the purchaser of plots 4 and 5 entered into negative covenants with the company and its assigns which included a covenant not to erect any building other than one dwelling house. A similar negative covenant was imposed on the purchasers of plots 2 and 3, but they also entered into substantially different covenants from those relating to plots 1, 4 and 5. In 1948, a deed was executed by the company and the four owners of plots 1 to 5 whereby, at the request of the owner of plots 4 and 5, who had built a house on plot 4, the other parties released him from the covenant in his 1938 conveyance so as to permit him to erect a house on plot 5. Clause 3 of the deed provided that apart from that nothing contained in the deed should be deemed to release any of the parties or their successors in title from any of the obligations imposed on them under the 1938 conveyances. The Claimant subsequently became the owner of plot 3 and the Defendant of plot 1. In 1983, the Defendant started to construct more than one house on plot 1. The Claimant brought a claim seeking to enforce against the Defendant the negative covenant in the 1938 conveyance of plot 1.

Decision

In order to establish a scheme of development giving rise to mutually enforceable rights, it was necessary to prove, inter alia, that:
(i)   the original common seller had laid out a defined part of its land for sale in plots subject to negative covenants intended to be imposed on all plots;
(ii)   this intention was consistent only with a general scheme of development; and
(iii)   the purchasers of all plots within the area of the scheme had known what that area was.

The Claimant had failed to prove that the purchasers in 1938 of plots 1, 2 and 3 had known that plot 5 had formed part of the area of land sold off by the seller. Accordingly, the requirements for establishing a scheme of development had not been satisfied. Further, the lack of uniformity in the negative covenants imposed on plots of a similar nature also indicated that there had been no intention to create reciprocally enforceable rights. The 1948 deed, although admissible as evidence of what the parties had intended in 1938, was too

117

equivocal to prove the requisite intention to create a scheme of development. Therefore, since no scheme of development had been created, the restriction imposed on the Defendant's predecessor in title in 1938 (not to build more than one dwelling house on plot 1) was unenforceable. The Claimant's claim would therefore be dismissed.

Federated Homes Ltd v Mill Lodge Properties Ltd (1980)

Facts

In 1970, Mackenzie Hill Ltd (MacKenzie), the owner of a site near Newport Pagnall in Buckinghamshire that comprised three areas of land – red, green and blue – obtained outline planning permission to carry out a residential development at the site. In February 1971, Mackenzie (as seller) transferred the blue land to the Defendant. By a negative covenant contained in the transfer, the Defendant covenanted with the seller that, in carrying out the development of the blue land, it would not build:

> 'at a greater density than a total of 300 dwellings so as not to reduce the number of units which the seller might eventually erect on the retained land under the existing planning consent.'

The 'retained land' was described as 'any adjoining or adjacent property' retained by Mackenzie and therefore included the red and green land. By a series of transfers the Claimant became the owner of the red and the green land. In the case of the green land, the transfers contained an unbroken chain of express assignments of the benefit of the negative covenant. However, in the case of the red land, the transfer to the Claimant did not contain any express assignment of the benefit of the covenant and the chain of assignments of the benefit of the covenant was therefore broken. In 1977, the Claimant discovered that the Defendant had obtained permission to develop the blue land at a higher density than permitted by the negative covenant, and that that density was likely to prejudice its proposed development of the red and green land. The Claimant therefore brought a claim to restrain the Defendant from building on the blue land at a density that would be in breach of the negative covenant. By its defence, the Defendant contended, inter alia, that, if the negative covenant was capable of assignment and was not extinguished on the lapse of the 1970 planning permission, the benefit of the covenant had not been passed to the Claimant.

Decision

Where there was a negative covenant that related to or touched and concerned the covenantee's retained land, section 78(1) of the *Law of Property Act* 1925 had the effect of annexing the benefit of the covenant to the covenantee's retained land, and did not merely provide a statutory shorthand for shortening a conveyance. The language of section 78(1) implied that such a negative covenant was enforceable by:
(i)   the covenantee and its successors in title;
(ii)   a person deriving title under either; and
(iii) the owner or occupier of the benefited land.

Since the transfer to the Defendant showed that the negative covenant was for the benefit of the red and green land and that both the red and green land were sufficiently described in the transfer for the purposes of annexation, the covenant related to, or touched and concerned, the red and green land. Section 78(1) had the effect of annexing the benefit of the covenant to the red and green land for the benefit of Mackenzie, its successors in title and the persons deriving title under it or them including the owners for the time being of the red and green land. Furthermore, if, on the proper construction of a document a restrictive covenant was annexed to land, prima facie it was annexed to every part of the land. It followed that section 78(1) had caused the benefit of the negative covenant to run with the red and green land and be annexed to it, and that the Claimant, as the owner of both the red and green land, was entitled to enforce the covenant against the Defendant. Accordingly, an injunction would be granted to restrain the Defendant from breaching the covenant.

Gafford v Graham (1999)

Facts

By a conveyance dated 31 December 1971, James Conwell became the freehold owner of a piece of land consisting of 22 acres at Hunston, near Chichester. At that time there was a two bedroom bungalow on the south-west corner of the land. Subsequently, Conwell built stables and a yard adjacent to the bungalow. He also built a new bungalow for his wife and himself.

By a conveyance made on 22 December 1976, Conwell conveyed to Margaret Mackie a part of his land consisting of 12 acres, which included the original two bedroom bungalow, the stables and the yard (the servient land). The 1976 conveyance imposed negative covenants (the covenants) on the servient land for the benefit of Conwell's retained land (the dominant land). The dominant land comprised ten acres and included the new bungalow. The covenants, which were duly registered as a land charge Class D(ii), were as follows:

'(i)   nothing shall be done or permitted to be done on the [servient land] which shall be or may grow to be a nuisance damage or annoyance to the owner or occupier for the time being of the [dominant land] or any part or parts thereof and at no time shall the [servient land] or any part thereof be used or permitted to be used other than as a livery yard and stabling for horses and one residential bungalow;

(ii)   not more than one caravan shall be allowed to remain on the [servient land] at any one time; and

(iii)   no building of any description shall be allowed on the [servient land] hereby conveyed or any part thereof until detailed plans thereof have been submitted to and approved in writing by [Conwell] provided always that this covenant shall not apply to the bungalow at present erected on the [servient land] hereby conveyed nor to any renovating or alterations necessary to make the same fit for habitation and use nor to the stables and outbuildings at present erected on the [servient land] hereby conveyed.'

By a conveyance dated 17 May 1978, Conwell sold part of the dominant land comprising two acres (Littlemead Farm) to Douglas Gafford. On 19 November 1980, Arthur Graham bought the remainder of the dominant land from Conwell. Further, on 12 July 1983, Graham became the owner of the servient land.

In 1986, Graham, without submitting plans for approval, converted the bungalow on the servient land into a two-storey house with loft above. That same year he also, without submitting plans for approval, extended the barn on the servient land. Later, in 1989, Graham, without submitting plans for approval, constructed an indoor riding school (the school building) and operated the business of a riding school, both indoors and outdoors, on the servient land. In August 1989, Gafford, as owner of Littlemead Farm, which enjoyed the benefit of the covenants, issued proceedings against Graham for breach of covenant. He wanted the school building taken down and the operation of the riding school business stopped. He was willing, however, to accept damages for the wrongful conversion of the bungalow and the wrongful extension of the barn in lieu of an injunction. At the trial of the proceedings that took place in October 1996, the judge found that Graham had breached the covenants. He rejected Graham's defence of acquiescence and awarded Gafford damages totalling £20,750. The judge refused to grant a mandatory injunction obliging Graham to demolish the school building. He stated that by failing to apply for an interim injunction:

> 'at the outset, [Gafford] or his advisers took the risk that the [school building] would be completed before the trial of the action could take place. Moreover, it has been in existence for seven and a half years. It would not be right to compel its destruction now when it could be used, or adapted for use, in a way which would not violate the covenant.'

The judge did, however, impose a prohibitory injunction restraining Graham from operating the business of a riding school. Gafford appealed the judge's decision not to grant a mandatory injunction for the demolition of the school building. Graham cross appealed the judge's decision to award Gafford damages.

Decision

As a general rule, someone who, with the knowledge that he has clearly enforceable rights and the ability to enforce them, stands by whilst a permanent and substantial structure is unlawfully erected, ought not to be granted a mandatory injunction to have it pulled down.

The test to determine whether there had been acquiescence on the part of the covenantee was whether the situation had become one where it would be dishonest or unconscionable for the covenantee to continue to seek to enforce its rights. The test applied irrespective of whether the rights that the covenantee was seeking to enforce were legal or equitable.

So far as the conversion of the bungalow and extension of the barn were concerned, Gafford had known what his rights were when these breaches of covenant took place in 1986. He failed to make any complaint to Graham at the time. Although

Gafford did object to the grant of planning permission for the conversion of the bungalow and the extension of the barn, he made no complaint to Gafford until 1989. Even then, this complaint was fuelled by Graham's threat to erect the school building. Before that, Gafford had effectively treated the conversion of the bungalow and the extension to the barn as closed issues. Gafford had undoubtedly acquiesced to the breaches of covenant relating to the bungalow and barn and he was therefore barred from seeking any relief in respect of those breaches. The award of damages made by the trial judge of £20,750 would be set aside.

So far as the construction of the school building was concerned, there had been no acquiescence on Gafford's part. He had acted promptly in 1989 and complained to Graham before the construction of the school building had started. However, Gafford had not applied for an interim injunction and to impose a mandatory injunction forcing Graham to demolish the completed building at this late stage, would, arguably, be oppressive and disproportionate.

Gafford had previously indicated to Graham that he would be willing to accept a cash payment in settlement of the dispute. It was therefore relevant to ask the question 'Why should Gafford not be held to that position and be granted damages in lieu of an injunction?' Damages would be adequate compensation for the loss and injury to Gafford's legal rights. Damages should equate to the sum that Gafford might have reasonably demanded for relaxing the covenants. £25,000 would have been a reasonable sum for Gafford to demand and this sum would be awarded in damages. The injunction granted by the trial judge would be discharged.

German v Chapman (1877)

Facts

In 1869, the Claimant purchased a 57-acre site near Sevenoaks with a view to selling it off in plots for development. In May 1872, the Claimant sold to the Defendant a 4-acre plot (the servient land), and by a deed of the same date as the conveyance, the Defendant covenanted with the Seller that he, his heirs and assigns:

> 'will not at any time erect or build or suffer to be erected or built upon the land purchased by him more than four

messuages or dwelling houses, and also that no messuage, dwelling house, or other building so to be erected or built upon the same land shall at any time hereafter be used or occupied otherwise than as and for a private residence only, and not for any purpose of trade.'

The rest of the site was sold off by the Claimant in plots subject to similar negative covenants. In February 1877, the Defendant contracted to sell the servient land to the Institution for the Education of Daughters of Missionaries, the sale being stated to be 'subject to certain restrictive covenants as to buildings.' In purchasing the servient land, the Institution intended to construct a large building capable of accommodating 100 girls who were to be boarded, lodged, and educated. This proposed building was opposed by the Claimant, and the owners of adjoining plots, on the ground that it would be a breach of the negative covenant contained in the deed of May 1872, and also would materially interfere with the privacy and enjoyment of their plots. On 15 May 1877, the Claimant started a claim against the Defendant and the Institution to restrain them from building or permitting to be built on the servient land any building intended, or adapted only for use and occupation as a school or institution, or otherwise than as a private residence, and from doing any other act in breach of the covenant contained in the deed of May 1872. In cross-examination, it became apparent that the Claimant had given permission to one of the other plot purchasers to open a boarding school for boys, which was capable of accommodating about 18 boys.

Decision

Where all the plot purchasers of a site were bound by negative covenants not to use their houses otherwise than as private residences, and the seller had given permission to one of the purchasers to open a school in his house, this would not be a waiver of the covenant as to another purchaser whose house was at some distance away.

Hall v Ewin (1888)

Facts

The Claimant was the owner of a house in Edgware Road, Paddington. On 3 November 1849, the Claimant granted a lease of the house to a tenant called Tarlington for 80 years. The lease imposed a negative covenant on the tenant for himself, his heirs, executors, administrators, and assigns, in the following terms:

> 'That he, his executors, administrators, and assigns, shall not at any time during the said term use, exercise, or carry on in or upon the said hereby demised premises, or permit or suffer any part thereof to be occupied by any person or persons who shall use, occupy, or carry on therein any noisome or offensive trade, business, or employment whatsoever without the like consent in writing of [the Claimant], his heirs or assigns, first obtained.'

On 11 January 1851, Tarlington entered into a deed mortgaging the house by granting an underlease to a person called Ruddach for the residue of the term of 80 years less 3 days. On 19 September 1865, the executors of Ruddach, under the power of sale contained in the mortgage deed of 11 January 1851, assigned the underlease to the Defendant. On 29 October 1885, the Defendant sub-underlet the house to a person called McNeff for 21 years. This sub-underlease contained the following covenant by McNeff:

> 'And also shall not at any time during the said term use, exercise, or carry on in or upon the said demised premises any noisome or offensive trade, business, or employment whatsoever without the like consent in writing of [the Defendant], his executors, administrators, or assigns, first obtained.'

In February 1886, McNeff purchased some lions, and opened an exhibition of wild beasts at the house. He exhibited pictures outside the house and employed men to parade in front of it with a gong and trumpet, so that the neighbours complained of the nuisance.

The Claimant started a claim for breach of covenant to restrain the Defendant and McNeff from:
(i)   using the house as an exhibition of wild animals, or otherwise so as to cause a nuisance to the Claimant; and
(ii)   carrying on at the house, or permitting or suffering any part of it to be occupied by any person carrying on, any noisome or offensive trade or business without the consent in writing of the Claimant.

In his defence, the Defendant asserted that, even if the factual allegations made against him were true, they did not give rise to a cause of action against him. None of the acts complained of had been committed by him, and he had not consented in writing to the exhibition. On the contrary, he had done all in his power, except for bringing proceedings against McNeff, to encourage McNeff to stop any acts which might cause annoyance to the neighbourhood.

Decision

As there was no privity of contract or estate between the Claimant and the Defendant, and as there was no evidence that the Defendant had permitted or suffered a breach of covenant, the claim against the Defendant could not be maintained; he was not liable either at law or in equity for not taking proceedings against McNeff to prevent him from opening the exhibition even though it was an offensive business.

Halsall v Brizell (1957)

Facts

On 3 May 1851, a 40-acre estate of freehold land at Cressington Park, Liverpool was purchased by developers. The developers subsequently sold off Cressington Park in 174 plots, but retained ownership of the roads, sewers, a promenade and the sea wall. In a deed dated 19 August 1851, several plot owners covenanted with the developers:

> ' ... seventhly, that each and every of them the said persons parties to these presents and his respective heirs executors administrators and assigns shall and will from time to time contribute and pay a due and just proportion in respect of the plot ... of land in the said plan [drawn upon the deed] marked with his name ... and of the dwelling house on each such plot erected or to be erected in common with the owners of the several other plots of land described in the said plan of all costs charges and expenses'

in maintaining and keeping in good repair the aforesaid roads, sewers, promenade and sea wall

> ' ... for the common use convenience and advantage of the owners for the time being of the several plots of land described in the same plan and of the dwelling houses

erected or to be erected thereon ... and that ... [if] any of the said persons parties hereto of the first part or his or their respective heirs or assigns or owner or owners for the time being of plots inscribed on the said plan ... or of the dwelling house or dwelling houses thereon erected who shall refuse or neglect to pay such proportionate share of such costs charges and expenses the [developers] or the survivor of them or his heirs executors administrators or assigns or other the trustee or trustees for the time being under these presents should have a right to distrain in the same manner as landlords are authorised to do for rent in arrear ... .'

In 1931, John Finney purchased a plot at Cressington Park. The plot came with a dwelling house. The conveyance to Finney was made subject to the covenants contained in the deed of 1851 so far as 'they related to and affected the said house and land and were subsisting and enforceable and capable of taking effect.' Subsequently, Finney adapted his dwelling house so as to make it fit for multi-occupation. He later let the house to five separate tenants. Until 1950, it had been the practice at the estate annual general meeting for the developers to levy an equal sum from each plot owner to defray the cost of maintaining the roads, sewers, promenade and sea wall, and Finney, and after his death his executor, had paid the levies. But in 1950 a resolution was passed empowering the developers to make additional levies against any plot whose dwelling house had been divided into two or more separate flats or dwellings. Pursuant to this resolution, additional levies were made against Finney's executor who had declined to pay them. A claim was issued to determine, inter alia, whether the deed of 1851 was valid and enforceable insofar as it purported to make the successors of the original contracting parties liable to pay levies.

Decision

The covenants contained in the deed were unenforceable because:
(i)   a positive covenant in the terms of the (seventh) covenant did not run with the land;
(ii)   the particular provisions in respect of payment of levies infringed the rule against perpetuities; and
(iii) the provision for distraining on failure to pay such levies was invalid, as a right to distrain could only be annexed to a rentcharge, which this provision plainly was not.

However, the Defendant was not entitled to take advantage (as he desired) of the right contained in the deed to use the roads, sewers, promenade, etc. without undertaking the corresponding obligation, namely, to contribute towards the cost of keeping them in repair, and that on this principle he was bound by the terms of the covenant to pay levies.

Harlow v Hartog (1977)

Facts

The Claimant applied to the Court for an injunction to prohibit the Defendant from constructing a building designed to enclose an existing swimming pool. The Claimant argued that the construction of this building would breach a negative covenant that 'no building other than private dwelling houses shall be erected.'

Decision

The proposed building, designed as it was, to enclose the swimming pool was an ancillary use to the Defendant's house and so did not breach the covenant.

Haywood v The Brunswick Permanent Benefit Building Society (1881)

Facts

By a deed dated 17 May 1866, Charles Jackson conveyed a plot of land to Edward Jackson at an annual rent of £11. Edward covenanted to pay the rent by two half-yearly instalments and to erect and keep in good repair buildings of the value of double the rent (the covenants). The obligation to pay the annual rent was annexed to a rentcharge. On 2 March 1867, Charles assigned to Haywood the benefit of the rentcharge and covenants. Edward conveyed the plot of land to MacAndrew who, in turn, mortgaged it on 8 September 1871 to the Brunswick Building Society subject to the rentcharge and the covenants. Later, the building society exercised the powers in its mortgage deed and took possession of the plot and the buildings on it. The buildings on the plot had not been kept in repair, and the question arose as to whether the building society was bound by the covenant to keep them in repair.

Decision

Where (as here) the performance of a covenant necessitates expenditure, it is unenforceable against a covenantor's assignee, even if it has notice of the covenant. The equitable doctrine laid down in *Tulk v Moxhay* has no application to positive covenants. Only a covenant that can be complied with without expenditure of money will be enforceable against an assignee in equity if he has notice of the covenant.

Holdom v Kidd (1991)

Facts

The Claimant sold a plot of land near Attleborough in Norfolk, comprising 2.5 acres to the Defendant's predecessor in title (the servient land). The transfer contained negative covenants that the buyer would:
(i)   use the land for agricultural purposes only; and
(ii)   not erect on the servient land any residential buildings.

The Defendant placed concrete slabs on the servient land for taking caravans. At one point in time there were 17 caravans or mobile homes belonging to gypsies on the servient land. The gypsies, although travellers, did work on local farms when 'residing' at the servient land. Further, the Defendant had permitted the servient land to be used by a friend for the repair of motor vehicles. The Defendant made an application for planning permission to use the servient land for accommodating gypsy caravans and he intended, in the event that his application was successful, to apply to the Lands Tribunal under section 84(1) of the *Law of Property Act* 1925 to have the negative covenants modified or discharged. The Claimant applied to the Court for an interim injunction to restrain the Defendant from breaching the negative covenants. When the Claimant's application for an injunction came to be heard, the Defendant's planning application had been refused by the local planning authority, although the Defendant had lodged an appeal to the Secretary of State. It was accepted that the Defendant's servient land was burdened by the negative covenants and that the Claimant's retained land enjoyed the benefit of the covenants. The judge of first instance granted the Claimant an interim injunction but the Defendant sought to overturn the judge's decision by appealing to the Court of Appeal.

Decision

The Defendant was undoubtedly in breach of the negative covenants. Although the gypsies did work on local farms, it could not be said that the servient land was being used for agricultural purposes or that there had not been any general relaxation or release of the negative covenants by the Claimant. There was no basis for interfering with the judge's exercise of his discretion. The judge was fully entitled to recognise that granting an interim injunction did not prevent the Defendant from pursuing the planning appeal. Further, the judge could take the view that the function of the Secretary of State was to decide, on planning considerations, whether the servient land should or should not be used for accommodating gypsies and that the Secretary of State was not obliged to determine, on considerations of humanity, whether the servient land should or should not be used to accommodate particular gypsy families who happened to be there. Accordingly, the appeal would be dismissed and the injunction granted by the judge would be left in place.

Ives v Brown (1919)

Facts

In 1876, George Durrant owned The Branksome Estate near Bournemouth (the estate). He let a small part of the estate to Sidney Brown for use as a workshop (the workshop). George Durrant also granted Brown an option to purchase the freehold of the workshop. George Durrant died in 1882, leaving the estate, including the reversion to the workshop, to Elizabeth Durrant and Frederick Fox on trust to pay the rents to Elizabeth for life, and after her death to upon trust for such persons as she should appoint by will. Soon after George Durrant's death, Brown exercised his option to purchase the freehold to the workshop, and this was conveyed to him by Elizabeth Durrant and Fox subject to certain negative covenants. The covenants were stated to run with the freehold to the workshop and prohibited Brown and all persons deriving title under him, without the written consent of Elizabeth Durrant and Fox, their heirs or assigns, or the persons deriving title under them or either of them from (inter alia):

(i)   carrying on or permitting to be carried on at the workshop any trade or business except that of a builder or coal merchant; and

(ii)   permitting at the workshop any act, matter or thing whatsoever which might be a nuisance, annoyance or disturbance to Elizabeth and Fox, or the persons deriving title under them or either of them.

Fox died in 1885. Elizabeth Durrant died in 1917, having by her will exercised her power of appointment so as to make Robert Ives tenant for life of (most) of the estate. Elizabeth Durrant also gave Ives one-half of her residuary personalty. Further, he was appointed one of her executors. Brown died in 1883, and his trustees let the workshop in 1915 to Elliott for a term of five years to be used, and which was used, for a business that was prohibited by the first covenant. Further, Elliott, in the course of this prohibited business, caused annoyance and disturbance to other tenants of the estate and thereby also committed breaches of the second covenant. Ives, in his capacities as tenant for life of the estate and Elizabeth's executor, brought (with his co-executor) a claim against Brown's trustees and Elliott for an injunction to restrain the breaches of covenant.

Decision

There was insufficient express wording in the conveyance to Brown to annex the benefit of the covenants to any part of the estate, which after the conveyance to Brown remained in the ownership of Elizabeth Durrant and Fox. Further, the dispositions made by Elizabeth Durrant's will did not amount to an assignment by her to Ives of the benefit of the covenants. However, the benefit of the covenants could pass by operation of law as well as by express assignment, and the covenants could be enforced therefore by Ives and his co-executor as representing both Elizabeth Durrant's real estate and personal estate. Accordingly, an injunction would be granted to restrain a breach of the first and second covenants.

Jaggard v Sawyer (1995)

Facts

In 1980 the Claimant and her husband purchased 1 Ashleigh Avenue, Maiden Newton, Dorset (no. 1) a house in a residential development of ten properties lining a private cul-de-sac. Each plot had been conveyed subject to negative covenants (which were binding on successive owners) not to use any part of the unbuilt land other than as a private garden. In 1987, the Defendants purchased 5 Ashleigh Avenue (no. 5) a house at the opposite end of the cul-de-sac from the Claimant's house. Subsequently, the Defendants purchased additional land behind no. 5 and obtained planning permission to build a new house, no. 5A, on that plot. The Claimant objected to the Defendants' proposal to provide access to and from no. 5A by means of a driveway to be constructed over part of the garden of no. 5, and threatened to bring a claim for an injunction to restrain this proposed use of the garden as a driveway on the ground that it would involve a breach of covenant. She did not however institute proceedings until the building work on no. 5A was at an advanced stage. The judge at first instance found that:

- although the proposed use of the garden as a driveway would involve breach of covenant, the Defendants had acted openly and in good faith and through inexperience had not appreciated the problem of the covenant;
- the Claimant had failed to seek an interim injunction at an early stage; and
- if an injunction was granted, no. 5A would have no access route.

In those circumstances, the judge refused to grant the injunction sought because it would be oppressive to the Defendants and instead decided that the Claimant should be awarded damages in lieu under section 50 of the *Supreme Court Act* 1981 in the modest sum of £694 representing one ninth of the sum that the Defendants might reasonably have paid for a release of the covenant. The Claimant appealed, contending that the judge had erred in refusing to grant an injunction.

Decision

The Court had jurisdiction to award damages instead of granting an injunction to restrain a breach of covenant where:
(i)   the injury to the Claimant's rights was small;
(ii)   its value was capable of being estimated in money;
(iii)   it was capable of being adequately compensated by a small money payment; and
(iv)   it would be oppressive to the Defendant to grant an injunction.

When considering the question of oppression the Court should not adopt a general balance of convenience test. Oppression had to be judged as at the date the Court was asked to grant an injunction, and the Court could not ignore the reality with which it was then confronted. The fact that the Claimant could at an early stage have sought an interim injunction was clearly relevant, as was the fact that the Defendant could have sought a declaration. Those considerations were not however decisive; for example, it would weigh against a finding of oppression if the Defendant had acted in blatant and calculated disregard of the Claimant's rights. On the facts, the judge had been correct in finding that conditions (i), (ii) and (iii) were satisfied. He had also been entitled to conclude, on the basis of the material before him at trial, that the grant of an injunction would be oppressive, and therefore to award the Claimant damages in lieu.

Further, where a Claimant's property rights were capable of being protected by an injunction, it was proper for the Court to make a 'once and for all' award of damages for future wrongs because the award was in substitution for the grant of an injunction and, therefore, to compensate for those future wrongs that an injunction would have prevented. There was no reason why damages in lieu should not be measured by the amount that the Claimant could reasonably have expected to receive for the release of the negative covenant. The judge's approach to the assessment of damages was correct on the facts and in accordance with established principles and the appeal would therefore be dismissed.

Jamaica Mutual Life Assurance Society v Hillsborough Ltd (1989)

Facts

The Seller owned the Constant Spring Estate in Jamaica (the estate) which it sold off in plots in 1956 for residential development. The plots were all sold subject to negative covenants not to:
(i)   divide any plot into subplots less than one acre each; or
(ii)   carry on any trade or business on the land.

The Claimant, as the successor in title of one of the plots (plot Y), wished to develop plot Y as a multi-unit residential complex, in contravention of covenant (i). The Claimant applied to a judge of the Supreme Court of Jamaica in Equity for a declaration pursuant to section 5 of the *Negative Covenants (Discharge and Modification) Act* 1960 as to whether plot Y was burdened by the negative covenants and, if so, the nature and extent of the covenants and by whom they were enforceable. The claim for a declaration was opposed by other owners of plots on the estate. The 1956 conveyances to the original plot purchasers did not state that the negative covenants were intended for the benefit of the land retained by the Seller, and there was no express assignment of the benefit of the covenants by the Seller to the Defendants' predecessors. The judge at first instance held that the covenants in the Claimant's title ran with the land and enured to the benefit of the original plot purchasers and their successors in title. The Court of Appeal of Jamaica dismissed the Claimant's appeal. The Claimant pursued a further appeal to the Privy Council.

Decision

Since there had been no express assignment from the Seller to the Defendants' predecessors in title of the benefit of the negative covenants burdening plot Y, and no inference could be drawn that, when the Seller imposed negative covenants on its several plot purchasers, it intended those covenants to benefit its retained land, the covenants burdening plot Y were personal to the Seller and, as such, could not benefit the owners of others plots comprising the estate. For a scheme of development (or building scheme) to exist, reciprocity of obligations between the original plot purchasers was essential. The Defendants had failed to establish that the original plot purchasers had accepted:

(i)   negative covenants that could be enforceable not only by the Seller but also by its other plot purchasers; and

(ii)   the benefit of and the right to enforce the negative covenants given by the Seller's other plot purchasers.

Accordingly, no scheme of development was created in 1956 and it followed that the negative covenants burdening plot Y were not enforceable by the Defendants.

J Sainsbury plc v Enfield LBC (1989)

Facts

In 1882, Alfred Walker inherited from his father an estate at Winchmore Hill, Enfield. Neither the father nor the son ever lived on the estate. On 5 April 1894, Walker sold part of the estate to the second Claimant's predecessor in title (the blue land). The conveyance of 5 April 1894 contained negative covenants prohibiting the use of the blue land by the purchaser or its successors in title for, inter alia, building purposes other than houses, or for trade or business. Under section 58(1) of the *Conveyancing and Law of Property Act* 1881, the covenants were deemed to have been made 'with the covenantee, his heirs and assigns' and had effect as if such heirs and assigns were expressed in the conveyance. Walker sold further parts of the estate to other purchasers and, after his death in 1898, his executors sold the remainder of the land. In 1985, the second Claimant entered into a contract for the sale of the blue land to the first Claimant, conditional on the Court declaring that the blue land was no longer burdened by the negative covenants. The first and second Claimants jointly applied to the Court for a declaration to that effect. The application was opposed by the present owners of the land that had remained in Walker's ownership immediately following the conveyance of 5 April 1894 (the retained land).

Decision

The declaration sought would be granted because:

(i) construing the conveyance of 5 April 1894 in the light of the surrounding circumstances, it could not be implied from the conveyance that the benefit of the negative covenants was intended to be annexed to the retained land, since it was clear that Walker intended to sell off the retained land as and when he could rather than keep it for himself;

(ii) there was no express reference in the conveyance of 5 April 1895 to the retained land or to Walker's successors in title; and

(iii) the deemed incorporation of Walker's heirs and assigns into the conveyance by section 58(1) of the 1881 Act was insufficient to give rise to the annexation of the benefit of the negative covenants to the retained land.

Lloyd's and Lloyd's Application (1993)

Facts

Richard and Penelope Lloyd (the Lloyds) owned a dwelling house known as 1 Charmandean Road, Broadwater, Worthing. 1 Charmandean Road was burdened by negative covenants imposed by a conveyance dated 31 July 1935. The negative covenants provided for:

(i) the maintenance of a building line;

(ii) the erection of dwelling houses to a minimum cost in accordance with plans approved by the seller;

(iii) flats or houses not to be erected for occupation by more than one family; and

(iv) no trade or business whatsoever to be carried on except any profession or a school or boarding house (the restrictions).

The Lloyds wished to be able to use 1 Charmandean Road as a 'community care home' for ten residents in accordance with planning permission they had obtained in August 1989. They made an application, therefore, to the Lands Tribunal under section 84(1) of the *Law of Property Act* 1925 to discharge or modify the restrictions. The Lloyds relied on grounds (a), (aa) and (c) in section 84(1).

Broadwater was a primarily residential suburb of Worthing about one mile away from the sea and town centre. Charmandean Road was part of a large residential area of mixed age and house types next to Broadwater's shopping centre. 1 Charmandean Road had originally been built in the 1930s as a four- or five-bedroom dwelling house. However, over the years, it had been extended significantly and the upstairs was readily adaptable for use by ten residents occupying single 'bedsits'. Downstairs, there was a large lounge, a dining room, a games room, a kitchen and storage space. 1 Charmandean Road also enjoyed a substantial rear garden and adequate parking space at the front for three or four vehicles.

It was not clear which properties in the locality had the benefit of the restrictions. The section 84(1) application had been widely advertised and, in response, several owners of properties in Charmandean Road lodged notices of objection. The Lloyds were willing to concede for the purposes of their section 84(1) application that the Objectors had the benefit of the restrictions and, therefore, were entitled to oppose it.

Decision

The restrictions should not be deemed obsolete. Although there had been relatively minor changes in the neighbourhood since the restrictions were imposed in 1935, the essential character of the neighbourhood as good-quality housing in a desirable residential area had been preserved. The preservation of that essential character had been due, in part, to the existence of the restrictions, and they were still capable of fulfilling that purpose by exercising control over inappropriate developments. Ground (a) must, therefore, fail.

It was common ground that the use of 1 Charmandean Road as a community care home for ten residents was a reasonable user that the restrictions impeded. Accordingly, ground (aa) was engaged. Moreover, the restrictions were contrary to the public interest. The evidence indicated that:

(i)   central government had a long established policy of discharging patients from mental hospitals and institutions for 'care in the community';

(ii)   this policy necessitated a range of residential facilities in a community setting for treating and rehabilitating those patients that were to be released;

(iii)   there was a desperate need in the Worthing area for a facility of the kind proposed at 1 Charmandean Road;

(iv)   1 Charmandean Road was, in all respects, suitable for meeting this desperate need; and

(v)   the Lloyds were well qualified, and able and willing to adapt 1 Charmandean Road for that need.

Furthermore, the section 84(1) application would also succeed on the alternative limb of ground (aa). When construing the restrictions as a whole, one could not ignore the fact that the use of 1 Charmandean Road as a boarding house or as a school or for the carrying on of any profession was expressly permitted. It was therefore difficult to see how the restrictions, in preventing the use of 1 Charmandean Road as a residential care home, secured to the Objectors any practical benefit of substantial advantage or value. Any fears and apprehensions that the Objectors might have as to the character of the residents who would live at 1 Charmandean Road were groundless. There was no evidence to suggest that the residents would be any more or less likely to be objectionable or anti-social than any other persons chosen at random from the wider community.

Ground (c) would succeed too. The modification of the restrictions so as to permit the Lloyds to implement their planning permission would not injure the Objectors. No real distinction could be drawn between any injury that the Objectors would suffer if 1 Charmandean Road was used as a residential care home or a use expressly permitted by the restrictions such as a school or boarding house. If anything, the use of 1 Charmandean Road as a school was likely to cause the Objectors more injury as it would, undoubtedly, generate more noise, disturbance, etc. than a residential care home. Further, there was no evidence that the use of 1 Charmandean Road as a residential care home would cause the value of the Objectors' neighbouring properties to diminish in value. As the Lloyds had succeeded on ground (c), the question as to whether compensation should be paid did not arise.

London County Council v Allen and Others (1914)

Facts

In November 1906, a builder applied to the Claimant, the London County Council, under section 7 of the *London Building Act* 1894, for its permission to lay out a new street (to be called Galloway Road) on land that he owned. The Claimant agreed to give its permission on condition that the builder entered into a negative covenant not to build at one end of Galloway Road (the strip) so that the Claimant could at a later date, if it so wished, extend the street to meet an existing road called Dunraven Street. The builder accordingly executed a deed whereby he covenanted with the Claimant

> 'for himself, his heirs and assigns, and any persons claiming under him, and so far as practicable to bind the land into whosesoever hands the same might come, not to erect or cause or permit to be erected upon [the strip] any building, structure, or other erection ... without the [Claimant's] previous consent in writing so to do'.

> The Claimant did not possess nor have an interest in any neighbouring land for the benefit of which the covenant was imposed. It was admitted that the negative covenant did not run with the land at law. The builder subsequently conveyed the strip to the Defendant who had notice of the negative covenant. The Defendant proceeded to build houses on the strip without the Claimant's consent. In response, the Claimant issued proceedings for an injunction and damages.

Decision

Where a negative covenant does not 'run with the land', a successor in title of the covenantor is not bound by the covenant in equity if the covenant was not imposed for the benefit of any adjoining or neighbouring land that was either owned or in the possession of the covenantee, even if he took the land with notice of its existence. In such a case, the doctrine of *Tulk v Moxhay* does not apply. Accordingly, as the Claimant did not own any land adjoining or neighbouring the strip that was intended to have the benefit of the negative covenant given by the builder, the Claimant could not enforce the covenant against the Defendant.

Lund v Taylor (1975)

Facts

In 1932, a company called W. A. Telling Ltd (Telling) purchased The Grange Estate, in Northwood, Middlesex (the estate) for development. The estate comprised a large house known as The Grange and six acres of grounds. Telling instructed an architect to prepare a plan of the estate. This plan split most, but not all, of the estate into 23 numbered plots. The part of the estate that, on the plan, was not split into plots was significant in size and included The Grange. The 23 plots were sold off by Telling between 1932 and 1938. Telling imposed negative covenants on each plot purchaser that were substantially the same although the form of the covenants varied from one conveyance to another. One of the negative covenants imposed on each plot purchaser prohibited the building of a block of flats. In or about 1970, the Defendant purchased plots 13, 14 and 15 with the intention of building a block of flats in breach of covenant. The Claimants, as successors in title of other plot purchasers on the estate, claimed the benefit of and the right to enforce the negative covenants burdening plots 13, 14 and 15. They argued that their plots and the plots owned by the Defendant were comprised in a scheme of development created by Telling and enforceable in equity. There was no extrinsic evidence to indicate that Telling had shown each of its plot purchasers the architect's plan or told them that similar negative covenants would be imposed on other plot purchasers.

Decision

Whatever scheme involving reciprocal rights and obligations Telling may have sought to establish, the necessary evidence that each plot purchaser intended to be bound by a scheme under which they were to have reciprocal rights and obligations was lacking. Without extrinsic evidence or anything in the conveyances to plot purchasers indicating that Telling intended to create a scheme of development relating to a defined area, or impose similar negative covenants on each plot purchaser, the contention that a scheme of development existed must fail.

Mander v Falcke (1891)

Facts

The Claimant was the freehold owner of 34 Poland Street, London (the premises). The premises were let to the first Defendant. The Claimant brought a claim for forfeiture of the first Defendant's lease and an injunction to restrain the first Defendant and his father, the second Defendant, from using the premises, or permitting the premises to be used as a brothel or disorderly house. The Claimant applied for and obtained an interim injunction against both the father and the son. The father, however, appealed against the imposition of an interim injunction on the ground that he had no 'interest' in the premises. The evidence indicated that the business relationship between the father and son was rather obscure, but there was no doubt that the father had much more to do with the business carried on at the premises than he was prepared to admit. Indeed, it was quite likely that the father had a substantial financial interest in the business and was managing the premises. It also appeared that the father had full notice of the terms of the son's lease which contained a covenant on the part of the tenant:

> 'not to do or cause or permit to be done upon the premises anything which might grow to the annoyance, damage, injury, prejudice, or inconvenience of the premises or of the adjoining property of the lessor or of the occupiers thereof.'

Decision

Although the father was not the tenant, he was, nevertheless, a person in occupation who had notice of the covenants contained in his son's lease. As a matter of principle, there is no reason why a simple occupier should not come within the decision of Lord Cottenham in *Tulk v Moxhay*. Accordingly, the father's appeal would be dismissed and the interim injunction that had been imposed on him by the judge below would remain in place pending the trial of the claim.

Marquess of Zetland v Driver (1939)

Facts

By a conveyance dated 10 September 1928 (the 1928 conveyance), the first Marquess of Zetland sold premises known as 200 Lord Street, Redcar (the premises) to David Goodswen. The 1928 conveyance imposed the following negative covenant:

> 'no intoxicating or spirituous liquors shall be sold from the premises and in particular that no part of the land hereby conveyed shall be used for the purpose of a club and that no act or thing shall be done or permitted

139

> thereon which in the opinion of the vendor may be a public or private nuisance or prejudicial or detrimental to the vendor and the owners or occupiers of any adjoining property or to the neighbourhood.'

The negative covenant was expressed to be for the benefit and protection of such part or parts of the first Marquess' retained land that:

(i) remained unsold; or
(ii) were sold with the express benefit of the negative covenant.

The negative covenant was duly registered as a Class D land charge. At the time of the sale of the premises to Goodswen, the land retained by the first Marquess included the land adjoining and neighbouring the premises. In 1929, the first Marquess died and the second Marquess became entitled to the first Marquess' retained land. In 1935, the premises were conveyed to the Defendant, and after that date, he used the premises for the sale of fried fish for consumption off the premises. The second Marquess received various complaints about the Defendant's business and he formed the opinion that the use of the premises for the sale of fried fish was detrimental to the amenities of the neighbourhood and his own land. The second Marquess brought a claim for an injunction to restrain the Defendant from, inter alia, using any part of the premises for frying fish for consumption off the premises.

Decision

When the second Marquess formed his opinion as to whether the sale of fried fish from the premises was detrimental to the amenities of the neighbourhood and of his own land, he was not performing a judicial or quasi-judicial function. This meant that he had no obligation to give the Defendant an opportunity to make representations. As there was no evidence to suggest that the second Marquess had acted capriciously or in bad faith, the Court could not interfere with the opinion that he had formed. Accordingly, an injunction would be granted in the terms sought.

Marten v Flight Refuelling Ltd (1962)

Facts

In July 1942, the Air Ministry requisitioned (under regulation 51 of the *Defence (General) Regulations* 1939) 200 acres of a

562-acre farm known as Cook Farm for use as an aerodrome (the blue land). Cook Farm formed part of the Crichel Estate in Devon – a large agricultural holding of approximately 7,500 acres (the estate). By a conveyance dated 25 March 1943 (the 1943 conveyance), the then owners of the estate, Hoares Trustees, in their capacity as executors of the late Baron Alington, conveyed Cook Farm to the sitting tenant, Donald Harding, who had been in occupation since 1920. Clause 2 of the 1943 conveyance imposed the following negative covenant:

> 'The purchaser hereby covenants with the vendor and its successors in title that no part of the land hereby conveyed nor any building or erection thereon shall at any time hereafter be used for any purpose other than agricultural purposes without the previous written consent of the vendor or its agent provided always that if the vendor should sell all or any part of its land immediately adjoining or adjacent to the land hereby conveyed either free from any restriction as to user or on terms permitting the same to be used for any purpose other than agricultural purposes or if the vendor should agree with the town or country planning authorities that all or any part of the land immediately adjoining the land hereby conveyed may be used for purposes other than agricultural purposes the purchaser shall be at liberty to use or sell all or any part of the land hereby conveyed either free from any restriction as to user or subject to the same conditions as to user as those imposed by the vendor on such sale or agreed with the town or country planning authorities as the case may be ... .'

The negative covenant was duly registered in April 1943 against Cook Farm under section 10(1) of the *Land Charges Act* 1925 as a Class D(ii) land charge.

In 1947, the Air Ministry let a commercial company called Flight Refuelling Ltd (FRL) into occupation of the blue land. The Air Ministry granted FRL rights over the blue land in the nature of a tenancy for which FRL paid a substantial rent. FRL's activities included maintaining the aerodrome and its facilities, the design and development of flight refuelling equipment and the fitting of that equipment to RAF aircraft. In September 1950, Mary Marten, the daughter of the late Baron Alington, and the person beneficially entitled to the estate following her father's death, attained the age of 21 whereupon

Hoares Trustees executed an assent to vest the estate in her name. The assent did not, however, contain any reference to the negative covenant imposed by clause 2 of the 1943 conveyance. On 1 July 1958, the Air Ministry exercised its powers under the *Defence Acts* 1842 to 1935 to compulsorily purchase the blue land. Following the compulsory purchase, the Air Ministry did not make use of the blue land itself, but retained an interest in it as a 'reserve' airfield to be available for use in an emergency. The effective occupier continued to be FRL. FRL had proposals to increase significantly its industrial activities on the blue land and Marten objected to these proposals.

A claim was brought against FRL and the Air Ministry by Marten and Hoares Trustees for declarations that:

(i)   the benefit of the negative covenant imposed by the 1943 conveyance was vested in Marten or, alternatively, in Marten and Hoares Trustees;

(ii)   FRL and the Air Ministry held the blue land subject to the negative covenant;

(iii)   the negative covenant prohibited the use of the blue land by FRL and the Air Ministry for any purpose other than an agricultural purpose unless the previous written consent of Marten and Hoares Trustees was obtained; and

(iv)   FRL's use of the blue land was in breach of the negative covenant.

Marten and Hoares Trustees also sought an injunction restraining FRL from using the blue land in breach of the covenant. They conceded, however, that the use and maintenance of the blue land as an aerodrome for the defence of the realm could not be interfered with.

Decision

In deciding whether Marten and Hoares Trustees were entitled to the benefit of the negative covenant, it was necessary to determine:

(i)   whether the negative covenant had been entered into for the benefit of any 'dominant' land belonging to the covenantees;

(ii)   whether that dominant land was sufficiently defined by permissible inference or evidence;

(iii)   whether that dominant land was, or had been, capable of being benefited by the negative covenant; and

(iv)   whether, since Marten was not an express assignee of the negative covenant, the claim could be brought by Hoares Trustees or Hoares Trustees and Marten jointly.

In determining questions (i) and (ii), the Court was not confined to a consideration of land whose existence was indicated in the 1943 conveyance, but could consider other land whose existence and situation could be shown with reasonable certainty by extrinsic material. Taking a broad and reasonable view of the evidence before the Court, the answers to questions (i) and (ii) were that the negative covenant was taken for the benefit of the whole estate, which could be clearly identified. The evidence before the Court also indicated that, in relation to point (iii), the negative covenant was of value to the estate. Taken together, Marten and Hoares Trustees represented the whole legal and equitable interest in the negative covenant and thus they were entitled to the benefit of the covenant. As the Air Ministry was a purchaser for value, and under section 198(1) of the *Law of Property Act* 1925 was deemed to purchase with notice of the negative covenant, it took subject to the negative covenant. Marten and Hoares Trustees were entitled therefore to a declaration that the negative covenant burdened the blue land in the hands of either of the Air Ministry or FRL. The Court could not interfere with any legitimate use made by the Air Ministry of the blue land for any of the statutory purposes for which it had been acquired, or with any work undertaken by FRL on its behalf pursuant to those statutory purposes. There was a definite threat, however, that, unless restrained, FRL would extend its industrial activities that were not related to the statutory purposes for which the blue land had been acquired. In these circumstances, Marten and Hoares Trustees were entitled to an injunction to restrain FRL from extending its industrial activities.

Miles v Easter (1933)

Facts

On June 24 1907, Shoreham and Lancing Land Company Ltd (SLL) purchased from Carr Lloyd a large estate in Shoreham, Sussex (the estate). By a conveyance dated 23 October 1908 (the 1908 conveyance), SLL sold a part of the estate comprising 515 acres to Nathaniel and Herbert Blaker (the Blakers). The part sold was shown on a plan annexed to the 1908 conveyance coloured pink (the pink land). SLL's retained land was shown on the same plan coloured green (the green land). The 1908 conveyance imposed covenants on both SLL and the Blakers. The following negative covenant was imposed on the Blakers:

'The purchasers for themselves their heirs and assigns covenant not to do anything on any of the land thereby conveyed which might be or might grow to be a nuisance or damage to [SLL] and not to erect or authorize to be erected on the hereditaments thereby conveyed any factory within 460 yards of the land coloured green therein referred to and not to erect any hotel public-house beer-house or beer-shop on the hereditaments thereby conveyed and not to authorize more than one grocer's licence for the sale of wine beer or spirits to be applied for or used within 460 yards of the land coloured green' (the Blakers covenant).

The following positive covenant was imposed on SLL:

'The vendors for themselves and their successors in title and assigns do hereby covenant with the purchasers their heirs and assigns or other the person or persons who shall for the time being be the owner or owners of the lands hereby conveyed or any part or parts thereof (all of whom are included under the expression 'the owner of the land coloured pink' as hereinafter used) to do certain things upon the land' (the SLL covenant).

Stephen Easter became the owner of the greater part of the green land some time after 1908. In or about 1911, SLL had gone into liquidation. By a deed of 19 January 1912 (the 1912 deed), SLL conveyed to Seaside Land Company (Seaside) all the unsold parts of the estate. Further, on 10 May 1909 the Blakers conveyed part of the pink land to Arthur Bury. Bury proceeded at once to divide up into plots the land he had purchased from the Blakers and to sell them off. One such plot (plot Z) was purchased by William Phillips on 11 May 1909. The conveyance to Phillips included the following negative covenant:

'The purchaser for himself his heirs and assigns owner or owners for the time being of the hereditaments hereby conveyed but not so as to make the purchaser or any person claiming under him personally liable after he or they shall have parted with the said hereditaments hereby covenants with the vendor his heirs and assigns not to do anything on any of the land hereby conveyed which may be or grow to be a nuisance or damage to the vendor or to the neighbourhood and not to erect or authorise to be erected on any of the said land any factory hotel public house beer house or beer shop and not to authorise any grocer's licence for the sale of wine beer or spirits to be applied for or used in respect of or on any part of the said land' (the Phillips covenant).

Frederick Miles purchased plot Z and, at the time of his purchase, he had notice of Phillips covenant. By a deed 15 October 1921, Easter took an assignment of the benefit of the Blakers covenant. On 10 April 1931, Easter also took an assignment from Bury of the benefit of the negative covenants that Bury had imposed on his plot purchasers (including the Phillips covenant). At the date of this assignment, Bury had sold all the land that had been conveyed to him by the Blakers on 10 May 1909. Miles brought a claim seeking declarations that Easter was not entitled to enforce the Blakers covenant or the Phillips covenant. At the date of the trial, Easter was still the owner of a substantial part of green land although he had sold off part of it in 15 plots. Further, and with the passage of time, it was not now possible to establish why the Blakers covenant had been imposed.

Decision

Where a negative covenant has been imposed by a seller on the sale of part of its land, but no building scheme has been created, a subsequent purchaser of part of the seller's retained land will be entitled to the benefit of the covenant, even if the benefit has not been expressly assigned to him, providing it is apparent from the conveyance that imposed the covenant that the covenant runs with part sold. In all other cases, a subsequent purchaser will not acquire the benefit of the covenant unless the benefit is expressly assigned to him. An express assignee of the benefit of a negative covenant that does not run with the seller's retained land can enforce the covenant only if, at the time the covenant was imposed, the assignor retained ascertainable land capable of enjoying, as against the land of the covenantor, the benefit of the negative covenant. Further, a negative covenant cannot be enforced by the covenantee against an assignee of the covenantor after the covenantee has parted with the whole of the land benefited by the covenant.

The express inclusion in the SLL covenant of the words:

> 'or other the person or persons who shall for the time being be the owner or owners of the lands hereby conveyed or any part or parts thereof (all of whom are

> included under the expression 'the owner of the land coloured pink' as hereinafter used)',

when contrasted with the omission of any similar wording in the Blakers covenant, showed that the benefit of the Blakers covenant was not intended to be annexed to the green land and, therefore, the benefit of the Blakers covenant did not run with the green land. Easter was not entitled to the benefit of the Blaker covenant, as an express assignee, since it had not been shown that his (green) land was intended to be benefited by that covenant. Further, at the date of the assignment by Bury to Easter of the benefit of the Phillips covenant, Bury no longer owned any land in respect of which the covenant was intended to benefit. Accordingly, Bury was then unable to assign to Easter the right to enforce the Phillips covenant.

Montague v Long (1972)

Facts

In February 1938, a licensor granted a licensee (and its assigns and successors in title) 'the right to erect and maintain in perpetuity' a timber footbridge at a specified point on the licensor's land over which the licensees were to have rights of way 'for the purpose of linking the east and west banks of the river Loddon.' The licensee covenanted with the licensor:

> 'to erect the said bridge in seasoned timber and of sufficient height in order that it will not interfere with normal river traffic and further to maintain it in good and substantial repair.'

The licensee paid a nominal sum for the grant of the licence. Prior to the grant of licence, the river was crossed at that specified point by boat. After a number of years, the bridge that had been erected by the licensee fell into disrepair and a new one was put up in its place. The new bridge was firmly affixed to the soil on which it stood, about 116 feet long and five feet wide and was fastened to eight piles driven six feet into the river bed with the ends embedded in concrete. In November 1971, the Claimant, Albert Montague, (who was the licensee's successor in title) issued a claim seeking a declaration that, on the true construction of the licence:

(i)   he was the owner of the bridge and the Defendant, Diana Long, (who was the licensor's successor in title) was not entitled to use it without his consent; or, alternatively

(ii) he was entitled to the sole use of the bridge to the exclusion of Long and those claiming through her.

Decision

As the bridge was fixed to Long's land, it had become part of her land. Further, on the true construction of the licence and the surrounding circumstances:

- the licensor, by permitting the licensee to erect the bridge on his land for a nominal sum, represented that the licensee was authorised to continue to use it in perpetuity providing the licensee maintained it; and
- the licensee, by fixing the bridge to the licensor's land and allowing him and others to use it without raising any objection, represented to the licensor that in common with the licensee's own rights of user, it was his bridge to use as and when he wished.

That arrangement bound the successors in title of both the licence and licensees because they had had explicit notice of the position when acquiring their respective interests. Accordingly, Montague's claim would be dismissed.

Mortimer v Bailcy & Anor (2005)

Facts

The Claimants, Martin and Jocelyn Mortimer, owned and occupied a residential property called 'The Heugh', Ainderby Steeple, Northallerton in North Yorkshire. The Defendants, Colin Bailey and Pamela Waterton-Bailey, owned and occupied the adjoining residential property called 'The Old Barn'. The Old Barn was burdened by negative covenants imposed by a deed dated 19 August 1992 including a covenant not to erect any building or structure of any kind and not to carry out additions or alterations thereto without the prior written approval of the Claimants, such approval not to be unreasonably withheld (the building covenant).

In early 2000, the Defendants decided to extend The Old Barn on the north side to provide an extra room on the ground floor. They instructed an architect to prepare drawings. In February 2003, the Defendants raised their proposed extension with the Claimants and the Defendants gave the Claimants a copy of their architect's drawings. The Claimants considered the Defendants' proposed extension and then gave their comments to the Defendants in writing. In their letter to the Defendants, the Claimants made clear that, in their view, the proposed extension to The Old Barn would have a terrible impact on The Heugh. Discussions between the Claimants and the Defendants followed but, after a time, the Defendants felt that the Claimants were not going to approve plans for any development of The Old Barn on the north side. They also felt that the Claimants were acting unreasonably and they decided to take legal advice following which they applied for planning permission for their proposed extension. The Claimants made representations to a local planning authority objecting to the grant of planning permission. Although the authority accepted that the proposed extension to The Old Barn would reduce direct sunlight into the Claimants' kitchen, it did not consider that this loss of amenity was sufficient to reject the Defendants' planning application.

The Defendants started to build their extension in early June 2003. The Claimants sought advice from their solicitors and, it was only at this point, that the Claimants appreciated that the Defendants were in breach of the building covenant. The Claimants' solicitors wrote to the Defendants stating that the Claimants had not approved the plans for the extension and the Defendants were asked to stop building works immediately. In response, the Defendants' solicitors referred to the fact that approval could not be unreasonably withheld, and they contended that the Claimants had unreasonably withheld their approval.

Further correspondence passed between the parties' solicitors and in one letter, dated 18 July 2003, the Claimants' solicitors stated that it was the Claimants' intention to have the extension demolished. Proceedings were not commenced by the Claimants until the end of July 2003. They applied for an interim injunction but this was refused as the extension was almost complete. The judge who heard the application intimated that he might have granted the application and imposed an interim injunction had the application been made earlier.

At the trial of the proceedings, the trial judge decided that the Defendant had carried out the extension to The Old Barn without obtaining the Claimants' approval and the Claimants had acted reasonably in withholding their approval. He found that the extension had adversely affected the Claimants' enjoyment of their kitchen because of the loss of light generally, the loss of direct winter sunlight and the loss of view. He accepted the Claimants' evidence that the overall effect of the extension to The Old Barn was to make their kitchen claustrophobic. He assessed the total sum that would have been payable to permit the extension at £40,000 but he concluded that a mandatory injunction ought to be imposed obliging the Defendants to demolish the extension. The Defendants appealed against the grant of a mandatory injunction. They argued that the delay on the part of the Claimants in pursuing an application for an interim injunction meant that they should not have been granted a mandatory injunction at trial.

Decision

Where a covenantee does not apply for an interim injunction, or delays in doing so, the Court can take this fact into consideration when deciding whether a (permanent) injunction should be granted. There was no general rule, however, that a failure to apply for an interim injunction, or a delay in making the application, precluded a covenantee from seeking a injunction at trial. The circumstances of the case might be such that it was entirely reasonable for the covenantee, having given the covenantor adequate warning, to proceed to trial without applying for an interim injunction.

In the present case, the injury to the Claimants' legal rights was not small; its value was not capable of being estimated in money; or of being adequately compensated by a small money payment. It was not, therefore, oppressive to the Defendants to grant a mandatory injunction. They had put up their extension in the full knowledge of the building covenant, and knowing that the Claimants objected strongly to the extension and were threatening to take proceedings. Further, there had been no indication on the part of the Claimants that they were willing to accept a sum of money as compensation for the breach of the building covenant. Despite any delay on the part of the Claimants in pursuing an application for an interim injunction, it remained open to the trial judge to grant a mandatory injunction and, on the evidence, he was justified in doing so. The appeal would be dismissed.

Newton Abbot Co-operative Society Ltd v Williamson & Treadgold (1952)

Facts

Bessie Mardon was the owner and occupier of premises known as 'Devonia', Fore Street, Bovey Tracey, Devon from which she carried on the business of an ironmonger. She also owned numbers 25 and 27 Fore Street and the adjacent cottage known as 'Swiss Cottage' and she sold these three properties (the three properties), which were adjacent to Devonia, on 9 May 1923. In the conveyance to the purchasers, the purchaser's gave the following negative covenant:

> 'The purchasers hereby covenants with the vendor that they the purchasers and the persons deriving title under them will not at any time hereafter carry on or cause to be carried on on any part of the hereditaments and premises hereinbefore expressed to be hereby conveyed any business of such a nature which will in any way affect or be in competition with the business of a furnishing ironmonger china dealer plumber sanitary or electrical engineer and that furnishing ironmongery shall mean that the purchasers and those deriving title under them shall not at any time hereafter sell or expose for sale any ironmongery or hardware brooms brushes baskets paints lamps and glasses of any description on any part of the hereditaments hereby conveyed' (the 1923 covenant).

Mardon died in 1941 and her executors executed an assent vesting Devonia in her son, Leonard. The assent made no mention of the 1923 covenant. In 1947, Williamson & Treadgold Ltd (WTL) became the owner of the three properties. In May 1948, Leonard granted Bovey Tracey Co-operative Society (BTC) a lease of Devonia for 21 years and assigned to it the goodwill of the ironmonger business and the benefit of the 1923 covenant. In April 1949, BTC amalgamated with Newton Abbot Co-operative Society Ltd (NAC). In 1950, WTL began to sell from one of the three properties articles of ironmongery and hardware. A dispute between NAC and WTL broke out which led to NAC commencing proceedings in April 1951. NAC claimed an injunction to restrain WTL from breaching the 1923 covenant. In its defence, WTL contended that NAC was not entitled to enforce the 1923 covenant.

Decision

There was no wording in the conveyance dated 9 May 1923 to identify Devonia as the land intended to benefit from the 1923 covenant so as to annex the benefit of the covenant to Devonia. Although the executors had not assigned the benefit of the covenant to Leonard, the benefit of the covenant was held by them as bare trustees for him, and as the covenant had not been imposed purely to protect Mardon's business, Leonard was therefore entitled to assign the benefit of the covenant in equity to BTC. Despite the statement in the case of *Re Union of London & Smith's Bank Ltd's Conveyance*, to the effect that, where a person is suing as an assignee of the benefit of a covenant, there must be wording in the deed creating the covenant to identify the land for the benefit of which the covenant was imposed, the Court was entitled to look at the surrounding circumstances to see if the land to be benefited could (without such wording) still be established with reasonable certainty. Bearing in mind the close juxtaposition of Devonia and the three properties, the only reasonable inference to draw from the circumstances that existed at the time of the 1923 conveyance was that Mardon took the covenant for the benefit of her own ironmonger business and Devonia. This fact must have been apparent to the purchasers in 1923. An injunction would be granted restraining WTL from breaching the covenant.

Oceanic Village Limited v United Attractions Ltd (2000)

Facts

By a lease dated 28 February 1997, the landlord of the Riverside Building (previously the old County Hall Building) next to the River Thames (the Building) let part of the Building for use as a high quality gift shop in connection with the London Aquarium. The lease contained a covenant by the landlord in favour of tenant not to permit any other gift shop to be operated 'in the Building', but the lease did not define the extent of 'the Building'. Between the facade of the Building and the river wall was a wide walkway forming part of Queen's Walk. The landlord proposed to erect two kiosks on Queen's Walk and use them for the sale of gift items, including items relating to the London Aquarium. The tenant brought proceedings claiming that the walkway formed part of the Building for the purposes of the landlord's covenant and that, in the alternative, the use of the proposed kiosks to sell items relating to the London Aquarium would be in derogation of the landlord's grant.

Decision

As the express provisions of the lease did not define what 'the Building' comprised, that question had to be answered by determining whether or not any particular area could properly be considered to be part of the Building. On the facts, Queen's

Walk was not part of the Building: although Queen's Walk was attached to the Building and provided shelter for part of the Building underneath, it did not pass through the Building and therefore, could not be said to form part of the Building. The landlord's covenant was restricted to not permitting other gift shops to be operated in the Building and that restriction could not be construed to extend to 'in or about' the Building. Accordingly, the landlord's covenant did not prevent the proposed construction and operation of two kiosks on Queen's Walk.

However, the evidence showed that the purpose for which the lease was granted was to operate the London Aquarium gift shop. That purpose carried with it the exclusive right to sell items relating to the London Aquarium. The fact that the parties had expressly negotiated a restriction prohibiting the landlord from operating competing gift shops in the Building did not prevent the lease from containing an implied term restricting the sale of items connected with the London Aquarium outside the area covered by the express restriction, if such an implied term was necessary to protect the business, which the parties intended would be exclusively carried on by the tenant. Under the principle of non-derogation from grant, a term would be implied into the lease restricting the landlord from permitting the sale of items related to the London aquarium from kiosks constructed anywhere on Queen's Walk.

Osborne v Bradley (1903)

Facts

On 31 October 1889, the Claimant purchased the Broadway, Leigh-on-Sea, Essex (the Broadway) from a gentleman called Smith. To the north, the Broadway abutted the High Road leading from Leigh-on-Sea to Southend. In the conveyance to him, the Claimant gave the following covenant: to the intent that the burden thereof might run with the hereditaments conveyed and every part thereof, that the purchaser, his heirs or assigns, that no building except a boundary wall or fence should be erected on the frontage of the land abutting the High Road except private dwelling houses, and that no such house should be of less cost than £300, and that all such houses should front the High Road and stand in a line parallel to the High Road, and should not be used or occupied for any trade or business unless a purely professional business (the 1889 covenant).

By a conveyance dated 3 May 1890, the Claimant sold to George Bavin part of the Broadway abutting the High Road (the blue land). The conveyance imposed a covenant on Bevan as follows: the purchaser hereby covenants to the intent that the burden of the covenant might run with the [blue land] and every part thereof that every house erected upon the land should be occupied as and for a private dwelling house only, and no manufacture, trade, or business should be carried on thereon, nor should any operative machinery be fixed or placed thereon (the 1890 covenant).

Bavin built two houses on the blue land and by a conveyance dated 23 December 1891 sold the blue land to John Hills subject to the 1890 covenant. Subsequently, by a conveyance dated 23 April 1897, Hills sold the blue land to the Defendant subject to the 1890 covenant. Until 1890 there had been only three shops at the Broadway but, owing to the construction in the vicinity of a large estate by a developer, the Broadway had become the principal business thoroughfare of the town. Further, large numbers of chars-à-bancs and other pleasure vehicles now passed along the Broadway every day throughout the summer and tramways running from Southend to Leigh-on-Sea had been introduced in 1901. The rails and overhead electric wires for the tramways ran alongside the Broadway. From about 1894 onwards, the Claimant built approximately 20 shops at the Broadway, all of which fronted the High Road in breach of the 1889 covenant. As Smith was an elderly man, he had not sought to police the 1889 covenant. One of these 20 shops was occupied by the Defendant from which he carried on the business of an ironmonger.

Since the Defendant had been the owner of the blue land, he had found it very difficult to let the two houses as private residences. He, therefore, considered the possibility of converting the two houses into shops, and, with a view to this, he made an application for planning permission to Leigh Urban District Council (the Council). According to the Defendant, there had been a great change in the neighbourhood from residential to commercial and families no longer found it an attractive place to live. By 1903, there were only 11 private houses in the vicinity and these were used variously as an estate agent's office, an auctioneer's business, a doctor's surgery, etc.

The Claimant was a member of the Council and in this capacity he learnt of the planning application. On 23 October 1902, the

Claimant's solicitors wrote to the Defendant bringing to his attention the 1890 covenant and objecting to the conversion of the two houses into shops. On 3 December 1902, the Defendant saw the Claimant and told him that, owing to the character of the neighbourhood having changed from a residential to a commercial one, and the fact that the Claimant himself had built approximately 20 shops on land intended for dwelling houses, the Claimant could not prevent him from going ahead with the proposed conversion of the two houses. In response, the Claimant stated that he still had the right to enforce the 1890 covenant, and he expressed the view that a release of the 1890 covenant would significantly increase the value of the blue land. Communications between the parties and their solicitors continued but, after an impasse was reached, the Claimant issued proceedings in March 1903 claiming an injunction to restrain the Defendant from converting the two houses on the blue land into shops in breach of the 1890 covenant.

Decision

Where a covenantor is in breach of a negative covenant, the Court has, when faced with a claim for an injunction, speaking generally, no discretion to consider the balance of convenience between the parties or other matters of that nature. Instead, the Court is bound to give effect to the covenant unless the covenantee has, by its own conduct, 'disentitled' itself from applying for an injunction. A negative covenant does not cease to have effect simply because circumstances change; however, a covenantee who is entitled to the benefit of a negative covenant may, by its acts or omissions, put itself in such an altered position in relation to the covenantor as to make it manifestly unjust for the covenantee to ask the Court to enforce the covenant through the imposition of an injunction. Further, a change in the character of a neighbourhood, even one brought about by a covenantee in developing its retained land (in breach of a negative covenant burdening the retained land), does not make it manifestly unjust for the covenantee to ask the Court to enforce a negative covenant that binds a covenantor, unless the purpose for which the negative covenant was imposed has, by the covenantee's own acts or acquiescence, become impossible to achieve. On the evidence, the Court could not conclude that the purpose for which the 1890 covenant had been imposed could no longer be achieved. Accordingly, the Claimant would be entitled to the injunction sought.

P&A Swift Investments v Combined English Stores Group plc (1989)

Facts

In 1959, P & A Swift (Investments) Ltd (Swift) became the assignee of a lease (the lease) for 99 years of premises at 58–60 Lime Street, Liverpool. On 26 July 1967, Swift granted an underlease (the underlease) to Dubarry (Liverpool) Ltd (Dubarry) for a term of 35 years at a substantial rent. Dubarry's obligations as subtenant were guaranteed by Combined English Stores Group plc (CES) which joined the underlease as surety only. In 1969, Swift went into voluntary liquidation and, with the concurrence of the liquidator, the lease was assigned to a partnership that traded under the name P & A Swift Investments (the partnership). The document of transfer to the partnership did not contain any specific assignment of the benefit of the guarantee given by CES. Dubarry failed to pay rent due under the underlease and later went into liquidation. The partnership brought an action against CES alleging that the benefit of the guarantee passed to it on taking an assignment of the lease.

Decision

The benefit under a covenant could be enforced by an assignee of the reversion without an express assignment if the covenant touched and concerned the land. Whether a covenant touched and concerned the land depended on the covenant satisfying the following three conditions:
(i)   it must benefit only the reversioner for the time being;
(ii)   it must affect the nature, quality, mode of user or value of the reversioner's land; and
(iii)   it must not be personal in nature.

If these three conditions were satisfied, a covenant for the payment of a sum of money could touch and concern the land if it was connected with something to be done on, to or in relation to the land. A covenant by a surety guaranteeing that a tenant's covenants that touched and concerned the land would be performed and observed was itself a covenant that touched and concerned the land. Accordingly, the partnership was entitled to recover from CES the outstanding rent payable under the underlease.

Price v Bouch (1987)

Facts

A deed dated 30 May 1895 established a cooperative pursuant to which 53 Victorian tradesmen would buy an estate in Northumberland for building purposes and subdivide the estate between them in plots. The deed contained a scheme of development that included negative covenants. Clause 14 of the deed made provision for the election of a committee and stated that no dwelling houses or other buildings were to be erected on the estate unless the plans were first submitted to and approved by the committee. Ernest and Myra Price (the Prices) were the successors in title to plot 32. In 1982, the Prices split their plot, sold part of it and retained the rest. They wished to build a house on the retained part and submitted plans to the committee. The plans were refused by the committee. Two further sets of plans were also refused by the committee.

The Prices brought proceedings claiming a declaration that the committee's approval had been unreasonably withheld and that they were entitled to proceed with their proposed house without the committee's consent. A trial was ordered to determine the following two preliminary issues:
(i)   whether the covenant at clause 14 included an implied term to the effect that the committee could not unreasonably withhold its consent; and
(ii)   whether the committee, when refusing consent, was obliged to give reasons for its decision.

Decision

There was no general principle of law that, whenever a contract obliges one party to obtain the consent of the other, there is an implied term that such consent was not to be unreasonably withheld. Whether such a term is to be implied depends on the circumstances of the particular contract. Where, as here, the covenantors had delegated to a committee (that they elected) authority to make decisions as to whether building plans should be approved, there was no implied term that such approval should not be withheld unreasonably. The implication of such a term was unnecessary as the committee was bound to act honestly and in good faith and not for some improper purpose. Further, to imply such a term would involve resting control from the forum that the covenantors had established to decide such matters and placing it with the Court.

Although it might be helpful for the committee to give reasons for its decision, there was no legal obligation on the committee to do so.

Re Azfar's Application (2002)

Facts

Adnan Azfar (the Applicant) made an application to the Lands Tribunal under section 84(1) of the *Law of Property Act* 1925 for a modification of restrictive covenants to enable him to use land that he owned – 34 Kensington Park Road, Selly Oak, Birmingham (number 34) – as a residential home for the elderly. Number 34 consisted of a two-storey detached house built in 1938 in the grounds of 1.25 acres. Number 34 was burdened by negative covenants imposed by a conveyance of 20 May 1864 and these covenants included the following restrictions:

(i)   'no ... buildings other than dwelling houses with suitable outbuildings and offices should be erected or allowed to be upon the said piece of land or any part thereof ... ';

(ii)   'every dwelling house whether detached or semi-detached should have attached to it at least one quarter of an acre of land including the site of such dwelling house ... '; and

(iii)   'not more than two dwelling houses attached together should be built on any part of the said piece of land thereby conveyed'.

Number 34 lay within Selly Hall Estate, an area predominantly residential in character. The estate was subject to a scheme of development so all properties within the estate were burdened by similar restrictions.

In making his section 84(1) application, the Applicant relied on grounds (a) 'obsolescence' and (aa) 'reasonable user impeded'. The Applicant had obtained planning permission from the local planning authority, Birmingham City Council (the Council), on 19 November 1998 to extend the two-storey house at number 34 and to change its use to a 30-bed residential home for the elderly. The extension envisaged an increase in the gross floor area of the house from 3,732 sq. ft to 9,188 sq. ft. At the trial of the application, the Applicant stated that, before the Council had granted planning permission, various employees of the Council who had expertise in such matters as noise, disturbance and traffic safety had given careful consideration to his proposed development, and none of them had raised any objections to it, and in his view, this was significant. The Applicant also contended that the estate itself was part of a larger residential area, Selly Park, within which there were about 30 'institutional type' properties such as care homes, nursing homes, hostels, hotels, schools, sheltered housing, a family support centre, a church, a convent, commercial premises, blocks of flats, and a hospice. The Applicant was also able to point to the fact that the convent was directly opposite number 34. He felt that the use of number 34 as a residential home for the elderly would not be out of place.

Numerous owners of residential properties within the estate objected to the section 84(1) application. They argued that the development proposed of number 34 would set an extremely undesirable precedent, as it would undermine the existing character and residential density of the estate. Further, the Objectors contended that, if number 34 was used as a residential care home for the elderly, this would generate a significant increase in traffic; staff and visitors' vehicles, catering deliveries and public service vehicles such as refuse lorries and ambulances could all be expected to add to daily traffic movements. Again, the construction of an extension of over 9,000 sq. ft on land currently used as a back garden would constitute an obtrusive and visually unacceptable building, adversely affecting the privacy and the quiet use and enjoyment of the rear gardens of neighbouring properties. There was also a potential threat if the proposed residential home turned out not to be financially viable, that number 34 might then be used for an even less acceptable purpose, such as a remand home or bail hostel.

Decision

Where an applicant applied for a modification of a negative covenant on ground (a), issue as to whether the covenant was obsolete must be considered in the context of the particular object of the covenant. In the present case, the restrictions were not obsolete. Most properties within the estate were still used as low-density housing. Although a number of properties had other uses, the object of the restrictions could still be attained if protection was given to those persons entitled to enforce them.

There was undoubtedly a need for residential homes for the elderly and the Council, in granting planning permission, had decided that the use of number 34 as such a home was appropriate. Accordingly, the restrictions did impede a reasonable use of number 34 and ground (aa) was engaged.

However, the restrictions, in impeding the use of number 34 as a residential home for the elderly, were not contrary to the public interest. No evidence had been adduced to the effect that it was in the public interest to have such a home on this particular site. The restrictions secured to the owners of neighbouring residential properties practical benefits of a substantial advantage to them, particularly since number 34 formed part of a scheme of development. The proposed development of number 34 would have a substantial adverse impact on the use and enjoyment of nearby residential properties by their owners. The owners would face traffic noise, cooking smells, parking difficulties, and the unsightliness of the large extension. Further, the value of the two adjoining residential properties would suffer a substantial diminution of a least £40,000, equating to 12–20 per cent of their present market value.

The application would be dismissed.

Re Hydeshire Ltd's Application (1994)

Facts

By a conveyance dated 13 January 1922, the Earl of Jersey sold to Lobjoit about two acres of land now known as numbers 180, 182, 184, 186 and 188 Jersey Road, Osterley, Hounslow (the site). The conveyance of 1922 imposed on the purchaser a negative covenant 'not to erect more than six dwelling houses on [the site] or more than twelve semi-detached houses in all' (the 1922 covenant).

By a conveyance dated 28 December 1922, Lobjoit sold part of the site to Bird. The part sold to Bird comprised what was now numbers 182 to 188 Jersey Road (nos. 182–188). At about the same time as the sale to Bird, Lobjoit sold the remainder of the site comprising what was now number 180 Jersey Road (no. 180) to Gardener.

On 23 January 1923, Gardener and Bird executed a deed that imposed a mutual covenant on no. 180 and nos. 182–188. The covenant stated that not more than four detached houses or eight semi-detached houses may be erected on nos. 182–188 and not more than two houses or four semi-detached houses may be erected on no. 180 (the 1923 covenant).

In 1990, there was a bungalow at no. 180, a detached house at no. 182, a pair of semi-detached houses at 184 and 186, and a detached house at 188. On 10 September 1990, the present owner of no. 180, Hydeshire Ltd (the Company), obtained planning permission to demolish the bungalow at no. 180 and, in its place, build five detached houses. In January 1992, the Company paid £15,000 to obtain a release of the 1922 covenant from the successors of the Earl of Jersey. The Company also entered into mutual releases of the 1923 covenant with the current owners of nos. 182, 184 and 186. To enable the Company to implement its planning permission, it made an application to the Lands Tribunal under section 84(1) of the *Law of Property Act* 1925 to modify the 1923 covenant. The owner of no. 188, a gentleman called Tuoma, objected to the section 84(1) application. He had obtained planning permission to demolish the detached house at no. 188 and, in its place, put up two new houses. Tuoma argued that, if the Company's proposed development went ahead before he carried out his proposed development, his development would (in effect) involve the erection of a ninth detached house on the site, and, thereby, put him in breach of the 1922 covenant. He would, therefore, lose the ability to build two houses on no. 188, which was a 'practical benefit' that the 1923 covenant secured to him. The Company contended that, even if Tuoma was able to erect two houses at no. 188 at the present time without breaching the 1922 covenant, this gave him a right to build that was not a practical benefit of the kind contemplated by section 84(1A)(a) of the 1925 Act.

Decision

As planning permission for the proposed development of no. 180 had been obtained, it was difficult to argue that the 1923 covenant did not impede a reasonable user of no. 180. The Company would, therefore, be able to rely on ground (aa) of section 84(1). Tuoma's claim that:
(i)   the 1923 covenant secured to him a 'right' to build on no. 188 within the constraints imposed by the 1922 covenant; and
(ii)   this right was a 'practical benefit' of substantial value or advantage within the meaning of section 84(1A)(a);

must be rejected. A restriction such as the 1922 covenant did not secure a right to build; rather, a right to build was simply an incident of land ownership that a restriction such as the 1922 covenant limited. A restriction that secured a practical benefit (properly so-called) must be capable in consequence of its wording and effect to preserve a view, protect against noise or traffic, etc. or, as in this case, maintain a pre-determined density. The Company's application would be granted.

Re Lee's Application (1996)

Facts

In the 1960s, a residential estate in Pontefract, West Yorkshire, known as 'Hardwick Court' was laid out in plots and built. The estate comprised terraced houses, detached houses and bungalows. The developer imposed a scheme of development that bound all the residential properties within the estate. The scheme consisted of various negative covenants one of which prohibited the erection of a second house on any plot (the restriction). In 1988, Ewart Bywater, the owner of number 14 Hardwick Court (number 14) obtained from the local planning authority, Wakefield Metropolitan District Council (the Council) permission to build a second house within the curtilage of number 14. Subsequently, he made an application to the Lands Tribunal pursuant to section 84(1) of the *Law of Property Act* 1925 to discharge the restriction so that he could implement his planning permission. No one objected to the section 84(1) application and the Lands Tribunal, therefore, discharged the restriction. Bywater proceeded to implement his planning permission and a two-storey house was built within the curtilage of number 14. The house was named 'Rosie' and was sold to Eileen Hyde.

In March 1994, Jean Lee, the owner of 13 Hardwick Court (number 13) obtained planning permission from the Council to build a detached house on land that formed part of her garden. As number 13 was burdened by the restriction, Lee, like Bywater before her, made an application to the Lands Tribunal to discharge the restriction so that she could proceed to implement her planning permission. Only one objection was lodged to Lee's section 84(1) application. The Objector was Hyde, whose house, Rosie, overlooked number 13. In support of her section 84(1) application, Lee argued that there had been extensive residential development within the estate that had changed its character to such an extent that the restriction should be deemed obsolete. Lee pointed out that Rosie, itself, had been built following a discharge of the restriction, and she contended that her proposed development would not cause Hyde any injury. Hyde argued that the erection of a second house at number 13 would cause her to lose privacy and peace and quiet, and the value of Rosie would diminish.

Decision

A scheme of development establishes a system of 'local law' and its effect is to:

(i)   make stronger the presumption that negative covenants imposed by the scheme will be upheld; and

(ii)   make more onerous the burden of proof that an applicant must discharge to show that the requirements of section 84(1) have been met.

The objective of the restriction was to limit development within the estate to one house per plot. That objective was still achievable and it was clearly desirable to prevent a division of plots on this attractive estate. It could not be said, therefore, that the restriction was obsolete.

Further, the restriction secured practical benefits of substantial value or advantage to Hyde. First, the restriction preserved a pleasant outlook from the front of Rosie. Number 13 had an attractive garden with a lawn, rockery and shrubs, which could be clearly seen from the front of Rosie and when Rosie was approached from along Hardwick Court. If a second house was built on number 13, this attractive view would be spoilt to the detriment of Rosie. Second, the restriction prevented an increase in traffic and possibly parking problems along Hardwick Court. A second house at number 13 was likely to generate additional traffic movements and more parking in Hardwick Court to the detriment of the enjoyment of Rosie. Third, and in general with all the owners on the estate, the restriction enabled Hyde to preserve the existing layout of the estate.

To prohibit Lee's proposed development was not against the public interest, as the erection of a second house within the curtilage of number 13 would make a negligible contribution to the local housing stock. Each section 84(1) application must be judged on its own merits and the discharge of the restriction in 1988 that enabled Rosie to be built did not, therefore, set a precedent. Bywater's section 84(1) application had been unopposed and Rosie had been built on land that was unsightly; in fact, the erection of Rosie had improved the street scene. Lee's section 84(1) application would be dismissed.

Re MCA East Ltd (2003)

Facts

In 1937, the Ministry of Defence (the MoD) purchased two separate plots of land ('the northern plot' and 'the southern plot') bounded by Horn Lane, Julian Avenue and Creswick Road, Acton.

The southern plot was subject to a negative covenant that had been imposed by a conveyance of 1883 as follows:

> ' ... the [purchaser], his heirs and assigns will not, nor shall at any time or times hereafter, build or cause or suffer to be built on the said piece or parcel of ground hereby granted and assured, or intended so to be, any messuage or dwelling house which with the outhouses and buildings that may be attached thereto shall of less annual rental value than the sum of £70 in the aggregate, and also that no building to be erected on the said piece or parcel of ground hereby granted and assured, or intended to be, shall extend southward or eastward further than the line marked 'building line' on the said plan, and also that [the purchaser], his heirs or assigns, will not, nor shall at any time or times hereafter without the previous consent in writing of the [seller], their heirs or assigns erect or suffer to be erected upon the said piece or parcel of land hereby granted and conveyed, or intended so to be, or upon any part thereof, any erection or building whatsoever which shall or may be used for any shop, beer shop, or public house, or for the sale of wine, beer or spirits, or for any trade, business or manufacture, or for any other purpose other than a private dwelling house, or private dwelling houses, with suitable stabling, outhouses or offices attached thereto and will not, nor shall permit, the sale of wines, beer or spirits to be made upon any such dwelling house or building as aforesaid, or exercise or carry on, or permit, or cause to be exercised or carried on in or upon the said piece or parcel of land, or any part thereof, or in or upon any of the buildings to be erected thereon, or in any part of the same, any trade or manufacture whatsoever' (the 1883 covenant).

The northern plot was subject to a negative covenant that had been imposed by a conveyance of 1912 as follows:

' ... the purchaser with the vendor his heirs, executors, administrators and assigns as to hereditaments thereby conveyed and with intent to bind all persons into whom the same should be vested for the time being, but not so as to be personally liable under that covenant after parting with the said hereditaments: (a) not to erect upon the land thereby conveyed, or any part thereof, any building, other than private dwelling houses, professional residences, or buildings comprising not more than two self-contained residential flats or maisonettes, or (as to such buildings only as have a frontage to Horn Lane aforesaid) shops, unless any such dwelling houses, residences or buildings or shops, either with or without stables, coach-houses, motor-houses, green-houses, conservatories and necessary outbuildings; (b) not to use any messuage or other building to be erected upon the land thereby conveyed, or any part thereof, any laundry or factory, or for any other purpose (as to buildings having a frontage to Julian Avenue aforesaid) than that of a private or professional dwelling house or residence, or (as to buildings having a frontage to Horn Lane aforesaid) than that of the private or professional dwelling house or residence or shop; and (c) not to do or suffer upon the land thereby conveyed or any part thereof, or in or upon any building to be erected thereon anything which might be a nuisance to the vendor, his heirs, executors, administrators or assigns, or the person or persons for the time being owning or occupying any of the land adjacent to or in the neighbourhood of the said land thereby conveyed' (the 1912 covenant).

In 1999, MCA East Limited (MCA) bought the northern plot and southern plot from the MoD. MCA applied to the local planning authority for permission to develop the northern plot and southern plot by converting an existing building into a number of flats and erecting seven town houses. The planning application, although granted, was met by a storm of protest from local residents who were opposed to MCA's proposed development. This led MCA to apply to the Court for a declaration under section 84(2) of the *Law of Property Act* 1925 that the 1883 and 1912 covenants were no longer enforceable. Steps were taken by MCA to inform all owners of properties in the vicinity of its proposed development and the existence of the 1883 and 1912 covenants. In the notice that these owners were sent, they were asked to indicate whether they wished to claim the benefit of and the right to enforce the 1883 and 1912 covenants. Despite the storm of protest that MCA's planning application had aroused, no one responded to MCA's notice expressing a desire to oppose the section 84(2) proceedings. Although the proceedings were 'undefended', it was still necessary for MCA to make good its claim before the Court as the declaration sought, if granted, would 'bind the world'.

Decision

If the benefit of a covenant is to be regarded as annexed to 'servient' land of the covenantor, there must be, inter alia, an intention that the covenant should benefit identifiable 'dominant' land belonging to the covenantee. That intention may be apparent from express wording in the deed or implied if, on a true construction of the deed as a whole when viewed in the light of surrounding circumstances as they existed at the time the deed was made, such an intention can be inferred. The 1883 covenant was not expressed to have been imposed for the benefit or protection of any dominant land; it was consistent with an intention on the part of the covenantee that the benefit of the restrictions contained in the covenant should remain with him personally rather than attach to any of his retained land.

Further, where a covenant (such as the 1912 covenant) was imposed for the benefit of a particular area of land and that land and the land subject to the covenant fall into common ownership, the restrictions contained in the covenant automatically cease to be enforceable, and will not revive on a subsequent severance of the land unless the restrictions are re-imposed.

Re New Ideal Homes Ltd's Application (1978)

Facts

On 6 September 1973, the Applicant purchased from Banstead Urban District Council (the District Council) a plot of land at Merland Rise and Headley View, Banstead, Surrey comprising 9.66 acres (the blue land) for the price of £801,000. In the transfer to the Applicant, the Applicant covenanted with the District Council not to use the plot or permit it to be used for any purposes other than the erection of private dwelling houses of which there were not to be more than 75 (the 1973 covenant). Subsequently, on 14 August 1974, the District Council's successor, Reigate and Banstead Borough Council (the Borough

Council) granted planning permission for the erection of 4 extra dwelling houses. On 27 May 1976, the Secretary of State, on appeal, granted a further planning permission allowing the blue land to be developed at a density of 16 dwelling houses to the acre; this had the effect of increasing the number of dwelling houses there could be erected on the plot from 79 to 156. To enable the Applicant to implement its latest planning permission, it applied to the Lands Tribunal under section 84 (1) of the *Law of Property Act* 1925 for a modification of the 1973 covenant. The Applicant relied on ground (aa) in section 84(1). The Borough Council, which enjoyed the benefit of the 1973 covenant, objected to the section 84(1) application. The 1973 covenant was annexed to three parcels of land which the Borough Council had inherited from the District Council:

- a parcel of land comprising 13 acres adjoining the blue land (the red land);
- a parcel of land that housed a pumping station for an underground oil pipe; and
- a parcel of land some distance away that comprised woodland, part of which was zoned for industry.

The Applicant and the Borough Council agreed that, if at trial, the section 84(1) application was successful, the quantum of compensation payable to the Borough Council should be £51,000. This sum represented, for the purposes of paragraph (ii) of section 84(1), compensation:

> 'to make up for any effect which the restriction had, at the time when it was imposed, in reducing the consideration then received for the land affected by it.'

In opposing the section 84(1) application, the Borough Council contended, inter alia, that if the 1973 covenant was modified, the modification would deprive it, as owner of the red land, of the opportunity of selling part of the red land for low-density housing to private developers at a high price.

Decision

The evidence did not indicate that there was a shortage of land within the Borough that could be developed for residential housing. The 1973 covenant, in restricting the density of houses that could be built on the blue land, was not contrary to the public interest merely because, if the Applicant was obliged to carry out a development of low density housing, part of the blue land would be 'wasted'; the same would apply even if, on the evidence, there was a shortage of land available for residential development within the Borough. The contention advanced by the Borough Council that a modification of the 1973 covenant would deprive it of the opportunity to sell a part of the red land for low-density housing to residential developers at a high price was misplaced. The truth of the matter was that the Secretary of State, in granting planning permission for 156 dwelling houses, had deprived the Borough Council of this opportunity. The effect of the planning permission was to give residential developers an expectation that they could develop the red land at a density at or about 16 dwelling houses to the acre. Even if the 1973 covenant was left unmodified, there was no likelihood of the Borough Council selling the red land to private developers for low-density housing at a high price. Accordingly, it could no longer be said that the 1973 covenant, in restricting the use of the blue land to 75 dwelling houses, secured to the Borough Council a practical benefit of substantial advantage or value. Alternatively, if the 1973 covenant did secure such a practical benefit, a money payment would be adequate compensation for any loss or injury suffered. It would be inappropriate for the Lands Tribunal, in this case, to decline to exercise its discretion to grant a modification of the 1973 covenant because the Applicant, who was the original covenantor, had entered into the covenant only four years ago. The decision in *Jones v Rhys Jones* applied.

The modification sought by the Applicant would be granted and an award would be made in favour of the Borough Council in the agreed sum of £51,000.

Re Page's Application (1996)

Barbara Page owned Kingswood Cottage Stables, Kingswood Lane, Warlingham, Surrey, a site comprising 0.17 acres upon which there was an L-shaped row of single-storey buildings, originally constructed in 1535 and used for stabling horses (the Stables). The Stables had a floor area of approximately 240 square yards and were constructed of brick and flint with a pitched roof covered with tiles. The remainder of the site was an open yard with a flint surface and, on part of this yard, there was a caravan in which Page lived. There had been an outbreak of attacks on horses in the general locality and to protect the horses stabled on the site, Page felt it necessary to live there. In March 1994 however, the local planning authority, the London Borough of Croydon (the Council) served Page with an enforcement notice obliging her to remove the caravan from the site. This prompted Page to apply to the Council for permission to convert one of the Stables for use as a one-bedroom dwelling (the conversion). Although the Council granted permission for the conversion in January 1995, it was highly arguable that its decision to grant permission did not sit comfortably with the planning policies for the area.

The Stables were previously part of a larger piece of land that included an adjacent residential property known as Kingswood Lodge (the Lodge). The Lodge comprised an early 18th century listed building in approximately three acres of grounds. When the Stables and the Lodge were fragmented in 1985, a negative covenant, for the benefit of the Lodge, was imposed on the Stables (the covenant). The covenant stated that the Stables should only be used for horses. To enable Page to carry out the conversion, she needed to obtain a modification of the covenant and, therefore, she made an application to the Lands Tribunal pursuant to section 84(1) of the *Law of Property Act* 1925. Her application was opposed by the owners of the Lodge, Joseph and Graziella Muscat (the Objectors). In opposing the section 84(1) application, the Objectors argued that:

(i)   the Stables were both within the North Downs Area of Special Character and the Metropolitan Green Belt and, thus, in planning terms, any development within the area should be severely restricted; and

(ii)   the covenant secured benefits including the preservation of the historic nature of the neighbourhood, and the preservation of privacy and seclusion and peace and quiet for which a money payment could not adequately compensate them. The Objectors also drew attention to the fact that the covenant had only recently been imposed.

Decision

To use one of the stables as a one-bedroom dwelling was a reasonable use of the land and as the covenant prohibited this use section 84(1)(aa) was engaged. If the conversion went ahead, the Objectors, as owners of the Lodge, would only suffer a marginal loss of privacy and there would be little change in the character of the neighbourhood. Nevertheless, the covenant still secured practical benefits of substantial value or advantage to the Objectors as the covenant gave them the right to prevent further residential development and to maintain the status quo. The 'thin edge of the wedge' argument was relevant. If the covenant was modified to permit the conversion to be carried out, it would make it easier to seek further modifications of the covenant to permit other stables within the row of stables to be developed. This was not a situation where the public interest overrode private objections. The conversion would make a negligible impact on any need for additional housing stock. Further, the fact that the covenant had only been imposed relatively recently – ten years ago – was relevant since 'the sanctity of contract must have some relevance' (per Danckwerts L.J. in *Cresswell v Proctor*).

Re Shaw's Application (1994)

Facts

A preliminary question was raised for determination by the Lands Tribunal under section 84(3A) of the *Law of Property Act 1925* as to whether Objectors who had filed a notice of objection were entitled to oppose an application to discharge a negative covenant. The Applicant wished to build a bungalow in the garden of a property known as Crimbles Court House, Scalby Road, Scalby near Scarborough that had been converted into three flats by local builders, G. Wright and Sons (Scarborough) Ltd (Wrights) in 1961. Crimbles Court House consisted of a main house, an outbuilding and a large garden. The main house was split between flats 1 and 2 and the outbuilding housed flat 3. Wrights sold flat 1 on 19 April 1961 and 'mutual' covenants were given by the purchaser for the benefit of Wrights and the (eventual) purchaser of flat 2. Flat 2 was sold on 8 January 1962 and the same mutual covenants were given by the purchaser in favour of Wrights and flat 1. Neither the conveyance of flat 1 or flat 2 made any mention of flat 3. On 6 June 1962, flat 3 and a significant portion of the large garden (upon which the Applicant wished to build the bungalow) were sold subject to a covenant in favour of Wrights not to carry out alterations or additions:

> 'without first submitting plans to the seller or its successors in title the owners and occupiers of the adjoining properties and obtaining written consent thereto.'

The Objectors were Mr and Mrs Snowdon (the Snowdons) who became the owners of flat 1 in 1976 and the owners of flat 2 in 1987. Having acquired flats 1 and 2, the Snowdons restored the main house to a single dwelling. They now wanted to prevent the present owner of flat 3, Moira Shaw, building her proposed bungalow.

The Snowdons contended that, as Wrights did not own any 'adjoining properties', the reference in the covenant to 'adjoining properties' must be a reference to flats 1 and 2, and although Wrights had already sold flats 1 and 2 when selling flat 3, section 56(1) of the *Law of Property Act* 1925 – enabling an individual to take an interest in land to which covenants are attached without being named in the conveyance – was engaged, as the covenant in the conveyance of 6 June 1962 was obviously intended to benefit flats 1 and 2.

Decision

Section 56(1) of the 1925 Act did operate to enable the Snowdons to oppose the application for a discharge of the covenant. They fell within the scope and benefit of the covenant according to the true construction of the conveyance dated 6 June 1962. Although the term 'adjoining properties' was not specifically defined in the conveyance, the term could only be construed as referring to the owners of flats 1 and 2 and as intending to confer the benefit of the covenant upon them. 'Adjoining' must mean 'touching' and the only properties adjoining flat 3 whose owners and occupiers could be described as successors in title to Wrights were flats 1 and 2.

Re Snaith and Dolding's Application (1996)

Facts

The Applicants, Peter Snaith and Elizabeth Dolding, owned a residential property on the Wildernesse Estate, Sevenoaks (the estate) known as 'Westwood'. The estate had been laid out as a substantial low-density residential estate in the 1920s. The Applicants wished to build a second house – for which they had obtained planning permission – in the curtilage of Westwood but this was prohibited by a negative covenant contained in a scheme of development that bound the whole estate. They made an application to the Lands Tribunal under section 84(1) of the *Law of Property Act* 1925 to modify the negative covenant so as to permit them to proceed with their proposed development. The Applicants relied on ground (aa), i.e. that the negative covenant impeded a reasonable user of Westwood without securing to those persons entitled to the benefit of the negative covenant any practical benefits of substantial value or advantage. The application generated hostility from owners of other residential properties on the estate and 14 of them lodged notices of objection.

The Applicants conceded that the scheme of development (which imposed a collection of negative covenants on each owner of a residential property within the estate) was a practical benefit of substantial value or advantage to the Objectors; however, they argued that the particular modification sought posed no threat to the scheme as a whole. In their view, the Objectors could be compensated for any loss of benefit by a money payment. Further, it was apparent from the evidence that, within the estate, there were several extant planning permissions to build a second house within the curtilage of an existing one, which if erected, would breach the scheme of development. The Objectors argued that, as planning policies were unable to protect the established character of the estate, it was essential not to undermine the scheme of development if that character was to be preserved.

At the trial of the application, the principal issue between the Applicants and the Objectors was whether the negative covenant secured to the Objectors any practical benefits; if so, whether those benefits were of substantial value or advantage to them; if not, whether any loss or disadvantage that they might suffer from a modification of the negative covenant could be adequately compensated by a money payment.

Decision

By prohibiting the erection of a second house within the curtilage of an existing one the negative covenant secured to the Objectors and to other residents of the estate practical benefits of substantial value or advantage. The fact that houses had been laid out to a particular density made the scheme of development, in preserving this aspect of the estate, a practical benefit of substance to the estate as a whole. When confronted by the 'thin edge of the wedge' argument, the Lands Tribunal would consider each application on its merits. Where it was apparent that an application, if granted, would have the effect of undermining the integrity of a scheme of development that had been successfully maintained, this must be viewed as depriving the Objectors of a substantial benefit. The building of a second house within the curtilage of Westwood could materially affect how future applications under section 84(1) from other owners of residential properties within the estate were considered. Accordingly, the application would be dismissed.

Re Truman, Hanbury, Buxton & Co's Application (1956)

Facts

Truman, Hanbury, Buxton & Co. Ltd (the Company) owned a plot of land fronting on to London Road, Leigh-on-Sea (plot Y). At one time, London Road had been the principal road between Leigh-on-Sea and London but it was now an arterial road. Plot Y formed part of a large estate called the Leigh Park Building Estate (the estate) that had been laid out in plots in 1898. A large number of residential properties were built on the estate as well as several roads, of which London Road was one. Negative covenants were imposed on the plot purchasers of each residential property. These negative covenants were substantially in the same form and their purpose was to preserve the estate as a residential area. One of the negative covenants prohibited the use of any plot for the trade of a hotel keeper, innkeeper, victualler of wines, spirits or beer (the restriction).

The Company wished to build a public house or inn on plot Y, so it applied to the Lands Tribunal pursuant to section 84(1) of the *Law of Property Act* 1925 for a discharge or modification of the restriction. The Company founded its application on the ground specified in section 84(1)(a) namely:

> 'by reason of changes in the character of the property concerned or the neighbourhood, or otherwise, the restriction ought to be deemed obsolete'.

The application was opposed by owners and occupiers of nearby residential properties that fell within the estate. Most of the objecting owners and occupiers lived in a road called Gordon Road, which ran into London Road. The Company argued that the building of shops fronting to London Road had rendered the restriction obsolete so far as the London Road frontage of the estate was concerned. At the trial of the application, the judge found that the use of plot Y as on-licensed premises by casual visitors travelling by coach or motorcar to or from Southend would adversely affect the value of residential properties in Gordon Road, and would cause the owners and occupiers of those properties whose gardens abutted plot Y to suffer a serious loss of amenity. The judge decided that, whilst there undoubtedly had been a change in the character of the frontage of this part of London Road, it could not be said that the restriction was 'obsolete'. He therefore dismissed the application. The Company appealed.

Decision

If the character of an estate as a whole or of a particular part of it changed gradually, a time might come when the purpose for which a negative covenant had been imposed could no longer be achieved. For example, what was intended to be a residential area might become substantially a commercial area, and when this occurred, it might be said that the covenant had become 'obsolete' within the meaning of section 84(1)(a). In the present case, however, the judge had found that, although there had been a change in the character of the frontage of London Road where plot Y was located, a discharge of the restriction would severely injure persons entitled to enforce it. This finding of fact made it impossible to say that the restriction had become 'obsolete'. The appeal would be dismissed.

Reid v Bickerstaff (1909)

Facts

In 1840, Robert Rollo purchased a parcel of land comprising sixty-four acres fronting Beech Street on the outskirts of Liverpool (the blue land), which formed part of the Fairfield Estate held by the trustees of the late Edward Falkner (trustees). In a deed dated 20 November 1840, Rollo covenanted with the trustees, their heirs and assigns, that he, his heirs and assigns, would not at any time thereafter apply or use the blue land for:

> 'any purposes other than the erection of dwelling houses thereon, and that not more than three dwelling houses with necessary offices and outbuildings attached thereto should be erected or permitted to be erected on the [blue land], and that no buildings whatever (save and except fences, walls, or palisades) should at any time thereafter be erected on the [blue land] nearer the front of Beech Street than 12 yards, and that each dwelling house with the offices attached thereto should not cover or occupy less than 100 square yards of land, and should not exceed more than two storeys in height, and should be built of or fronted with white stone or be cemented in imitation of white stone on all four sides thereof' (the 1840 covenant).

A dwelling house known as 'The Lindens' was subsequently built on the blue land in compliance with the 1840 covenant.

Between 1843 and 1847, the trustees sold off the remainder of the Fairfield Estate and imposed on each plot purchaser a covenant similar to the 1840 covenant. These later plot purchasers, were not, however, aware of the existence of the 1840 covenant. With few exceptions, dwelling houses were built on all the plots sold off by the trustees between 1843 and 1847 so the Fairfield Estate was residential in character. In 1908, the blue land was sold to the Defendant subject to the 1840 covenant, and a copy of the covenant was annexed to the contract. In March 1908, the Defendant started to build, inter alia, large sheds on the blue land from which he intended to operate the business of a coach and car proprietor.

The Claimants, who were successors in title of plot purchasers who had bought their plots from the trustees between 1843 and 1847, issued a claim for:
(i)   a declaration that they had the benefit of and the right to enforce the 1840 covenant; and
(ii)   an injunction to restrain the Defendant building the proposed sheds in breach of the 1840 covenant.

In support of their claim, the Claimants made two contentions. First, there was a scheme of development (building scheme) affecting Fairfield Estate, and each plot purchaser from the trustees was under an implied covenant or obligation to every other plot purchaser to conform to the scheme. Second, apart from any scheme of development, the Claimants were entitled to the benefit of the 1840 covenant as it was entered into with the trustees, their heirs and assigns, and they were successors in title of the land for whose benefit the 1840 covenant had been imposed.

Decision

To establish the existence of a scheme of development there must be definite reciprocal rights and obligations extending over a defined area. If, on a sale of part of an estate, the purchaser covenants with the seller, his heirs and assigns, not to deal with the purchased property in a particular way, a subsequent purchaser from the seller of another part of the estate does not obtain the benefit of the covenant unless either:
(i)   he takes an express assignment of the covenant; or
(ii)   the covenant is expressed to be for the benefit and protection of the particular part of the estate purchased by the subsequent purchaser.

Further, the benefit of a covenant that is capable of being annexed to land, but is not expressly stated to be annexed to land in the deed creating the covenant (or in a later deed executed by the covenantee), does not pass as an incident of land on a subsequent conveyance.

On the facts, the Claimants had failed to establish the essential requisites of a scheme of development. The evidence did not suggest that all plot purchasers from the trustees had agreed to definite reciprocal rights and obligations extending over a defined area. Further, the benefit of the 1840 covenant was not expressly assigned to the Claimants' predecessors in title, or expressed in the deed of 20 November 1840 to be annexed to the land that the Claimants now owned. The mere fact that the Claimants' land was adjacent to the blue land belonging to the Defendant, and would be more valuable if the 1840 covenant was annexed to their land, was not sufficient justification for the Court to hold that the 1840 covenant was annexed to the Claimants' land. As the Claimants had not been able to make good either of the two contentions that they had advanced in support of their claim, the claim would be dismissed.

Renals v Cowlishaw (1878)

Facts

The trustees of the late Ann Swinburne (the trustees) were the owners of:
(i)   a mansion house and other residential properties comprising the 'Mill Hill Estate';
(ii)   a parcel of land adjoining the Mill Hill Estate (the blue land); and
(iii)   a second parcel of land adjoining the Mill Hill Estate (the red land).

By a conveyance dated 29 September 1845, the trustees sold the blue land to Francis Shaw. In this conveyance, Shaw covenanted for himself, his heirs, executors, administrators, and assigns, with the trustees, their heirs, executors, administrators and assigns, that:
(i)   he would not erect any buildings within eight yards of the centre of a certain road leading to the mansion house on the Mill Hill Estate;
(ii)   the garden walls of any houses which he might build along this road should stand back six yards from the centre of the road;

(iii)   every house to be erected on land adjoining the road should be of the value of not less that £800, and of a specified elevation; and

(iv)   no trade or business should be carried on in any such houses, which were to be used as private dwelling houses only (the 1845 covenant).

At about the same time as the sale to Shaw, the trustees sold off the red land in parts. A similar covenant was contained in each conveyance of part as the trustees wished to secure the residential character of the neighbourhood.

Shaw died and on 15 August 1867, his executor sold the blue land to John Gadsby. The conveyance to Gadsby contained a negative covenant (the 1867 covenant) substantially identical to the 1845 covenant. Subsequently, the blue land came into the ownership of the Defendant. When the blue land was conveyed to the Defendant, he knew of the existence of the 1867 covenant.

By a conveyance dated 5 December 1854, the trustees had sold the Mill Hill Estate to Bainbrigge. After he died, his executors, by a conveyance dated 29 September 1870, sold the Mill Hill Estate to the Claimant. The conveyances of 5 December 1854 and 29 September 1870 made no mention of the conveyance to Shaw or the 1845 covenant.

In 1878, the Defendant began to erect a large chimney and other buildings, and to carry on the trade of wheelwrights, smiths, and timber merchants on the blue land. The Claimant brought proceedings claiming an injunction to restrain the Defendant from breaching the 1845 covenant. From the pleadings and evidence given at trial, there was no indication that Brainbrigge, on purchasing the Mill Hill Estate, had taken an assignment of the benefit of the 1845 covenant. The issue before the Court was whether the Claimant was entitled to sue on the 1845 covenant.

Decision

To enable a subsequent purchaser of land to take the benefit of a negative covenant imposed by a seller on a previous purchaser, there must be (in the absence of an express assignment) something in the deed that creates the covenant to define the retained land which is to benefit from the covenant. It was impossible to say what land, if any, the trustees had intended should benefit from the 1845 covenant. Accordingly, the Claimant could not claim the benefit of the 1845 covenant and the proceedings would be dismissed.

Rhone v Stephens (Executrix) (1994)

Facts

In 1960, the owner of Walford House, Brook Street, Combwich, Somerset, divided the property into two separate dwellings. Part of the roof of the larger dwelling (the Lodge) lay above a bedroom in the smaller dwelling (the Cottage). The owner retained the Lodge but, by a conveyance dated 27 August 1960, sold the Cottage. In the conveyance to the purchasers of the Cottage, the owner covenanted:

> 'for himself and his successors in title ... to maintain to the reasonable satisfaction of [the purchasers] and their successors in title such part of the roof of [the Lodge] as lies above [the Cottage] in a wind and watertight condition' (the 1960 covenant).

In 1981, Ronald and Hazel Rhone (the Rhones) purchased the Cottage and, in the conveyance to them, they took an express assignment of the benefit of the covenant. In 1984, the condition of the roof deteriorated so that water leaked through into the Cottage bedroom. The then owner of the Lodge, Jean Stephens, refused to make the roof watertight. This led to the Rhones issuing a claim to enforce the 1960 covenant. Stephens argued that, as the 1960 covenant was 'positive' (as opposed to 'negative') in nature, it could not be enforced by a successor in title of the Cottage.

Decision

The 1960 covenant was a positive covenant as the covenantor would need to incur expenditure to comply with it.

The enforceability of positive covenants was governed by the common law. As such, a positive covenant could not be enforced against a successor in title of the covenantor as this would contradict the common law rule that a person could not be made liable for breach of a contract unless he was a party to it.

Although negative covenants were enforceable in equity against a successor in title of the covenantor under the doctrine laid down in *Tulk v Moxhay*, the equitable doctrine did not extend to positive covenants. Equity's willingness to intervene to enable a negative covenant to be enforced against a successor in title of the covenantor was justified on the ground that a negative covenant deprived the covenantor of a right to use the servient land in a particular way, and his successor in title was to be prevented from exercising a right which he had never acquired.

There was no principle requiring a covenantee deriving a benefit from a conveyance to accept any burden in the same conveyance (such as an obligation to contribute towards repairs to be carried out by the covenantor), and although a condition to this effect could be attached to the exercise of a power in express terms or by implication, that condition had to be relevant to the exercise of the right. The 1960 covenant to keep the roof watertight was, however, an independent provision in the conveyance dated 27 August 1960 which, on its true construction, did not impose any reciprocal rights or benefits in favour of the covenantor.

Accordingly, although Stephens was the owner of the roof, the burden of the 1960 covenant did not run with the land and the Rhones could not enforce it against her.

Roake v Chadha (1984)

Facts

In March 1930, Wembley (C&W) Land Company Ltd (the Company) bought part of Sudbury Court Estate in North Wembley, laid it out in building plots and sold off the plots using a standard form of transfer. By a transfer dated 4 April 1934, plot 4 was bought by William Lambert. In this transfer, Lambert covenanted with the Company to observe and perform all the provisions, conditions and stipulations contained in the schedule thereto:

> 'to the intent and so as to bind (so far as practicable) the land hereby transferred into whosesoever hands the same may come ... but so that this covenant shall not enure for the benefit of any owner or subsequent purchaser of any part of [the Company's] retained land unless the benefit of this covenant shall be expressly assigned ... ' (the 1934 covenant).

Stipulation 5 of the schedule to the transfer stated:

> 'No building or other erection of any kind except fences
> ... shall at any time be erected on any plot other than
> one private dwelling house with usual out-offices and not
> more than one house with or without a private garage
> shall be erected on any plot ... .'

By stipulation 10 the Company reserved the right to:
(i)   sell any part of its retained land free from the
      stipulations and subject to such restrictions and
      stipulations (if any) as it might think fit; and
(ii) with the written consent of the purchaser of any plot
      already sold, to vary or release the restrictions and
      stipulations affecting the plot purchased by him.

Following the sale to Lambert, the Company sold off the
neighbouring plots.

In 1982, the then owner of plot 4, Manmohan Chadha,
expressed an intention to build a second house on plot 4. The
owners of two neighbouring plots, Dorothy and Margaret Roake
and Arthur and Phyllis Taylor (the neighbours), objected to
Chadha's proposed development and they issued proceedings
claiming a declaration to the effect that they had the benefit of
and the right to enforce the 1934 covenant and an injunction to
restrain Chadha from breaching the 1934 covenant. Chadha
conceded that his proposed development would contravene
stipulation 5 and, by extension, breach the 1934 covenant. The
neighbours admitted that, when they purchased their
respective plots, they did not take an express assignment of the
benefit of the 1934 covenant. At an early stage in the
proceedings, the neighbours applied for summary judgment.

Decision

Even where a covenant is deemed to be made with successors in
title pursuant to section 78 of the *Law of Property Act* 1925, it is
still necessary to construe the covenant as a whole to see
whether the benefit of the covenant is annexed to the land.
Where, as here, the 1934 covenant itself stated that it 'shall not
enure for the benefit of any owner or subsequent purchaser of
any part of [the Company's] retained land unless the benefit'
was expressly assigned, it was plain that the benefit was not
annexed.

Further, since the 1934 covenant precluded the benefit passing unless it was expressly assigned, it could not be 'a right appertaining or reputed to appertain to land' within the meaning of section 62(1) of the 1925 Act and thus could not be transmitted pursuant to this statutory provision into subsequent transfers.

Accordingly, the neighbours' application for summary judgment would be dismissed and Chadha would be granted unconditional leave to defend the proceedings.

Robins v Berkeley Homes (Kent) Ltd (1996)

Facts

In 1890, a developer purchased the Camden Park Estate, Chislehurst, Kent (the estate). The estate comprised 124 acres. In 1894, the developer started to sell off the estate in plots subject to negative covenants. The Claimant was the successor in title to the plot called 'Fairacre', and the Defendant was successor in title to part of the rear garden of the adjoining plot called 'Camla'. Camla was burdened by a negative covenant imposed by a conveyance dated 14 April 1938 prohibiting the building of more than one house on the plot (the 1938 covenant). The 1938 covenant was expressed to be made with the 'vendor, his heirs executors administrators and assigns and other owners for the time being of all or part of the Camden Park Estate'.

The Claimant brought a claim to enforce the 1938 covenant against the Defendant who had obtained permission from the local planning authority to build a dwelling house on its part of the rear garden of Camla. The Defendant resisted the claim contending that the Claimant did not have the benefit of the 1938 covenant or, if he did, the 1938 covenant was obsolete and therefore should not be enforced by the grant of an injunction.

Decision

In deciding whether the benefit of the 1938 covenant was annexed to Fairacre, the Court had to look at the conveyance of 14 April 1938 as a whole to ascertain the parties' intention. There were clear indications in the conveyance that the 1938 covenant was intended to benefit the entire estate. Although the benefit of the 1938 covenant was not stated to be expressly annexed to each and every plot on the estate, section 78(1) of the *Law of Property Act* 1925 would have this effect if it applied.

It was common ground that section 78(1) applied to covenants that 'touched and concerned' the land, and it was apparent that if the 1938 covenant had been breached in 1938, that breach would have had a significant adverse effect on the value of Fairacre. There could be no doubt, therefore, that the 1938 covenant touched and concerned Fairacre. The developer had sold as trustees implying that the adjoining land also received the benefit of the 1938 covenant. It was not necessary for the Claimant to prove that, in 1938, the parties intended that the 1938 covenant should be annexed to each and every part of the estate. The Claimant merely had to establish that the 1938 covenant was one that touched and concerned Fairacre and, from the language of the conveyance as a whole, he was not prevented from enforcing it.

Whether a negative covenant had become obsolete because of a change in the neighbourhood was a question of fact in each case. A heavy burden lay on a covenantor to establish that a covenant was obsolete in the sense that it no longer afforded the dominant land any benefit or protection. The Defendant had not discharged this heavy burden. The Claimant would be entitled to the grant of an injunction to restrain the Defendant breaching the 1938 covenant.

Rogers v Hosegood (1900)

Facts

In 1869, the first Claimant was a partner in the firm of Cubitt & Co (the firm) carrying on the business of builders. The firm owned land at Palace Gate, Kensington, which it had laid out in plots suitable for the building of large private dwelling houses. On 31 May 1869, one of the plots (plot A) was conveyed by the firm to William, Duke of Bedford (Duke William). In the conveyance to him, Duke William covenanted:

> 'with intent that the covenant thereinafter on his behalf contained might so far as possible bind [plot A] thereby conveyed and every part thereof, into whosesoever hands the same might come, and might enure to the benefit of [the partners of the firm] their heirs and assigns and others claiming under them to all or any of their lands adjoining or near to [plot A], for himself, his heirs and assigns, with [the partners of the firm], their heirs and assigns, that no more than one messuage or dwelling house, with such suitable outhouse and stabling (if any)

181

as it might be thought fit to erect in connection therewith, should at any one time be erected or be standing on [plot A], and that such messuage should be used as and for a private residence only, and that no trade or business should at any time be carried on in or upon [plot A] (the May covenant).

Two months later, Duke William purchased a second plot (plot B) from the firm which abutted plot A. In a conveyance to him of 31 July 1869, Duke William gave a covenant in favour of the firm (the July covenant). The July covenant was in the same terms as the May covenant.

By a conveyance dated 25 March 1873, Sir John Millais purchased from the firm a plot at Palace Gate (plot D) together with 'all the rights, easements, or appurtenances belonging or reputed to belong thereto'. Plot D was separated from plots A and B by an intervening plot (plot C) about 60 feet in width. In the conveyance dated 25 March 1873, Sir John Millais entered into a negative covenant not to build more than two messuages or dwelling houses or carry on any trade or business on plot D. At the time of his purchase, Sir John Millais had no knowledge of the May or July covenants.

In 1872, Duke William died and ownership of plots A an B passed to his heir, Francis, Duke of Bedford (Duke Francis). By two deeds dated 30 October 1876, the firm, so far as they lawfully could, released Duke Francis and plots A and B from the May and July covenants and a new covenant (the October covenant) was imposed in their place. The October covenant stated, inter alia, that every messuage or dwelling house to be erected on plots A and B should at all times thereafter be adapted for and used as and for a private residence only, and that no trade or business should at any time be carried on, in, or upon plots A and B.

Subsequently, the first Claimant took a conveyance from his three fellow partners of plots F and G at Palace Gate, which were near to plots A and B. Sir John Millais died on 13 August 1896, and the second and third Claimants, were the executors of his estate. The Defendant became the owner of plots A and B and at the time when he purchased those plots he had notice of the May, July and October covenants. The Defendant proposed to construct on plots A and B one large block of flats consisting of thirty to forty self-contained flats, eight on each floor.

The first, second and third Claimants issued proceedings claiming:

(i)   a declaration that the erection on plots A and B of a block of flats would be a breach of the May, July and October covenants; and

(ii)   an injunction to restrain the Defendant from erecting his proposed block of flats.

Decision

When the benefit of a negative covenant has been annexed to land, there is a presumption that the covenant passes with a transfer of the land; there is no need for a future purchaser of the dominant land who is seeking to enforce the covenant to prove that he has taken an 'express' assignment of the benefit of the covenant. The covenant runs with the land in equity as well as at law because the transferee has purchased something that was inherent in or was annexed to the land which he bought. A purchaser's ignorance of the existence of the negative covenant does not defeat the presumption, although the presumption may be rebutted by the covenantor establishing facts that are inconsistent with it.

A declaration would be made to the effect that the first, second, and third Claimants were entitled to the benefit of the May, July, and October covenants, and an injunction would be granted to restrain the Defendant from erecting his proposed development.

Shropshire County Council v Edwards (1983)

Facts

In 1908, Samuel Atherton owned Nobold House in Shropshire together with substantial parcels of land within the neighbourhood (the estate). By a conveyance dated 10 February 1908 (the 1908 conveyance), Atherton conveyed to the Borough of Shrewsbury (the Borough Council) part of the estate:

> 'for the purpose of providing and maintaining the supply of water for their district and other purposes incidental thereto ... .'

The land conveyed to the Borough Council included:

> 'all springs streams wells cozings and percolations of water upon or in the hereditaments hereby conveyed ... .'

183

In the 1908 conveyance, the Borough Council covenanted that they:

> 'their successors and assigns will not erect any dwelling house on any part of the said land or hereditaments hereby conveyed except one cottage not exceeding two storeys in height to be erected at the point marked X on the attached plan ... ' (the negative covenant).

The 1908 conveyance stated that the negative covenant was to run with the land.

On 13 June 1982, Shropshire County Council (the County Council) acquired part of the land that had been conveyed by Atherton to the Borough Council (the blue land). It was the County Council's intention to use the blue land as a caravan site for gypsies. The County Council proposed to develop the blue land so that it could be used as a permanent site for approximately 14 caravans. At the time that the County Council acquired the blue land, it was aware of the existence of the negative covenant.

Over a number of years, Atherton, and following his death his executors, sold the remainder of the estate. Nobold House was purchased by Mr and Mrs Edwards (the Edwards) on 29 October 1956. The conveyance to the Edwards did not contain an express assignment of the benefit of the covenants.

The Edwards objected to the County Council's proposal to use the blue land as a caravan site for gypsies. In response to this objection, the County Council issued proceedings pursuant to section 84(2) of the *Law of Property Act* 1925 seeking a declaration as to the meaning, nature and effect of the negative covenant.

Decision

Before the benefit of a covenant could run with the land the following conditions must be met:
(i)   the covenant must be a negative one;
(ii)   at the time the covenant was imposed, the covenantee must have retained other adjoining or neighbouring land capable of benefiting from the covenant;
(iii) the retained land must be ascertainable with reasonable certainty; and
(iv) the covenant must 'touch and concern' the retained land.

It was clear that, at the time the negative covenant was imposed, there was retained land belonging to Atherton that was capable of benefiting from the negative covenant. With the assistance of extrinsic evidence, Atherton's retained land was ascertainable with reasonable certainty. Although it was highly desirable that the 1908 conveyance contained express words to annex the benefit of the negative covenant to the land with which it was to run, such words were in fact unnecessary. If, on the construction of the deed creating a negative covenant, both the land that was intended to benefit from the covenant and an intention by the parties to benefit that land (as distinct from benefiting the covenantee only) could be established, the benefit of the covenant would be annexed to that land and run with it despite the absence of any express words of annexation. Looking at the 1908 conveyance as a whole, it was clear that the negative covenant had been proposed to protect Nobold House from unwanted development. Accordingly, the negative covenant was enforceable by the Edwards.

Smith and Snipes Hall Farm v River Douglas Catchment Board (1949)

Facts

In 1938, Ellen Smith was the owner of a large piece of land known as 'Lower Meadows' situated between the Eller Brook (the brook) and the River Douglas in Lancashire. Lower Meadows was liable to flooding. On 25 April 1938, Ellen Smith and ten other landowners in the locality entered into a deed (the Deed) with the local drainage board, River Douglas Catchment Board (the Board), pursuant to the *Land Drainage Act* 1930. Under the Deed, the Board would widen, deepen and make good the banks of the brook and thereafter maintain the brook for all time. In return, the landowners would contribute towards the cost of these works. In order that the Board should have the necessary powers under the 1930 Act to carry out the works, it applied to the Minister of Agriculture and Fisheries to designate the brook a 'main river'. The Minister acceded to the Board's request. The Deed included the following recitals:

> 'Whereas (i) certain lands belonging to the parties of the first eleven parts hereto (hereinafter called 'the landowners') situate between the Leeds and Liverpool Canal and the River Douglas and adjoining the Eller Brook in the parish of Lathom in the county aforesaid are liable to flooding; (ii) the Board is a drainage board

duly constituted under the *Land Drainage Act* 1930 and the lands subject to flooding lie within the catchment area of the Board; (iii) a proposal has been made that the Board in order to improve the drainage of the land liable to flood and to prevent future flooding should undertake the widening, deepening, improvement and future maintenance of the Eller Brook from its junction with the River Douglas to Brook Bridge, Carr Lane, Burscough aforesaid, to which the Board have agreed subject to the landowners paying a proportion of the cost thereof; (iv) the landowners have agreed to contribute towards the cost of the works to be carried out by the Board as hereinafter contained; and (v) for the purpose of giving effect hereto the Board has applied to the Minister of Agriculture and Fisheries to make Eller Brook a 'main river' under the control of the Board.'

The work envisaged by the Deed was carried out by the Board in accordance with a plan prepared by its engineer. The work was completed by August 1940.

On 1 April 1940, John Smith purchased Lower Meadows from Ellen Smith. In the conveyance to John Smith, Lower Meadows was expressly stated to be conveyed with the benefit of the Deed. In May 1944, Snipes Hall Farm Ltd, a company controlled by John Smith (the Company), was incorporated and occupied that part of Lower Meadows which was used for arable farming under a yearly tenancy. The arable farmland comprised approximately 250 acres. In September 1946, owing to the severe weather conditions, the brook burst its banks, and Lower Meadows was flooded. The crops growing on the arable farmland were ruined. John Smith and the Company brought a claim against the Board seeking damages in tort and contract. They argued that the Board was in breach of its obligations under the Deed because it had constructed the banks of the brook using soil taken from the bed of the river which contained a large amount of sand; this made the banks unable to withstand the pressure of the greater volume of water flowing into the brook as a result of the drainage work. According to John Smith and the Company, the banks should have been given a clay core but the Board did not do this because it wished to save money. Further, Smith and the Company contended that the obligations on the part of the Board contained in the Deed ran with the land, and pursuant to section 78(1) of the *Law of Property Act* 1925, those obligations could be enforced by both of them.

Decision

The Board was in breach of its obligations under the Deed and this breach had caused John Smith and the Company to suffer loss and damage. The obligations contained in the Deed were such that they affected the value of Lower Meadows, and the language of the Deed showed an intention that those obligations should attach to Lower Meadows whoever was the owner of the land. The obligations on the part of the Board ran with the land, and by virtue of section 78(1) of the *Law of Property Act* 1925, they could be enforced by the covenantee, her successors in title and persons deriving title from them.

Stockport Metropolitan Borough Council v Alwiyah Developments (1986)

Facts

Stockport Metropolitan Borough Council owned a housing estate at Romiley in Stockport, which was adjacent to a four-acre plot of land (the plot) owned by Alwiyah Developments (the Company). The plot was burdened by a negative covenant prohibiting its use to anything other than agriculture. The housing estate enjoyed the benefit of the covenant. In September 1979, the Company obtained planning permission to build 42 houses on part of the plot. To enable it to implement the permission, the Company made an application under section 84(1) of the *Law of Property Act* 1925 to the Lands Tribunal for a modification of the negative covenant. The Lands Tribunal granted the Company's application and, as part of its claim for a monetary award under section 84(1A), the Council asked for £150,000 to reflect the sum of money that, in free negotiations between the Council and the Company, the Council might reasonably expect to obtain for a relaxation of the covenant. The Lands Tribunal rejected this head of claim and the Council appealed.

Decision

An award to the covenantee under section 84(1A) was intended to compensate the loss of a practical benefit that the negative covenant had secured. It was not intended to compensate the loss of a 'financial' benefit such as the loss of bargaining power to negotiate a relaxation or discharge of the covenant.

Tamares (Vincent Square) Ltd v Fairpoint Properties (Vincent Square) Ltd (2007)

Facts

The Claimant, Tamares (Vincent Square) Ltd, was the owner of 'Olsen House', situate at 64–65, Vincent Square, Westminster, London SW1. The Defendant, Fairpoint Properties (Vincent Square) Ltd, owned an adjoining site that comprised the former site of Rochester Row Magistrates' Court and police station (the site). The Defendant redeveloped the site. Part of the redevelopment involved demolishing a single-storey flat-roofed building and erecting a three-storey pitched-roofed building in its place. The Claimant claimed that the redevelopment had interfered with its right to light through, inter alia, two windows located near the basement staircase of Olsen House. The Claimant contended that the interference was sufficient to give rise to a claim in nuisance.

The Claimant issued proceedings. At the trial, the judge decided that the Defendant was liable to the Claimant in nuisance. However, the judge refused to grant the Claimant a mandatory injunction as this would necessitate the Defendant demolishing a significant part of its development. He considered that the imposition of a mandatory injunction would be oppressive and unjust and create a loss to the Defendant out of all proportion to any loss suffered by the Claimant. The judge decided that the Claimant should be awarded damages in lieu of an injunction and the amount of damages payable should be assessed at a further hearing.

At this further hearing, the evidence indicated that the profit that the Defendant was likely to make from the relevant part of the development was about £174,500.

Decision

In assessing damages in lieu of an injunction, the following principles were applicable:
(i)   the Court had to attempt to find a 'fair' result of a hypothetical negotiation between the parties;
(ii)   the background to the dispute, including the nature and seriousness of the infringement, had to be considered;
(iii)   the right to prevent a development, or part of it, gave the owner of the right a significant bargaining position;

(iv)   the owner of the right with such a bargaining position could be expected to receive a share of the profit for the development or the relevant part of it;

(v)   if there was no evidence as to the likely amount of the profit that the development or the relevant part of it would generate, the Court could assess damages by awarding a multiple of the damages that would be payable for loss of amenity;

(vi)   if there was evidence as to the likely amount of the profit that would be generated, the Court should normally award a sum that took into account a fair percentage of that profit;

(vii) the size of the award should not be so large that the development, or relevant part of it, would not have taken place had such a sum been payable; and

(viii) after arriving at a sum that took into consideration all these factors and any other ones that the Court considered to be relevant, the Court had to decide whether that sum was one that 'feels right'.

In the present case, had a negotiation between the Claimant and the Defendant taken place, the Claimant could have been expected to negotiate a one-third share of the profit derived from the relevant part of the development. This would produce a sum payable of £58,166, which would be reduced to £50,000 to take into account the fact that the infringement of the right of light had been relatively modest. Judgment would be entered for the Claimant for damages in the sum of £50,000.

Tod-Heatley v Benham (1888)

Facts

Catherine Lee was the freehold owner of land at Gloucester Terrace, Brompton, London (the freehold estate). By a lease dated 12 November 1821 (the 1821 lease), Catherine Lee let to Harriet Loyd number 6 Gloucester Terrace for a term of 98¼ years. In the lease, Loyd covenanted that:

> 'she, her executors, administrators, or assigns, would not during the term thereby granted, use, exercise, or carry on, or permit or suffer any other person or persons whomsoever to inhabit, dwell in, use, or occupy the said messuage or premises, or any part thereof, who should use or exercise therein or thereupon the trades or businesses of a tallow-chandler, or melter of tallow, soap

boiler, slaughterman, distiller, brewer, lampblack maker, sal ammoniac manufacturer, or any other noisome, obnoxious, or offensive trade or business, without the express licence and consent of Catherine Lee, her heirs or assigns, nor do, of wittingly or willingly cause or suffer to be done, any act, matter, or thing, in, upon, or about the said premises, which should, or might be, or grow to the annoyance, nuisance, grievance, or damage of Catherine Lee, her heirs or assigns, or the inhabitants of the neighbouring or adjoining houses' (the covenant).

At some time prior to 1888, Tod-Heatley had become the owner of the freehold estate, and Joseph Elliott and Edward Fry had become the lessees and occupiers of numbers 7 and 8 Gloucester Terrace respectively. In or about 1888, Benham, who was a doctor, took an assignment of the 1821 lease when he became the lessee of 6 Gloucester Terrace. Todd-Heatley, Elliott and Fry complained that Benham was operating a hospital called 'The Queen's Jubilee Hospital' for the treatment of diseases of the throat, nose, and ear, skin, eye, rectum, etc. at 6 Gloucester Terrace in breach of covenant. They considered the hospital to be a noisome, obnoxious, and offensive business causing them to suffer annoyance, nuisance, grievance and damage.

Todd-Heatley, Elliott and Fry brought proceedings claiming an injunction to restrain Benham from using 6 Gloucester Terrace as a hospital. The evidence adduced by the Claimants showed that the hospital attracted numerous poor people as outpatients suffering from infectious diseases, and that it diminished the value of neighbouring residential properties. Benham argued that:
- there was not the slightest risk of infection;
- no patients suffering from infectious or contagious diseases had visited the hospital;
- there was no crowding or loitering about of patients;
- there was a great need for a hospital such as his in the neighbourhood;
- the hospital was well operated and did not cause a nuisance or annoyance within the meaning of the covenant; and
- the hospital had not diminished the value of residential properties nearby as the houses were not of a high-class character.

Decision

The expression 'annoyance' has a wider meaning than 'nuisance'. If something:

> 'reasonably troubles the mind and pleasure of a person, not of a fanciful person, or of a skilled person who knows the truth, but of the ordinary sensible English inhabitant of a house, if there is anything which disturbs his reasonable peace of mind, that is an annoyance, although it may not appear to amount to physical detriment to comfort'.

The Claimants had a reasonable apprehension of risk of infection, which was an 'annoyance' within the covenant, and it was not necessary for them to prove pecuniary loss or damage. Benson had breached the covenant and an injunction would be imposed.

Tulk v Moxhay (1848)

Facts

The Claimant owned part of Leicester Square, London, including several houses that formed part of the square. In 1808, the Claimant sold part of his land (the square garden) to a gentleman called Elms subject to the following negative covenant:

> 'Elms, for himself, his heirs, and assigns, covenants with [the Claimant], his heirs, executors, and administrators that [Elms], his heirs, and assigns should, and would from time to time, and at all times thereafter at his and their own costs and charges, keep and maintain the square garden and the iron railing round the same in its then form, and in sufficient and proper repair as a square garden and pleasure ground, in an open state, uncovered with any buildings, in neat and ornamental order; and that it should be lawful for the inhabitants of Leicester Square, tenants of [the Claimant], on payment of a reasonable rent for the same, to have keys at their own expense and the privilege of admission therewith at any time or times into the said square garden and pleasure ground' (1808 covenant).

The square garden came in to the ownership of the Defendant. Although the conveyance to the Defendant made no mention of the 1808 covenant, he was, however, aware of its existence at the time of his purchase. The Defendant wished to build houses on the square garden and he thought that he had the right to do this. The Claimant, who was still the owner of several houses in Leicester Square that benefited from the 1808 covenant, objected to the Defendant's proposed development and he applied to the Court for an injunction.

Decision

A covenant between a seller and purchaser that imposed an obligation on the purchaser and his successors in title to use or refrain from using the land sold in a particular way will be enforceable in equity against all future purchasers who take with notice of the covenant. The enforcement of the covenant in equity is separate from the issue of whether the covenant is one that runs with the land so as to bind future purchasers at law.

The presiding judge, Lord Cottenham, established that if an equity is attached to property by the owner, no one purchasing with notice of that equity can stand in a different situation from that of the party from whom he purchased.

The Claimant was entitled to an injunction prohibiting the Defendant from implementing his proposed development.

Wakeham v Wood (1982)

Facts

By a conveyance dated 13 January 1930, Sidney Rodcliff conveyed to Amy Seltham land that lay between his house 'Cornelly' at Holywell Bay, Cubert and the sea (the blue land) subject to a negative covenant. The covenant prohibited the erection on the blue land of any building of a height that would obstruct the present view of the sea and beach enjoyed by Cornelly. Arthur Wakeham became the owner of Cornelly in 1946 and Arnold Wood became the owner of the blue land in 1979. Shortly after his purchase, Wood started to construct a building on the blue land and he continued his building operations despite protests from Wakeham and Wakeham's solicitors. To preserve his view of the sea and beach, Wakeham was forced to issue a claim for:
(i)   a declaration that he was entitled to the benefit of the negative covenant imposed by the conveyance of 13 January 1930; and

(ii)   a mandatory injunction obliging Wood to take down the building.

The evidence given at trial established that the building Wood had erected on the blue land breached the negative covenant; it had seriously obstructed the view of the sea and beach from Cornelly that had been enjoyed since 1930. The evidence also showed that Wood knew of the covenant but, when instructing his architect to prepare drawings for the building, did not bring the covenant to the architect's attention. It also became apparent at trial that Wakeham had spoken to Wood's builder who, in turn, had informed Wood that, if the building got too high, it would have to come down.

The trial judge refused to grant Wakeham a mandatory injunction but, instead, awarded him damages as compensation for the loss of view. Wakeham decided to appeal against the judge's refusal to grant an injunction.

Decision

As a general rule, where a covenantor committed a breach of a negative covenant with his eyes open and after receiving a warning, the Court would grant a mandatory injunction. An exception to the general rule might arise where the injury to the covenantee's legal rights:
(i)   was small;
(ii)   was capable of being estimated in money;
(iii)   could be adequately compensated by a small money payment; and
(iv)   it would be oppressive to the covenantor to grant a mandatory injunction.

Where the exception did arise, damages in substitution for an injunction could be awarded.

Wood had acted in flagrant disregard of Wakeham's legal rights and there had been a serious interference with those rights; namely, a serious obstruction of a scenic view of the sea and beach. Further, it was difficult, if not impossible, to estimate the loss of this view in money terms, and it could not be adequately compensated by a small money payment. Accordingly, the judge was wrong to award damages instead of granting a mandatory injunction because this had the effect of enabling Wood to buy his way out of his wrong. The judge's order would be set aside and a mandatory injunction obliging Wakeham to take down the building would be granted.

Williams & Anor v Kiley (t/a CK Supermarkets Ltd) (2003)

Facts

The Claimants, John and Hetty Williams, carried on the business of newsagents, confectioners and tobacconists from a shop in a parade of shops at Parkway, Sketty in Swansea. The Claimants' shop was number 4 Parkway (no. 4). The Claimants had a lease of no. 4 granted in 1964 by the County Borough of Swansea (the Council). The lease contained a covenant restricting the use of no. 4 to a newsagents, confectioners and tobacconists. The Defendant, Christopher Kiley, carried on business at the adjoining shop, numbers 6–8 Parkway (nos. 6–8). He had a lease from the Council granted in 1963. His lease contained a covenant that prohibited the use of nos. 6–8 as 'newsagents, sugar confectioners and tobacconists'. The Defendant ran a supermarket from nos. 6–8 and he sold a range of merchandise that a supermarket would ordinarily sell, including tobacco and cigarettes, confectionery and stationery items. The Claimants issued a claim against the Defendant seeking an injunction and damages. The Claimants argued that the Defendant's use of nos. 6–8 was in breach of the covenant in his lease, and, as tenants within the same 'letting scheme', they were entitled to enforce that covenant directly without having to rely on the intervention of the Council as landlord.

Decision

The legal principles that apply to determine whether a scheme of development (building scheme) exists affecting freehold land apply equally to leasehold land. In practice, however, the Court is likely to have less reason to infer an intention to create a scheme of mutually enforceable obligations in the case of leasehold land.

There were five shops that made up the parade of shops and there was clear evidence of an intention to create the reciprocal obligations necessary for a scheme to exist. Each lease imposed a covenant that had been drafted to dovetail with the covenants contained in other leases. Each tenant not only had a positive obligation to carry on a particular business, but also was protected against competition from other shops in the parade. There were terms in the leases for resolving disputes between tenants, and the absence of any right on the part of the tenants to oblige the Council to intervene in a dispute also indicated an intention to create covenants that were to be policed by the tenants themselves. The covenants were not directed simply to protecting the interests of the Council. The general character of the parade had been fixed since 1961 and it was reasonable to suppose that the original tenant of each shop was aware of the intention to create reciprocal obligations because of the unusually precise covenants in their respective leases. The area to which the scheme applied was apparent not only from the plans to the leases, but also from the fact that references to the uses in the leases all directly related to the others in the parade. The correct test in deciding whether the Defendant was using nos. 6–8 in breach of covenant was whether he could be said to be carrying on only the trade of a supermarket or some other composite trade, or differing trades in addition. This was a matter of fact and degree. The use of nos. 6–8 as a general store in 1963 would not have prevented the Defendant from selling confectionery and tobacco, providing it was not sufficiently great to amount to a distinct trade or business. If it crossed that line, then the fact that nos. 6–8 might still qualify as a 'general store' would not assist the Defendant, in view of the specific prohibition against carrying on the business of a tobacconist or confectioner. The covenant in the Defendant's lease could be breached even though the prohibited trades had not become the dominant ones. There was sufficient evidence to conclude that the tobacco and confectionery trades carried on by the Defendant, both in themselves, and in relation to the Claimants' business, amounted to a breach of covenant. The injunction sought by the Claimants would be granted and they would be entitled to an award of damages.

Wrotham Park Estate Co v Parkside Homes Limited (1974)

Facts

On 10 April 1935, the 6th Earl of Strafford sold to Aubrey Blake 47 acres of land (plot 14) situate in South Mimms, Hertfordshire. Plot 14 comprised part of the Earl's Wrotham Park Estate (the estate). In the conveyance to him, Blake covenanted at clause 3:

> 'with the vendor and his assigns owner or owners for the time being of the vendor's Wrotham Park Estate using that term in the broad and popular sense so as to bind the owner or owners for the time being of the property hereby conveyed and to the intent that the restrictions and stipulations hereinafter referred to shall run with

the land and be for the benefit of the vendor's said Wrotham Park Estate that he the purchaser and all persons deriving title under him the owner and occupiers for the time being of the property hereby conveyed will observe and perform the restrictive covenants and provisions contained in the second schedule hereto, provided that the said covenant shall bind the purchaser or other the owner or owners for the time being of the property hereby conveyed only so long as he or they shall be the owner or owners thereof.'

Further, clause 5 of the conveyance declared that there was no general building scheme affecting the estate and the clause also stated that a purchaser of a part of the estate should not be entitled to enforce any covenant unless the benefit had been expressly assigned to him and that the 6th Earl might release any stipulations. The second schedule to the conveyance contained, inter alia, the following restrictive covenant:

'Not to develop [plot 14] for building purposes except in strict accordance with a layout plan to be first submitted to and approved in writing by the vendor or the surveyors such plan to indicate thereon the roads, sewers and drains to be constructed' (the 1935 covenant).

The 1935 covenant was duly registered as a land charge Class D(ii) under the *Land Charges Act* 1925.

For a long period of time, the Strafford family had had an extensive land holding in and around the village of South Mimms and the towns of Potters Bar, Barnet and Elstree. This holding comprised approximately 4,000 acres and consisted of three separate parcels of land. The first parcel of land, which lay between Potters Bar and Barnet, contained the family mansion house and home farm of Wrotham Park; it was substantially larger than the second and third parcels of land. The second parcel of land lay to the northeast of Elstree, while the third parcel of the land, which was the smallest, lay to the northwest of South Mimms.

After 1917, outlying parts of the Strafford family's land holding had been sold off for development, particularly along the southern edge of Potters Bar. The development that had taken place comprised predominantly of detached houses. Covenants had been imposed in each conveyance that prohibited:
(i)   the construction of particular types of building;

(ii)   the use of land for an offensive purpose; and
(iii)   development of land except in accordance with layout plans approved by the vendor.

Plot 14 was developed and as built-out consisted entirely of private dwelling houses, most of which were semi-detached. Plot 14 was surrounded by other plots that had either already been developed for housing or were to be developed for housing in due course. In the middle of plot 14, there was a triangular wedge of land (the wedge). The sides of the wedge were approximately 100 yards, 170 yards and 170 yards. No buildings had been erected on the wedge. The only access to the wedge was via a path about ten feet wide running alongside a dwelling house called 11 Brooklands Gardens. One corner of the wedge had recently been used as a playground for children. Except for this corner, the wedge was unkept and, although it was not a rubbish dump, it was overgrown and used by the owners of adjoining dwelling houses for bonfires to burn garden waste.

In 1938 and 1940, the 6th Earl sold a significant part of his land holding to the east and west of Wrotham Park to the Middlesex County Council. In the conveyances to the Council, covenants were imposed to preserve the green belt. The 6th Earl died in 1951, following which the estate passed to his daughter, Lady Elizabeth Byng, who, in turn, sold the estate to Wrotham Park Estate Co Ltd (the Company) in 1964.

In or about 1955, Potters Bar Urban District Council (the District Council) became the owner of the wedge, for which it paid £225. In 1969, the District Council decided to sell off the wedge and, having purchased 11 Brooklands Gardens for £6,500 to improve access, it obtained permission from the local planning authority, Hertfordshire County Council, to erect 13 houses on the wedge. On 9 September 1971, the District Council offered to sell the wedge and 11 Brooklands Gardens (the site) with the benefit of its planning permission by public auction. The proposed sale was advertised and the particulars of sale stated that negative covenants burdened the site.

Parkside Homes Ltd (Parkside) bought the site at auction for £90,000. Before buying the site, neither Parkside nor their solicitors investigated the restrictive covenants. In October 1971, Parkside obtained permission from Hertfordshire County Council to build an extra dwelling house on the site and building operations then started. By the end of January 1972,

11 Brooklands Gardens had been demolished and preliminary building work, including footings, had begun on several of the dwelling houses, and holding deposits had been paid by several prospective purchasers.

On 5 January 1972, the Company's managing agents wrote to Parkside giving notice of the 1935 covenant and asking for confirmation that building operations at the site would cease. Parkside instructed its solicitors to respond to this letter. In their letter of 6 January 1972, the solicitors stated that they were aware of the 1935 covenant but considered it to be unenforceable. On 14 February 1972, the Company issued proceedings against Parkside claiming a prohibitory injunction to restrain it from building on the site other than in accordance with a layout plan approved by the Company and a mandatory injunction obliging Parkside to demolish any buildings that it had put up in breach of the covenants. The Company did not seek an interim injunction.

Despite the commencement of proceedings, Parkside continued its building operations. By July 1972, the access road to the site had been built and all 14 dwelling houses were at different stages of construction. Several dwelling houses were nearly complete. Parkside was keen to exchange contracts with its prospective purchasers but the solicitors acting for the prospective purchasers advised against it whilst the dispute with the Company remained unresolved. This led Parkside to take out insurance with Eagle Star Insurance Co Ltd. Under the insurance policy, each prospective purchaser would be given cover for losses up to £20,000 in the event of the Company's claim succeeding at trial. Backed by the insurance policy, the prospective purchasers exchanged contracts and all 14 dwelling houses were sold by the end of November 1972. By the end of January 1973, all the purchasers were in occupation. In April and May 1973, all the purchasers and their mortgagees were joined as Defendants to the proceedings.

Decision

On its natural construction, the 1935 covenant was a prohibition against development without obtaining prior approval from the owner of the estate, or his surveyor, of a layout plan that showed building plots as well as roads and the line of sewers and drains. The 1935 covenant had been entered into for the benefit of the estate, which was sufficiently identifiable. At the time that the 1935 covenant was imposed, it was capable of benefiting and continuing to benefit the estate, and its validity should be upheld so long as the estate owner might reasonably take the view that it remained of value to the estate. The Company, as the present owner of the estate, did take this view, which was a reasonable one, and the 1935 covenant was therefore enforceable.

Although the Company had failed to apply for an interim injunction, this was not a bar to the grant of a mandatory injunction at trial. However, as the grant of any injunction was always at the discretion of the Court, and since, in the present circumstances, an order to demolish the 14 dwelling houses would result in an inexcusable loss of much needed housing, a mandatory injunction would not be imposed.

Under the *Chancery Amendment Act* 1858 (Lord Cairns' Act), the Court could award damages in substitution for an injunction and this was a case when it would be appropriate for the Court to make use of the Act. An award of damages would be made against Parkside in respect of the construction of the roads that it still owned. An award of damages would also be made against the individual householders in respect of the erection of the dwelling houses that they now owned because the householders had aided and abetted in the breach of the covenant.

The quantum of damages should be the sum that the Company might reasonably have demanded as a quid pro quo for relaxing the 1935 covenant had Parkside approached the Company for a relaxation. It would be appropriate to award the Company a sum equal to five per cent of Parkside's anticipated profits from the development to be split equally between Parkside and the individual householders.

Appendix C: Specimen forms

Specimen forms 1–4 relate to the procedure for progressing a claim for breach of covenant seeking an injunction or damages in the High Court or County Court (see chapter 10 and flow chart 2).

Specimen forms 5–9 relate to the procedure for progressing a claim under section 84(1) of the *Law of Property Act* 1925 to discharge or modify a negative covenant in the Lands Tribunal (see chapter 14 and flow chart 4).

Further information on completing forms 5–7, including templates, is available at www.landstribunal.gov.uk

1   SPECIMEN PARTICULARS OF CLAIM

Claim no.: HC

IN THE HIGH COURT OF JUSTICE
CHANCERY DIVISION

BETWEEN:

1. DWAYNE PIPE

2. PATTY O'DORES   Claimants

– and –

RAPACIOUS DEVELOPMENTS LTD   Defendant

PARTICULARS OF CLAIM

1. Attached to these particulars of claim is a paginated bundle of true copy documents marked PC1. References to page numbers in these particulars of claim are to the page numbers of PC1.

2. The claimants and the defendant are all registered proprietors of freehold residential properties situate at the Scenic Wood Estate, Dorchester ('the estate'). The estate comprises three roads: namely, Scenic Wood Drive, Scenic Wood Crescent and Scenic Wood Lane. The first claimant is the registered proprietor of 2 Scenic Wood Drive, which is registered at the Land Registry with title number NH 7544322; the second claimant is the registered proprietor of 3 Scenic Wood Drive, which is registered at the Land Registry with title number NH 7544323; the defendant is the registered proprietor of 4 Scenic Wood Crescent, which is registered at the Land Registry with title number NH 7544321. Official copy entries obtained from the Land Registry for each of these properties are at pp. 1–9.

3. The estate was laid out in or about 1964. As and when the developer, Bulldozer Developments Ltd ('Bulldozer'), came to sell a residential property comprising part of the estate, a common form of conveyance was used. The common form of conveyance imposed a 'scheme of development'. A copy of the conveyance to the original purchaser of 4 Scenic Wood Crescent dated 22 March 1965 ('the defendant's conveyance') is at pp. 10–20.

4. The following restrictive covenants contained at clause 4 of the defendant's conveyance are relevant to the claim:

   - not more than one private dwelling house shall be erected on any part of the land hereby conveyed; and

201

- not to do or suffer to be done on any part of the land hereby conveyed anything of whatsoever nature which may be or become a nuisance or annoyance to the owners or occupiers for the time being of the estate or the neighbourhood.

5. The defendant obtained planning permission from Dorchester Borough Council on 1 April 2008 under reference 4545/08/FUL ('the permission') to build two detached houses at 1 Scenic Wood Drive ('the development'). A copy of the permission is at pp. 21–26. In or about early May 2008, the Defendant started to demolish the existing house at 1 Scenic Drive with the intention of implementing the permission.

6. The defendant's proposed development will breach the restrictive covenants referred to at paragraph 4 and cause the claimants to suffer annoyance and loss and damage. At trial, the claimants will adduce expert evidence to the effect that the defendant's proposed development, if implemented, will cause them to suffer a significant loss of amenity and/or a diminution in the value of their residential properties.

7. By reason of the matters referred to in paragraphs 5 and 6, the defendant is in breach of or is threatening to breach the covenants set out in paragraph 4. At pp. 21–25 is a copy of the claimants' letter of claim and the defendant's response thereto. It is evident from the defendant's response that unless restrained by an injunction the defendant will breach or continue to breach the covenants set out in paragraph 4.

The claimants claim:

1. an injunction prohibiting the defendant from building the development;

2. alternatively, damages in lieu of an injunction;

3. interest thereon pursuant to statute;

4. further and/or other relief; and

5. costs.

Statement of truth

I believe that the facts stated in these particulars of claim are true.

Signed:

....

DWAYNE PIPE and PATTY O'DORES

Date:

Served by IBB solicitors, Capital Court, 30 Windsor Street, Uxbridge, Middlesex UB8 1AB. DX 45105 Uxbridge. Telephone number: 08456381381. Fax number: 08456381351. Email address: andrew.olins@ibblaw.co.uk

Solicitors for the claimants.

2 SPECIMEN DEFENCE

Claim no.: HC

IN THE HIGH COURT OF JUSTICE
CHANCERY DIVISION
BETWEEN:

1. DWAYNE PIPE

2. PATTY O'DORES   Claimants

– and –

RAPACIOUS DEVELOPMENTS LTD   Defendant

DEFENCE

---

1. Reference to paragraph numbers in this defence are to the paragraph numbers of the particulars of claim. Further, the defence adopts the abbreviations used in the particulars of claim.

2. Paragraph 2 is admitted.

3. The allegation at paragraph 3 that the residential properties comprising the estate are bound by a scheme of development is denied. There is no express statement in the common form of conveyance creating a scheme of development, nor did circumstances exist at the time the estate was sold off in plots by Bulldozer in or about 1965 from which the creation of a scheme of development could be implied.

4. It is admitted that the restrictive covenants contained in clause 4 of the defendant's conveyance ('the restrictive covenants') were imposed for the benefit of Bulldozer's retained land of which 2 and 3 Scenic Wood Drive formed part. Accordingly, it is admitted that the claimants have the benefit of the restrictive covenants.

5. Paragraph 5 is admitted.

6. It is admitted that the development will breach the restrictive covenants but it is denied that the breach of the restrictive covenants will cause the claimants to suffer any annoyance or loss or damage as alleged or at all. The defendant will adduce expert evidence at trial to this effect.

7. As the development will not cause the claimant to suffer any annoyance or loss or damage, the defendant denies that the claimants are entitled to enforce the restrictive covenants by means of an injunction. Further, if, which is denied, the claimants are entitled to damages for breach of the restrictive covenants, such damages should be nominal only.

8. Paragraph 7 is admitted.

9. Further, and without prejudice to its contentions in the paragraphs above, the defendant intends to make an application to the Lands Tribunal pursuant to section 84(1) of the *Law of Property Act* 1925 for a modification of the restrictive covenants so as to permit the defendant to carry out the development. The application will rely on grounds (aa) and (c). The defendant believes that its application to the Lands Tribunal has good prospects of success and, therefore, this Action should be stayed pursuant to section 84(9) of the 1925 Act.

Statement of truth

The defendant believes that the facts stated in this defence are true. I am duly authorised by the defendant to sign the statement.

Signed:

....

Maximilian Stirling Silver
Director of Rapacious Developments Ltd

Date:

Served by Bill Large, Rookie & Green solicitors, 11 Doggy Avenue, Bow, London. DX 1234 Bow.

Solicitors for the defendant.

3 SPECIMEN INTERIM INJUNCTION

Claim no.: HC

IN THE HIGH COURT OF JUSTICE
CHANCERY DIVISION

Mr Justice Blackadder
Thursday 15 May 2008

BETWEEN:

1. DWAYNE PIPE

2. PATTY O'DORES   Claimants

– and –

RAPACIOUS DEVELOPMENTS LTD   Defendant

INJUNCTION

To the respondent:

Rapacious Developments Ltd whose registered office is situated at 7 Felling Lane, Dorchester DR6 7ND.

PENAL NOTICE

If you, Rapacious Developments Ltd, disobey this order you may be held in contempt of Court and may be imprisoned, fined or have your assets seized.

Any other person who knows of this order and does anything that helps or permits the respondent to breach the terms of this order may also be held to be in contempt of Court and may be imprisoned, fined or have their assets seized.

THIS ORDER

1. This is an injunction made against Rapacious Developments Ltd ('the respondent') on 15 May 2008 by Mr Justice Blackadder on the application of Dwayne Pipe and Patty O'Dores ('the applicants'). The Judge read the affidavits listed in Schedule A and accepted the undertakings set out in Schedule B at the end of this order.

2. This order was made at a hearing without notice to the respondent. The respondent has a right to apply to the Court to vary or discharge the order – see paragraph 7 below.

3. There will be a further hearing in respect of this order on 22 May 2008 ('the return date').

4. If there is more than one respondent:

- unless otherwise stated, references in this order to 'the respondent' mean both or all of them; and
- this order is effective against any respondent on whom it is served or who is given notice of it.

INJUNCTION

5. Until the return date or further order of the Court, the respondent shall cease building operations at 1 Scenic Drive, Dorchester.

COSTS

6. The costs of this application are reserved to the judge hearing the application on the return date.

VARIATION OR DISCHARGE OF THIS ORDER

7. Anyone served with or notified of this order may apply to the Court at any time to vary or discharge this order (or so much of it as affects that person), but they must first inform the applicants' solicitors. If any evidence is to be relied upon in support of the application, the substance of it must be communicated in writing to the applicants' solicitors in advance.

INTERPRETATION OF THIS ORDER

8. A respondent who is an individual and is ordered not to do something must not do it himself or in any other way. He must not do it through others acting on his behalf or on his instructions or with his encouragement.

9. A respondent which is not an individual and is ordered not to do something must not do it itself or by its directors, officers, partners, employees or agents or in any other way.

PARTIES OTHER THAN THE APPLICANTS AND RESPONDENTS

10. It is a contempt of Court for any person notified of this order knowingly to assist in or permit a breach of this order. Any person doing so may be imprisoned, fined or have their assets seized.

COMMUNICATIONS WITH THE COURT

11. All communications to the Court about this order should be sent to: Room TM 505, Royal Courts of Justice, Strand, London WC2A 2LL quoting the case number. The telephone number is 020 7947 6754. The offices are open between 10am and 4.30pm Monday to Friday.

SCHEDULE A

Affidavits

The applicants relied on the following affidavits:

1. first affidavit of Dwayne Pipe sworn on 14 May 2008 filed on behalf of the applicants; and

2. first affidavit of Patty O'Dores sworn on 15 May 2008 filed on behalf of the applicants.

SCHEDULE B

<u>Undertakings</u>

1. If the Court later finds that this order has caused loss to the respondent, and decides that the respondent should be compensated for that loss, the applicants will comply with any order the Court may make.

2. The applicants will as soon as practicable issue and serve a claim form claiming the appropriate relief.

3. The applicant will as soon as practicable serve upon the respondent:

    3.1. this order;

    3.2. copies of the affidavits and exhibits containing the evidence relied upon by the applicants, and any other documents provided to the Court on the making of the application;

    3.3. the claim form; and

    3.4. an application notice for continuation of the order.

4. Anyone notified of this order will be given a copy of it by the applicants' legal representatives.

5. The applicants will pay the reasonable costs of anyone, other than the respondent, that have been incurred as a result of this order and if the Court later finds that this order has caused such person loss, and decides that such person should be compensated for that loss, the applicants will comply with any order the Court may make.

NAME AND ADDRESS OF APPLICANT'S LEGAL REPRESENTATIVES

The applicant's legal representatives are:

IBB solicitors, Capital Court, 30 Windsor Street, Uxbridge, Middlesex UB8 1AB. DX 45105 Uxbridge. Telephone number: 08456381381. Fax number: 08456381351. Email address: andrew.olins@ibblaw.co.uk

4 SPECIMEN PROPOSALS FOR DIRECTIONS
(to accompany their allocation questionnaire)

Claim no.: HC

IN THE HIGH COURT OF JUSTICE
CHANCERY DIVISION
BETWEEN:

1. DWAYNE PIPE	
2. PATTY O'DORES	Claimants
– and –	
RAPACIOUS DEVELOPMENTS LTD	Defendant

CLAIMANT'S PROPOSALS FOR DIRECTIONS

- Trial: Week beginning 7 December 2008. Estimated length 3 days.
- Permission to amend as follows: The claimants to have permission to amend the particulars of claim in accordance with the draft initialled by the Judge. Re-service of the particulars of claim shall be deemed to have been effected today. The defendant to have permission to amend the defence by 4pm on 1 September 2008 limited to amendments consequential upon the amendment for which permission is first given above. The claimants to pay in any event the costs of and consequential upon that amendment, or thrown away thereby [and of this application].
- Disclosure of documents by 4pm on 14 September 2008. Standard disclosure.
- Signed statements of witnesses of fact to be served (and filed) by 4pm on 14 October 2008.
- Permission for expert evidence on the following terms:

Individual or Joint	Field	Name	Date for exchange	Whether permission for oral evidence
Claimants	Planning	William Smith of Town & Country Planners	5 November 2008	Yes
Claimants	Valuation	Douglas Jones of Dorchester Surveyors	5 November 2008	Yes

Defendant	Planning	?	5 November 2008	Yes
Defendant	Valuation	?	5 November 2008	Yes

- Reports to be exchanged (and filed) by 4pm on the dates specified.
- Experts in like fields to hold discussions in accordance with rule 35.12 by 5pm on 14 November 2008 on all the issues arising in their common fields.
- Statements under rule 35.12(3) to be prepared and filed by 4pm on 21 November 2008.
- The parties are to consult with each other and the court with a view to arranging service and (where required) filing of statements of case, witness statements, experts' reports, disclosure lists and other documents in computer readable form as well as in hard copy. [Format for court disks:]
- Time under paragraphs [2, 3, 4, 5 and 6] above not to be extended without permission.
- Pre-trial review date: 28 November 2008. Time allowed 1 hour. Parties to complete, file and serve pre-trial questionnaire, after consultation, by 2pm on 25 November 2008.
- The claimant shall prepare and file a trial bundle in compliance with CPR 39PD.3.
- Permission to restore.
- Costs in case.

5 SPECIMEN APPLICATION UNDER SECTION 84(1)

Crown copyright material is reproduced with the permission of the Controller of HMSO and the Queen's Printer for Scotland.

Case number: LP/ /

Application under section 84 of the *Law of Property Act* 1925 to discharge or modify a restrictive covenant

(Attached to this application marked 'A' is a bundle of true copy documents. References to page numbers in this application are to the page numbers of bundle A.)

1. **Applicant**
   Sympathetic Developments Ltd whose registered office is situate at 1 Conservation Wood, London. Telephone number: 02071234567.

2. **Applicant's representative**
   Andrew Olins of IBB solicitors, Capital Court, 30 Windsor Street, Uxbridge, Middlesex UB8 1AB. DX 45105 Uxbridge. Telephone number: 08456381381.   Fax   number: 08456381351.   Email   address: andrew.olins@ibblaw.co.uk

3. **Application land**
   Freehold land known as and situate at 1 Tumbledown Wood, London. The application land is registered at the Land Registry with title number ZT 654321 and official copy entries including the filed plan to the title are at pp. 1–4. The application land is shown edged red on the filed plan. The application land has the following ordnance survey number: TS 123456789.

4. **Applicant's interest in the land**
   The applicant is the registered freehold proprietor of the application land.

5. **Land in which the applicant has an interest**
   - The application land.
   - The land shown edged green on the plan at p. 5 ('the neighbouring land'), which adjoins the application land. The applicant is the freehold registered proprietor of the neighbouring land which is registered at the Land Registry with title number ZT 654322.

6. **Land subject to the burden of the restrictive covenants**
   The applicant believes that the land edged blue on the plan at p. 6 (which includes the application land and the neighbouring land) is burdened by the restrictive covenants.

7. **Land to which the benefit of the covenant is believed to attach**
   The applicant believes that the land edged brown on the plan at p. 6 may have the benefit of the restrictive covenants. The applicant has undertaken searches at the Land Registry and has identified that the land coloured yellow (comprising part of the land edged brown) is owned by the following registered freehold proprietors:

- Ivor Heap of 2 Tumbledown Wood, London; and

- Joe King of 3 Tumbledown Wood, London.

The land coloured orange (comprising the balance of the land edged brown) appears to be unregistered land. The applicant does not know the persons who own an interest in the land coloured orange. However, the land coloured orange appears to comprise the following:

- 4 5 Tumbledown Wood, London;

- 1–9 Tumbledown Cresent, London; and

- open space known as Tumbledown Green, London.

Nothing under this heading is intended to prejudice any contentions that the applicant may later wish to advance as to the entitlement of any persons to object to this section 84(1) application.

8. **The legal instrument under which the restrictive covenants were imposed**
   The covenants were imposed by a conveyance dated 1 January 1926 made between (1) Bulldozer Developments Ltd and (2) Yuri Nimbey. The applicant does not have a copy of the conveyance although an extract from the conveyance that includes the restrictive covenants appears at entry 1 of the charges register to the registered title of the application land (p. 3).

9. **Whether the applicant is in breach of any of the restrictions imposed by the legal instrument under which the covenant was imposed**
   At present, the applicant is not in breach of the restrictive covenants imposed by the conveyance dated 1 January 1926. However, the applicant wishes to carry out a development at the application land which, if implemented, will breach the restrictive covenants.

10. **The negative covenants the subject of this application**

    (i)   No building of any description be erected upon any part of the land hereby conveyed without the vendor's prior permission in writing;

    (ii) not more than five private dwelling houses to the acre shall be erected on any part of the land hereby conveyed;

    (iii) not to use any buildings erected on the land hereby conveyed for any purpose other than as a private dwelling house or as garage or outhouse to be used only in connection with such private dwelling house; and

    (iv) no trade or business shall be carried on at any time upon the land hereby conveyed but this shall not prevent the use of any private dwelling house for professional purposes of a medical practitioner dentist architect lawyer or surveyor.

11. **Whether the application is for a discharge or modification of the negative covenants**
    The applicant seeks a modification of the negative covenants.

12. **If the application is for modification of the restriction:**
   - **set out the modification that is sought;**
   - **specify which of grounds (a), (aa), (b) and (c) of section 84(1) of the Law of Property Act 1925 (as amended) are relied on; and**
   - **set out under each of the grounds relied on, relevant particulars of the grounds.**

(i) The applicant seeks a modification of the restrictive covenants burdening the application land so as to permit it to redevelop the application land as a four-storey block of flats with underground parking in accordance with a planning permission obtained from Diminster Council on 1 March 2008 under reference 9876/08/FUL ('the planning permission')(pp. 7–12).

(ii) The applicant relies on grounds (aa) and (cc).

As to ground (aa), the applicant contends that:
   - the restrictive covenants burdening the application land (to the extent that such restrictive covenants prevent a development of the application land in accordance with the planning permission) impede a reasonable user of the application land;
   - the restrictive covenants burdening the application land do not afford the persons who have the benefit of the restrictive covenants any practical benefit;
   - for at least five years, owners of residential properties within the vicinity of the application land have obtained planning permission for and implemented developments comparable to the one that the applicant wishes to carry out at the application land; and
   - if (which is denied) the persons who have the benefit of the restrictive covenants burdening the application land would suffer a practical loss by a modification of the restrictive covenants in the terms sought, the payment of money would be adequate compensation for such loss.

As to ground (cc), the applicant contends that the persons who have the benefit of the restrictive covenants burdening the application land will not suffer any injury if the restrictive covenants are modified in the terms sought.

13. **Fees**
   I have paid the setting-down fee of £200 and I accept responsibility for the conduct of the case and the payment of later fees.

   .... Date: ....

   Signed by IBB solicitors for and on behalf of the applicant

   Capital Court, 30 Windsor Street, Uxbridge, Middlesex UB8 1AB. DX 45105 Uxbridge. Telephone number: 08456381381. Fax number: 08456381351. Email address: andrew.olins@ibblaw.co.uk

6 SPECIMEN PUBLICITY NOTICE

Crown copyright material is reproduced with the permission of the Controller of HMSO and the Queen's Printer for Scotland.

Case number: LP/ /

Restrictive covenant application: publicity notice

1. TAKE NOTICE that an application under section 84 of the *Law of Property Act* 1925 to modify restrictive covenants affecting the land referred to below has been made to the Lands Tribunal. If you are legally entitled to the benefit of the covenant and you wish to object to the application, you should object within 28 days of the date of this notice.

2. The application relates to land at 1 Tumbledown Wood, London.

3. The applicant is Sympathetic Developments Ltd whose registered office is situate at 1 Conservation Wood, London.

4. The restrictive covenants contained in a conveyance dated 1 January 1926 made between (1) Bulldozer Developments Ltd and (2) Yuri Nimbey in respect of which the application is made, contains the following restrictions:

    (i) no building of any description be erected upon any part of the land hereby conveyed without the vendor's prior permission in writing;

    (ii) not more than five private dwelling houses to the acre shall be erected on any part of the land hereby conveyed;

    (iii) not to use any buildings erected on the land hereby conveyed for any purpose other than as a private dwelling house or as garage or outhouse to be used only in connection with such private dwelling house; and

    (iv) no trade or business shall be carried on at any time upon the land hereby conveyed but this shall not prevent the use of any private dwelling house for professional purposes of a medical practitioner dentist architect lawyer or surveyor

5. The application seeks the modification of the restrictions so as to permit it to redevelop the application land as a four-storey block of flats with underground parking in accordance with a planning permission obtained from Diminster Council under reference 9876/08/FUL ('the planning permission'). Modification is sought on the following grounds:

    - (aa) – that unless modified the covenant would impede the use of the land in accordance with the planning permission; that such use is a reasonable use; that in impeding that use the restriction does not secure to the persons entitled to the benefit of it any practical benefits of substantial value or advantage; and that money will be an adequate compensation for the loss or disadvantage (if any) which any such person will suffer from the modification; and

- (c) – that the proposed modification will not injure the persons entitled to the benefit of the restriction.

6. You may inspect the application, plan and other documents at the offices of IBB solicitors at Capital Court, 30 Windsor Street, Uxbridge, Middlesex UB8 1AB during normal working hours by prior appointment. IBB's telephone number is 08456381381. A copying charge may be payable if copies of any documents are required.

7. If you are a person legally entitled to the benefit of the restrictive covenant and you wish to object to the application, either download a form of objection (Form LPD) from www.landstribunal.gov.uk or request one from The Registrar, Lands Tribunal, Procession House, 55 Ludgate Hill, London EC4M 7JW. The Lands Tribunal's telephone number is 020 7029 9780. The form of objection should be completed, signed and posted to the Lands Tribunal within 28 days of the date of this notice.

8. Persons who lodge objections become parties to the case, and, provided they are entitled to object, they may appear at the hearing of the application, if there is one. In asking the Lands Tribunal to discharge or modify a restrictive covenant, the applicant may be seeking to have a property right removed from someone who is entitled to the benefit of that covenant. For this reason, successful objectors may normally expect to have their legal costs paid by the unsuccessful applicant. Likewise, although they will usually pay their own costs, unsuccessful objectors will not normally be ordered to pay the costs of successful applicants. However, an objector who acts unreasonably may be required to pay some or all of the applicant's costs where they behaved unreasonably in the course of the proceedings, in rejecting a reasonable offer to settle made by the applicant, or in objecting to the proposed change.
   In support of the application, the applicant may rely on a lack of objections, or a failure on the part of any particular person to object.
   You may wish to seek legal advice from a suitably qualified solicitor about these matters.

9. Signed .... Dated: ....

   (Applicant's solicitors) IBB solicitors, Capital Court, 30 Windsor Street, Uxbridge, Middlesex UB8 1AB. DX 45105 Uxbridge. Telephone number: 08456381381. Fax number: 08456381351. Email address: andrew.olins@ibblaw.co.uk

7 SPECIMEN NOTICE OF OBJECTION

Crown copyright material is reproduced with the permission of the Controller of HMSO and the Queen's Printer for Scotland.

Case number: LP/ /

Notice of objection to a restrictive covenant application

Concerning the application to discharge or modify restrictive covenants:

- made by Sympathetic Developments Ltd whose registered office is situate at 1 Conservation Wood, London; and
- concerning land at 1 Tumbledown Wood, London.

A. Objector

A1. Objector's name: Yuri Nimbey

A2. Status: Individual

A3. Postal address: 8 Tumbledown Wood, London

A4. Phone number: 02076786789

A5. Representative: Bill Large, Rookie & Green

A6. Status: Solicitors

A7. Postal address: 11 Doggy Avenue, Bow, London. DX 1234 Bow

A8. Phone number: 02073999988

A9. Reference number: AR/Nimbey/01

B. Legal entitlement

B1. Basis of objector's claim to be legally entitled to the benefit of the restriction:

There is a scheme of development and the application land and the objector's land fall within the area covered by the scheme.

B2. Land owned by the objector:

The objector is the freehold owner of 8, Tumbledown Wood, London.

C. Grounds of objection

C1. Is this an objection to the discharge wholly of the restrictive covenants?

No

C2. **If YES, give a brief statement of the objector's response to the grounds of the application for discharge [(a), (aa), (b) or (c) as the case may be].**

C3. Is this an objection to the modification of the restrictive covenants?

Yes

C4. **If YES, give a brief statement of the objector's response to the grounds of the application for modification.**

As to ground (aa), the objector contends that the negative covenants confer on his property, 8 Tumbledown Wood, a practical benefit of substantial value or advantage; in particular, the restrictive covenants protect the objector against loss of amenity and a diminution in the value of his property. The objector believes that, if the restrictive covenants are modified so as to permit the applicant to implement the development for which it has obtained planning permission, he will suffer the following detriment and injury: a loss of privacy and seclusion; a loss of peace and quiet; an increase in traffic flows; an increase in housing density within the residential estate thereby undermining the integrity of the existing scheme of development; and a diminution in the value of his property. The objector will adduce evidence from witnesses of fact and experts to make good his contentions.

As to ground (c), the objector repeats the comments made in the preceding paragraph.

C5. Any other reasons why the objector opposes the application.

None

D. Claim for compensation

D1. If in the event the application is successful, is this also a claim for compensation from the applicant?

Yes

D2. Approximate amount of compensation claimed: £10,000

E. Consequences of objecting or not objecting

IMPORTANT: An objector becomes a party to the case, with the rights and responsibilities this entails including attending the hearing.

In asking the Lands Tribunal to discharge or modify a restrictive covenant, the applicant may be seeking to have property rights removed from someone who is entitled to the benefit of that covenant. For this reason, successful objectors may normally expect to have their legal costs paid by the unsuccessful applicant. Likewise, although they will usually pay their own costs, unsuccessful objectors will not normally be ordered to pay the costs of successful applicants. However, an objector may be required to pay some or all of the applicant's costs if they behaved unreasonably in the course of the proceedings, in rejecting a reasonable offer to settle made by the applicant, or in objecting to the proposed change.

Anyone unsure of their position should take professional legal advice.

If no objections (or no valid objections) are made, the applicant may rely on the lack of objections in support of the application.

F. <u>Signature</u>

....

Signed: Bill Large, Rookie & Green
Dated:

....

Status: Solicitors for the objector

8 SPECIMEN LETTER OF INSTRUCTION TO EXPERT

My ref   ARO. Sympathetic/001

Your ref

Date

Ivor Meadow
Fallowfield Planning Consultants
Fallowfield Road
London

Dear Ivor

Formal letter of instruction

Lands Tribunal case number LP/ /

My firm acts for Sympathetic Developments Ltd. My client is the applicant in an Action before the Lands Tribunal.

My client would like to instruct you to act as its expert in the Action. This will necessitate you:

1. preparing an expert report by 29 March;

2. if appropriate, preparing a supplemental report in response to your opponent's report by 15 April;

3. holding without prejudice discussions with your opponent by 1 May with a view to resolving, or at least narrowing, the issues in dispute within your discipline;

4. preparing a joint statement with your opponent to record the outcome of these discussions by 7 May; and

5. attending the trial of the Action presently fixed for week commencing 1 June.

In the Action, my client is applying for a modification of restrictive covenants burdening freehold property which it owns at 1 Tumbledown Wood, London. The application is made pursuant to grounds (aa) and (c) of section 84(1) of the *Law of Property Act* 1925. The Lands Tribunal has given permission for the parties to adduce expert evidence from a planning consultant. This expert evidence is intended to assist the Lands Tribunal, at the trial of the Action, in determining the following issues:

1. whether the restrictive covenants burdening 1 Tumbledown Wood confer a practical benefit of substantial value or advantage on adjoining or neighbouring properties that have the benefit of the covenants; and

2. if so, to what extent (if at all) will that practical benefit be adversely affected if my client is able to build a four-storey block of flats with underground car park at 1 Tumbledown Wood in accordance with a planning permission that it has obtained from the local planning authority.

Before you accept this formal instruction, it is important that you satisfy yourself that you have the necessary skill and expertise to give an opinion on these issues.

Your duties as an expert

As an expert, it is important for you to appreciate that:

1. You have a duty to help the Lands Tribunal on the matters within your expertise, and this duty overrides any obligation that you may have to my client. Any failure on your part to comply with this overriding duty may lead to the Lands Tribunal ruling that your evidence cannot be relied upon.

2. Your evidence must not be influenced by the pressures of the litigation.

3. You must assist the Court by providing objective, unbiased opinions on the matters within your expertise, and you must not assume the role of an advocate.

4. You must consider all material facts, including those that might detract you from your opinions.

5. You must make clear in your report when:
    - a question or issue falls outside your expertise; or
    - you are not able to reach a definite opinion, for example, because you have insufficient information.

6. If, after producing your report, you change your view on any question or issue, such change of view must be communicated to the expert acting for the objectors.

Form and content of your report

I would like to give you general guidance as to the form and content of your report.

1. Your report should be addressed to the Lands Tribunal and not to my client or my firm.

2. Your report must:
    - give details of your qualifications;
    - give details of any literature or other material that you have relied on in making your report;
    - contain a statement setting out the substance of all facts and instructions given to you that are material to the opinions expressed in your report or upon which those opinions are based;
    - make clear which of the facts stated in your report are within your own knowledge;
    - state who carried out any examination, measurement, test or experiment which you have used in your report, giving the qualifications of that person, and stating whether or not the test or experiment has been carried out under your supervision;

- (where there is a range of opinion on the matters dealt with in your report), summarise the range of opinion and give reasons for your own opinion;
- contain a summary of the conclusions that you have reached;
- state if you are unable to give an opinion without qualification and state the necessary qualification;
- contain a statement that you understand your duty to the Lands Tribunal and you have complied and will continue to comply with that duty; and
- be verified by a statement of truth in the following form:
  'I confirm that insofar as the facts stated in my report are within my own knowledge, I have made clear which they are and I believe them to be true, and that the opinions I have expressed represent my true and complete professional opinion.'

I am obliged professionally to point out to you that proceedings for contempt of Court may be brought against an expert if he makes a false statement in his report without an honest belief in its truth.

Questions

I can advise you that the objector's expert is entitled to ask you questions for the purpose of clarifying your report. Usually, these questions must be put to you within 28 days after your report has been served. You must endeavour to answer any such questions within 14 days of receipt. I would like to emphasise that your answers must be verified by a statement of truth and comply with your duties to the Lands Tribunal.

You are likewise entitled to put questions to the objector's expert for the purpose of obtaining clarification of his/her report.

Directions

If, at any time, you consider that you require the assistance of the Lands Tribunal to carry out your functions, you are entitled to apply directly to the Lands Tribunal for directions. If you intend to make such an application, please let me know.

Enclosures

I enclose for your use:

1. the application;
2. the notices of objection;
3. the parties' factual witness statements;
4. the parties' disclosure documentation;
5. the order dated 1 February permitting the parties to adduce expert evidence;
6. my client's planning permission, reference 9876/08/FUL, together with the architectural drawings referred to therein; and

7. a map showing the location of I Tumbledown Wood and the adjoining or neighbouring properties owned by the objectors.

If you need any further information to enable you to carry out your instructions, please let me know.

Yours sincerely

Andrew Olins

Partner, IBB solicitors

9 SPECIMEN FINAL ORDER WITHOUT A HEARING

Case number: LP/ /

In the matter of an application under section 84 of the *Law of Property Act* 1925

Applicant: Sympathetic Developments Ltd

FINAL ORDER

The Lands Tribunal having read:

(i) the application dated **[INSERT DATE]** made under section 84(1) of the *Law of Property Act* 1925 ('section 84(1)') by Sympathetic Developments Ltd ('the originating applicant') who claims to be entitled to freehold interest in the land described in the first schedule hereto ('the application land');

(ii) the instrument referred to in the second schedule hereto containing the restrictions set out in the third schedule hereto affecting the application land ('the restrictions');

(iii) the certificate of compliance dated **[INSERT DATE]** by which the originating applicant satisfied the Tribunal that the application was advertised and notice given to persons who appeared to be entitled to the benefit of the restrictions;

and no objections to the application having been lodged and no claims for compensation having been made

and the originating applicant having consented to the Lands Tribunal determining the application without a hearing

and the Lands Tribunal being satisfied that the application should be modified as set out in the fourth schedule hereto under paragraphs (aa) and (c) of section 84(1)

it is ordered that the application be determined without a hearing

and it is ordered that the restrictions affecting the application land shall be modified as set out in the fourth schedule hereto pursuant to paragraphs (aa) and (c) of section 84(1).

First Schedule

Freehold land known as and situate at 1 Tumbledown Wood, London registered at the Land Registry with title number ZT 654321.

Second Schedule

Conveyance dated 1 January 1926 made between (1) Bulldozer Developments Ltd and (2) Yuri Nimbey.

Third Schedule

(i) No building of any description be erected upon any part of the land hereby conveyed without the vendor's prior permission in writing;

(ii) not more than five private dwelling houses to the acre shall be erected on any part of the land hereby conveyed;

(iii) not to use any buildings erected on the land hereby conveyed for any purpose other than as a private dwelling house or as garage or outhouse to be used only in connection with such private dwelling house; and

(iv) no trade or business shall be carried on at any time upon the land hereby conveyed but this shall not prevent the use of any private dwelling house for professional purposes of a medical practitioner dentist architect lawyer or surveyor.

Fourth Schedule

The restrictions be modified so as to permit the development of the application land as a four-storey block of flats with underground parking in accordance with a planning permission obtained from Diminster Council, reference 9876/08/FUL.

Dated

....

President, Lands Tribunal

Appendix D: Legislation

1 Online access

The legislation and statutory instruments referred to in this book can be freely accessed online. Please follow the instructions below; sections of particular importance have been highlighted for your ease.

Acts

An online database of revised UK primary legislation can be found at www.statutelaw.gov.uk, the UK Statute Law Database (SLD). The database is the official revised edition of UK primary legislation online. It contains primary legislation that was in force at 1 February 1991 and primary and secondary legislation that has been produced since that date. Note that there may be amendments which have not yet been applied. See the status statement at the top of each piece of legislation.

Using the search boxes at the top of the home page, legislation can be found by title and year. Links to individual sections are then available.

The relevant sections of the *Law of Property Act* 1925 and the *Town and Country Planning Act* 1990 are reproduced in full below.

Crown copyright material is reproduced with the permission of the Controller of HMSO and the Queen's Printer for Scotland.

Other Acts of particular importance that you may wish to refer to include:
- *Lands Tribunal Act* 1949
  - Section 1 – Establishment and jurisdiction of Lands Tribunal
  - Section 3 – Procedure, appeals, costs and fees
- *Supreme Court Act* 1981
  - Section 50 – Power to award damages as well as, or in substitution for, injunction or specific performance

Rules of Court

The *Civil Procedure Rules* can be found at www.justice.gov.uk/civil/procrules_fin/index.htm. Clicking on the 'Rules & Practice Directions' link in the top left-hand corner of the home page will provide a list of links to the various parts of the rules. Links to individual rules and paragraphs are then available.

The *Lands Tribunal Rules* can be found at www.landstribunal.gov.uk. The links at the top of the home page provide access to the rules and further details on the Lands Tribunal, including its jurisdiction, procedures and fees.

2 Law of Property Act 1925

Section 56 – Persons taking who are not parties and as to indentures

(1)   A person may take an immediate or other interest in land or other property, or the benefit of any condition, right of entry, covenant or agreement over or respecting land or other property, although he may not be named as a party to the conveyance or other instrument.

(2)   A deed between parties, to effect its objects, has the effect of an indenture though not indented or expressed to be an indenture.

Section 78 – Benefit of covenants relating to land

(1)   A covenant relating to any land of the covenantee shall be deemed to be made with the covenantee and his successors in title and the persons deriving title under him or them, and shall have effect as if such successors and other persons were expressed.
For the purposes of this subsection in connexion with covenants restrictive of the user of land 'successors in title' shall be deemed to include the owners and occupiers for the time being of the land of the covenantee intended to be benefited.

(2)   This section applies to covenants made after the commencement of this Act, but the repeal of section fifty-eight of the *Conveyancing Act* 1881, does not affect the operation of covenants to which that section applied.

Section 79 – Burden of covenants relating to land

(1) A covenant relating to any land of a covenantor or capable of being bound by him, shall, unless a contrary intention is expressed, be deemed to be made by the covenantor on behalf of himself his successors in title and the persons deriving title under him or them, and, subject as aforesaid, shall have effect as if such successors and other persons were expressed.
This subsection extends to a covenant to do some act relating to the land, notwithstanding that the subject-matter may not be in existence when the covenant is made.

(2) For the purposes of this section in connexion with covenants restrictive of the user of land 'successors in title' shall be deemed to include the owners and occupiers for the time being of such land.

(3) This section applies only to covenants made after the commencement of this Act.

Section 80 – Covenants binding land

(1) A covenant and a bond and an obligation or contract made under seal after 31st December 1881 but before the coming into force of section 1 of the *Law of Property (Miscellaneous Provisions) Act* 1989 or executed as a deed in accordance with that section after its coming into force, binds the real estate as well as the personal estate of the person making the same if and so far as a contrary intention is not expressed in the covenant, bond, obligation, or contract.
This subsection extends to a covenant implied by virtue of this Act.

(2) Every covenant running with the land, whether entered into before or after the commencement of this Act, shall take effect in accordance with any statutory enactment affecting the devolution of the land, and accordingly the benefit or burden of every such covenant shall vest in or bind the persons who by virtue of any such enactment or otherwise succeed to the title of the covenantee or the covenantor, as the case may be.

(3)   The benefit of a covenant relating to land entered into after the commencement of this Act may be made to run with the land without the use of any technical expression if the covenant is of such a nature that the benefit could have been made to run with the land before the commencement of this Act.

(4)   For the purposes of this section, a covenant runs with the land when the benefit or burden of it, whether at law or in equity, passes to the successors in title of the covenantee or the covenantor, as the case may be.

Section 84 – Power to discharge or modify restrictive covenants affecting land

(1)   The Lands Tribunal shall (without prejudice to any concurrent jurisdiction of the court) have power from time to time, on the application of any person interested in any freehold land affected by any restriction arising under covenant or otherwise as to the user thereof or the building thereon, by order wholly or partially to discharge or modify any such restriction on being satisfied:
        (a)   that by reason of changes in the character of the property or the neighbourhood or other circumstances of the case which the Lands Tribunal may deem material, the restriction ought to be deemed obsolete, or
        (aa) that in a case falling within subsection (1A) below the continued existence thereof would impede some reasonable user of the land for public or private purposes or, as the case may be, would unless modified so impede such user; or
        (b)   that the persons of full age and capacity for the time being or from time to time entitled to the benefit of the restriction, whether in respect of estates in fee simple or any lesser estates or interests in the property to which the benefit of the restriction is annexed, have agreed, either expressly or by implication, by their acts or omissions, to the same being discharged or modified; or
        (c)   that the proposed discharge or modification will not injure the persons entitled to the benefit of the restriction:
        and an order discharging or modifying a restriction under this subsection may direct the applicant to pay to any person entitled to the benefit of the restriction such sum

by way of consideration as the Tribunal may think it just to award under one, but not both, of the following heads, that is to say, either:

    (i)   a sum to make up for any loss or disadvantage suffered by that person in consequence of the discharge or modification; or

    (ii) a sum to make up for any effect which the restriction had, at the time when it was imposed, in reducing the consideration then received for the land affected by it.

(1A) Subsection (1)(aa) above authorises the discharge or modification of a restriction by reference to its impeding some reasonable user of land in any case in which the Lands Tribunal is satisfied that the restriction, in impeding that user, either:

    (a) does not secure to persons entitled to the benefit of it any practical benefits of substantial value or advantage to them; or

    (b) is contrary to the public interest;

and that money will be an adequate compensation for the loss or disadvantage (if any) which any such person will suffer from the discharge or modification.

(1B) In determining whether a case is one falling within subsection (1A) above, and in determining whether (in any such case or otherwise) a restriction ought to be discharged or modified, the Lands Tribunal shall take into account the development plan and any declared or ascertainable pattern for the grant or refusal of planning permissions in the relevant areas, as well as the period at which and context in which the restriction was created or imposed and any other material circumstances.

(1C) It is hereby declared that the power conferred by this section to modify a restriction includes power to add such further provisions restricting the user of or the building on the land affected as appear to the Lands Tribunal to be reasonable in view of the relaxation of the existing provisions, and as may be accepted by the applicant; and the Lands Tribunal may accordingly refuse to modify a restriction without some such addition.

(2)   The court shall have power on the application of any person interested:

(a) to declare whether or not in any particular case any freehold land is or would in any given event be affected by a restriction imposed by any instrument; or

(b) to declare what, upon the true construction of any instrument purporting to impose a restriction, is the nature and extent of the restriction thereby imposed and whether the same is or would in any given event be enforceable and if so by whom.

Neither subsections (7) and (11) of this section nor, unless the contrary is expressed, any later enactment providing for this section not to apply to any restrictions shall affect the operation of this subsection or the operation for purposes of this subsection of any other provisions of this section.

(3) The Lands Tribunal shall, before making any order under this section, direct such enquiries, if any, to be made of any government department or local authority, and such notices, if any, whether by way of advertisement or otherwise, to be given to such of the persons who appear to be entitled to the benefit of the restriction intended to be discharged, modified, or dealt with as, having regard to any enquiries notices or other proceedings previously made, given or taken, the Lands Tribunal may think fit.

(3A) On an application to the Lands Tribunal under this section the Lands Tribunal shall give any necessary directions as to the persons who are or are not to be admitted (as appearing to be entitled to the benefit of the restriction) to oppose the application, and no appeal shall lie against any such direction; but rules under the *Lands Tribunal Act* 1949 shall make provision whereby, in cases in which there arises on such an application (whether or not in connection with the admission of persons to oppose) any such question as is referred to in subsection (2)(a) or (b) of this section, the proceedings on the application can and, if the rules so provide, shall be suspended to enable the decision of the court to be obtained on that question by an application under that subsection, or by means of a case stated by the Lands Tribunal, or otherwise, as may be provided by those rules or by rules of court.

(4) [repealed]

(5)　Any order made under this section shall be binding on all persons, whether ascertained or of full age or capacity or not, then entitled or thereafter capable of becoming entitled to the benefit of any restriction, which is thereby discharged, modified, or dealt with, and whether such persons are parties to the proceedings or have been served with notice or not.

(6)　An order may be made under this section notwithstanding that any instrument which is alleged to impose the restriction intended to be discharged, modified, or dealt with, may not have been produced to the court or the Lands Tribunal, and the court or the Lands Tribunal may act on such evidence of that instrument as it may think sufficient.

(7)　This section applies to restrictions whether subsisting at the commencement of this Act or imposed thereafter, but this section does not apply where the restriction was imposed on the occasion of a disposition made gratuitously or for a nominal consideration for public purposes.

(8)　This section applies whether the land affected by the restrictions is registered or not.

(9)　Where any proceedings by action or otherwise are taken to enforce a restrictive covenant, any person against whom the proceedings are taken, may in such proceedings apply to the court for an order giving leave to apply to the Lands Tribunal under this section, and staying the proceedings in the meantime.

(10)　[repealed]

(11)　This section does not apply to restrictions imposed by the Commissioners of Works under any statutory power for the protection of any Royal Park or Garden or to restrictions of a like character imposed upon the occasion of any enfranchisement effected before the commencement of this Act in any manor vested in His Majesty in right of the Crown or the Duchy of Lancaster, nor subject to subsection (11A) below to restrictions created or imposed:

(a) for Naval, Military or Air Force purposes;

(b) for civil aviation purposes under the powers of the *Air Navigation Act* 1920, of section 19 or 23 of the *Civil Aviation Act* 1949 or of section 30 or 41 of the *Civil Aviation Act* 1982.

(11A) Subsection (11) of this section:

(a) shall exclude the application of this section to a restriction falling within subsection (11)(a), and not created or imposed in connection with the use of any land as an aerodrome, only so long as the restriction is enforceable by or on behalf of the Crown; and

(b) shall exclude the application of this section to a restriction falling within subsection (11)(b), or created or imposed in connection with the use of any land as an aerodrome, only so long as the restriction is enforceable by or on behalf of the Crown or any public or international authority.

(12) Where a term of more than forty years is created in land (whether before or after the commencement of this Act) this section shall, after the expiration of twenty-five years of the term, apply to restrictions affecting such leasehold land in like manner as it would have applied had the land been freehold:

Provided that this subsection shall not apply to mining leases.

(13) [repealed]

3 Town and Country Planning Act 1990

Section 106 – Planning obligations

(1) Any person interested in land in the area of a local planning authority may, by agreement or otherwise, enter into an obligation (referred to in this section and sections 106A and 106B as 'a planning obligation'), enforceable to the extent mentioned in subsection (3):

(a) restricting the development or use of the land in any specified way;

(b) requiring specified operations or activities to be carried out in, on, under or over the land;

(c) requiring the land to be used in any specified way; or

(d) requiring a sum or sums to be paid to the authority (or, in a case where section 2E applies, to the Greater London Authority) on a specified date or dates or periodically.

(2) A planning obligation may:
  (a) be unconditional or subject to conditions;
  (b) impose any restriction or requirement mentioned in subsection (1)(a) to (c) either indefinitely or for such period or periods as may be specified; and
  (c) if it requires a sum or sums to be paid, require the payment of a specified amount or an amount determined in accordance with the instrument by which the obligation is entered into and, if it requires the payment of periodical sums, require them to be paid indefinitely or for a specified period.

(3) Subject to subsection (4) a planning obligation is enforceable by the authority identified in accordance with subsection (9)(d):
  (a) against the person entering into the obligation; and
  (b) against any person deriving title from that person.

(4) The instrument by which a planning obligation is entered into may provide that a person shall not be bound by the obligation in respect of any period during which he no longer has an interest in the land.

(5) A restriction or requirement imposed under a planning obligation is enforceable by injunction.

(6) Without prejudice to subsection (5), if there is a breach of a requirement in a planning obligation to carry out any operations in, on, under or over the land to which the obligation relates, the authority by whom the obligation is enforceable may:
  (a) enter the land and carry out the operations; and
  (b) recover from the person or persons against whom the obligation is enforceable any expenses reasonably incurred by them in doing so.

(7) Before an authority exercise their power under subsection (6)(a) they shall give not less than twenty-one days' notice of their intention to do so to any person against whom the planning obligation is enforceable.

(8)   Any person who wilfully obstructs a person acting in the exercise of a power under subsection (6)(a) shall be guilty of an offence and liable on summary conviction to a fine not exceeding level 3 on the standard scale.

(9)   A planning obligation may not be entered into except by an instrument executed as a deed which:
   (a)   states that the obligation is a planning obligation for the purposes of this section;
   (b)   identifies the land in which the person entering into the obligation is interested;
   (c)   identifies the person entering into the obligation and states what his interest in the land is; and
   (d)   identifies the local planning authority by whom the obligation is enforceable and, in a case where section 2E applies, identifies the Mayor of London as an authority by whom the obligation is also enforceable.

(10)   A copy of any such instrument shall be given to the local planning authority so identified and, in a case where section 2E applies, to the Mayor of London.

(11)   A planning obligation shall be a local land charge and for the purposes of the *Local Land Charges Act* 1975 the authority by whom the obligation is enforceable shall be treated as the originating authority as respects such a charge.

(12)   Regulations may provide for the charging on the land of:
   (a)   any sum or sums required to be paid under a planning obligation; and
   (b)   any expenses recoverable by a local planning authority or the Mayor of London under subsection (6)(b);
   and this section and sections 106A and 106B shall have effect subject to any such regulations.

(13)   In this section 'specified' means specified in the instrument by which the planning obligation is entered into and in this section and section 106A 'land' has the same meaning as in the *Local Land Charges Act* 1975.

Section 106A – Modification and discharge of planning obligations

(1) A planning obligation may not be modified or discharged except:

    (a) by agreement between the appropriate authority (see subsection (11)) and the person or persons against whom the obligation is enforceable; or

    (b) in accordance with this section and section 106B.

(2) An agreement falling within subsection (1)(a) shall not be entered into except by an instrument executed as a deed.

(3) A person against whom a planning obligation is enforceable may, at any time after the expiry of the relevant period, apply to the appropriate authority for the obligation:

    (a) to have effect subject to such modifications as may be specified in the application; or

    (b) to be discharged.

(4) In subsection (3) 'the relevant period' means:

    (a) such period as may be prescribed; or

    (b) if no period is prescribed, the period of five years beginning with the date on which the obligation is entered into.

(5) An application under subsection (3) for the modification of a planning obligation may not specify a modification imposing an obligation on any other person against whom the obligation is enforceable.

(6) Where an application is made to an authority under subsection (3), the authority may determine:

    (a) that the planning obligation shall continue to have effect without modification;

    (b) if the obligation no longer serves a useful purpose, that it shall be discharged; or

    (c) if the obligation continues to serve a useful purpose, but would serve that purpose equally well if it had effect subject to the modifications specified in the application, that it shall have effect subject to those modifications.

(7) The authority shall give notice of their determination to the applicant within such period as may be prescribed.

(8)   Where an authority determine that a planning obligation shall have effect subject to modifications specified in the application, the obligation as modified shall be enforceable as if it had been entered into on the date on which notice of the determination was given to the applicant.

(9)   Regulations may make provision with respect to:
       (a)   the form and content of applications under subsection (3);
       (b)   the publication of notices of such applications;
       (c)   the procedures for considering any representations made with respect to such applications; and
       (d)   the notices to be given to applicants of determinations under subsection (6).

(10)   Section 84 of the *Law of Property Act* 1925 (power to discharge or modify restrictive covenants affecting land) does not apply to a planning obligation.

(11)   In this section 'the appropriate authority' means:
       (a)   the Mayor of London, in the case of any planning obligation enforceable by him;
       (b)   in the case of any other planning obligation, the local planning authority by whom it is enforceable.

(12)   The Mayor of London must consult the local planning authority before exercising any function under this section.

Section 106B – Appeals

(1)   Where an authority:
       (a)   fail to give notice as mentioned in section 106A(7); or
       (b)   determine that a planning obligation shall continue to have effect without modification;
       the applicant may appeal to the Secretary of State.

(2)   For the purposes of an appeal under subsection (1)(a), it shall be assumed that the authority have determined that the planning obligation shall continue to have effect without modification.

(3)   An appeal under this section shall be made by notice served within such period and in such manner as may be prescribed.

(4)   Subsections (6) to (9) of section 106A apply in relation to appeals to the Secretary of State under this section as they apply in relation to applications to authorities under that section.

(5)   Before determining the appeal the Secretary of State shall, if either the applicant or the authority so wish, give each of them an opportunity of appearing before and being heard by a person appointed by the Secretary of State for the purpose.

(6)   The determination of an appeal by the Secretary of State under this section shall be final.

(7)   Schedule 6 applies to appeals under this section.

(8)   In the application of Schedule 6 to an appeal under this section in a case where the authority mentioned in subsection (1) is the Mayor of London, references in that Schedule to the local planning authority are references to the Mayor of London.

Glossary

Acquiescence: a covenantee is guilty of acquiescence if there has been an overt and continuous breach of covenant for a significant period and, in all the circumstances, it would be unconscionable after such a passage of time to permit the covenantee to enforce the covenant.

Alternative dispute resolution (ADR): the voluntary participation in a non-litigation procedure designed to encourage the settlement of a dispute through the promotion of a constructive dialogue between the parties. Mediation and case evaluation by an independent third party are examples of alternative dispute resolution. A party that unreasonably refuses to participate in alternative dispute resolution may be penalised by the court in costs.

Annexation: the means by which the benefit of a negative covenant is attached to dominant land in such a way that, when the covenantee transfers the dominant land, the successor in title obtains the benefit of the covenant.

Building scheme: *see* scheme of development.

Commonhold land: a form of freehold land introduced by the *Commonhold and Leasehold Reform Act* 2002. All owners of commonhold units, which comprise the commonhold land, are bound by a commonhold community statement that may include positive and negative covenants.

Common law: the body of law that has been declared in decisions of the courts since time immemorial.

Constructive notice: knowledge that ought to come into the possession of a lawyer if the lawyer makes normal and customary enquiries; such knowledge is 'imputed' to the client.

Contract: an agreement between two or more persons that is legally enforceable in law.

Costs on indemnity basis: costs that are proportionate to the issues in dispute; where there is any doubt as to whether the receiving party's costs have been reasonably incurred or are reasonable and proportionate in amount, such doubt is to be determined in favour of the receiving party.

Costs on the standard basis: costs that are proportionate to the issues in dispute; where there is any doubt as to whether the receiving party's costs have been reasonably incurred or are reasonable and proportionate in amount, such doubt is to be determined in favour of the paying party.

Covenant: a promise usually contained in a deed whereby one party (the covenantor) promises another party (the covenantee) that it will or will not carry out a particular activity on its servient land for the benefit and protection of the covenantee's neighbouring or adjoining dominant land.

Covenantee: a person who is a party to a deed that imposes a covenant on the other party's servient land for the benefit of its own adjoining or neighbouring dominant land. The other party will be the covenantor.

Covenantor: a person who is a party to a deed that imposes a covenant on its own servient land for the benefit of the other party's adjoining or neighbouring dominant land. The other party will be the covenantee.

Cross undertaking in damages: an undertaking that a covenantee gives to the court when it applies for an interim injunction to restrain the covenantor from breaching its covenants. The covenantee promises that if, at trial, its claim against the covenantor is unsuccessful, it will pay the covenantor damages to compensate the covenantor for any loss suffered by reason of the imposition of the interim injunction.

Damages: a sum of money awarded by the court to compensate a person for loss or injury suffered. An award of damages is a common law remedy.

Declaration: a judgment that states the court's opinion on a question of law or as to the respective (property) rights of the parties.

Disclosure: the obligation imposed on litigants by the *Civil Procedure Rules* to disclose to each other all documents that they have (or have had) in their possession, custody or control relating to the dispute that either advance their own case and on which they rely or, alternatively, that may be detrimental to their own case and support their opponent's case.

Dominant land: land owned by the covenantee (or its successors in title) that has the benefit of a covenant.

Equity: the body of doctrines and procedures that have developed alongside the common law; intended to remedy some of the common law's harshness.

Estate rentcharge: a rentcharge created specifically for the purpose of ensuring the enforceability of covenants affecting land to which the rentcharge relates or of ensuring payments towards the provision of services or the carrying out of maintenance or repair or any other financial liability relating to the land charged.

Freehold: a legal estate in land of unlimited duration that implies absolute ownership.

Imputed notice: knowledge in possession of a lawyer that is 'imputed' to the client.

Injunction: an order of the court compelling a person to do or, alternatively, to restrain from doing, a particular act or acts. An injunction is an equitable remedy and, as such, the grant of an injunction is always at the discretion of the court.

Interim injunction: a temporary injunction imposed by the court at or shortly after the start of a claim usually to maintain the status quo between the parties pending the outcome of the trial. *See* injunction.

Leasehold: a legal estate in the land of limited duration created on the making of a lease.

Local land charges: particular types of covenant imposed by central or local government that are registrable under the *Local Land Charges Act* 1975. Such covenants should be entered in the Register of Land Charges maintained by local authorities and are enforceable against future owners of the burdened land.

Negative covenant: a covenant that prohibits a covenantor from carrying out a particular activity on its servient land for the benefit and protection of adjoining or neighbouring dominant land owned by the covenantor.

Part 36 offer: a formal offer made either before or after the start of litigation that is intended to promote a settlement of a dispute and that is likely to cause the offeree to suffer an adverse order as to costs if it rejects the offer and fails to secure a better result at the trial of the litigation.

Planning obligations: *see* section 106 agreement.

Positive covenant: a covenant that obliges a covenantor to carry out a particular activity that necessitates the covenantor incurring expenditure to comply with its terms.

Pre-Action Protocol: the procedural steps imposed on the parties by the *Civil Procedure Rules* aimed at encouraging a resolution of the dispute without recourse to litigation through an early exchange of information and documentation. A party that unreasonably refuses to follow the procedural steps set out in the *Pre-Action Protocol* is likely to be penalised by the court in costs.

Presumption: an assumption that the law makes until the contrary is proven.

Privity of contract: the relationship existing between the parties to a contract.

Privity of estate: the relationship existing between persons holding different estates in the same land such as a landlord and tenant.

Registered land: freehold or leasehold land registered at the Land Registry the ownership of which is established by producing a copy of the registered title to the land. Each registered title is assigned its own unique title number.

Restrictive covenant: *see* negative covenant.

Scheme of development: an arrangement whereby a developer imposes on each of its plot purchasers the same (or substantially the same) negative covenants with the intention that all plot purchasers and their respective successors in title will in equity be bound by the covenants and will be able to enforce them against each other.

Section 106 agreement: an agreement made between a local planning authority and a landowner (usually a developer) under section 106 of the *Town and Country Planning Act* 1990 that imposes planning obligations upon the landowner as a condition of granting the landowner planning permission. Planning obligations contained in a section 106 agreement typically include an obligation on the part of the landowner to contribute towards the cost of off-site infrastructure or to transfer land to the local authority as open space.

Servient land: land owned by the covenantor (or its successors in title) that is burdened by a covenant.

Successor in title: a future owner.

Third party: a person unconnected with the making of a contract.

Touch and concern: A covenant will be presumed to touch and concern the dominant land if its breach adversely affects the nature, quality, mode of use or value of the dominant land.

Transfer: a document that transfers ownership of land.

Transferee: a person to whom property is transferred, usually, but not necessarily, pursuant to a contract.

Transferor: a person who transfers property, usually, but not necessarily, pursuant to a contract.

Unregistered land: freehold or leasehold land that is not registered at the Land Registry, the ownership of which is established by the production of title deeds.

References

Cases that are followed by an asterix (*) have been included in appendix B.

Chapter 2

1   *Murray v Dunn* [1907] AC 283, HL

2   *National Trust v Midlands Electricity Board* [1952] Ch 380

Chapter 3

3   *Haywood v The Brunswick Permanent Benefit Building Society* (1881) LR 8 QBD 403*; *Rhone v Stephens (Executrix)* [1994] 2 AC 310, HL*

4   *Smith and Snipes Hall Farm v River Douglas Catchment Board* [1949] 2 KB 500, CA*

5   *Bedwell Park Quarry Co v Hertfordshire County Council* [1993] JPL 349, CA*

6   *Wrotham Park Estate Co v Parkside Homes* [1974] 1 WLR 798, HC*

7   *C&G Homes Ltd v Secretary of State for Health* [1991] Ch 365, CA*; *Holdom v Kidd* (1991) 61 P&CR 456, CA*; *Jaggard v Sawyer* [1995] 1 WLR 269, CA*

8   *Elliott v Safeway Stores plc* [1995] 1 WLR 1397, HC*

9   *Hall v Ewin* (1888) LR 37 ChD 74, CA*

10   *Bedwell Park Quarry Co v Hertfordshire County Council* [1993] JPL 349, CA*

11   *German v Chapman* (1877) LR 7 ChD 271*

12   *Foster v Fraser* [1893] 3 Ch 158

13   *Cryer v Scott Brothers (Sunbury) Ltd* (1988) 55 P&CR 183, CA*

14   *Cryer v Scott Brothers (Sunbury) Ltd* (1988) 55 P&CR 183, CA*

15   *Frederick Berry Ltd v Bank of Scotland* [1949] 1 KB 619 (non-UK case); *Price v Bouch* (1987) 53 P&CR 257, HC*

16   *Cryer v Scott Brothers (Sunbury) Ltd* (1988) 55 P&CR 183, CA*

17   *Goldman v Abbott* [1989] 48 EG 151

18   *Bray v Fogarty* (1870) 4 IR Eq 544

19   *C&G Homes Ltd v Secretary of State for Health* [1991] Ch 365, CA*

20   *Devonshire v Brookshaw* (1899) 81 LTR 83

21   *Derby Motor Cab Co v Crompton and Evans Union Bank* (1915) 31 TLR 185

22   *Texaco Antilles v Kernochan (Dorothy)* [1973] AC 609

23   *Tod-Heatley v Benham* [1888] 40 ChD 80, CA*

24   *Berton v Alliance Economic Investment Co Ltd* [1922] 1 KB 742, CA*; *Commercial General Administration Ltd v Thomsett* (1979) 250 EG 547, CA

25   *Berton v Alliance Economic Investment Co Ltd* [1922] 1 KB 742, CA*

Chapter 4

26   *London County Council v Allen and Others* [1914] 3 KB 642, CA*

27   *Berton v Alliance Economic Investment Co Ltd* [1922] 1 KB 742, CA*;
      P&A Swift Investments v Combined English Stores Group plc [1989] AC
      632, HL*

28   *Smith and Snipes Hall Farm v River Douglas Catchment Board* [1949]
      2 KB 500, CA*

29   *Smith and Snipes Hall Farm v River Douglas Catchment Board* [1949]
      2 KB 500, CA*

30   Section 78(1) of the *Law of Property Act* 1925 (see appendix D);
      Federated Homes Ltd v Mill Lodge Properties Ltd [1980] 1 WLR 594, CA*

31   *Amsprop Trading Ltd v Harris Distribution Ltd* [1997] 1 WLR 1025, HC*;
      Re Shaw's Application (1994) 68 P&CR 591, LT*

32   *Re Distributors & Warehousing* [1986] 1 EGLR 90; *Re Ecclesiastical
      Commissioners for England Conveyance* [1936] Ch 430

33   *J Sainsbury plc v Enfield LBC* [1989] 1 WLR 590, CA*

34   Section 1(3) of the *Contracts (Rights of Third Parties) Act* 1999

35   Section 1(1) and 1(2) of the *Contracts (Rights of Third Parties) Act* 1999

Chapter 5

36   *Rhone v Stephens (Executrix)* [1994] 2 AC 310, HL*

37   *Clem Smith Nominees Pty Ltd v Farrelly & Farrelly* (1980) 20 SASR 227
      (non-UK case)

38   *Halsall v Brizell* [1957] Ch 169, HC*

39   *Montague v Long* (1972) 24 P&CR 240, HC*

40   *Rhone v Stephens (Executrix)* [1994] 2 AC 310, HL*

Chapter 6

41   *Pirie v Registrar-General* (1963) 109 CLR 619 (non-UK case); *Rogers v
      Hosegood* [1900] 2 Ch 388, CA*

42   *Drake v Gray* [1936] Ch 451; *Osborne v Bradley* [1903] 2 Ch 446, HC*

43   *Rogers v Hosegood* [1900] 2 Ch 388, CA*

44   *Renals v Cowlishaw* (1878) LR 9 ChD 125, CA*

45   *Ives v Brown* [1919] 2 Ch 314, HC; *Jamaica Mutual Life Assurance Society
      v Hillsborough Ltd* [1989] 1 WLR 1101, Privy Council*; *J Sainsbury plc v
      Enfield LBC* [1989] 1 WLR 590, CA*; *Reid v Bickerstaff* [1909] 2 Ch
      305, CA*

46   *Federated Homes Ltd v Mill Lodge Properties Ltd* [1980] 1 WLR 594,
      CA*; *Re Arcade Hotel Pty Ltd* [1962] VR 274 (non-UK case)

47   *Marten v Flight Refuelling* [1962] Ch 115, HC*

48   *Jamaica Mutual Life Assurance Society v Hillsborough Ltd* [1989] 1 WLR 1101, Privy Council*; *J Sainsbury plc v Enfield LBC* [1989] 1 WLR 590, CA*

49   *Robins v Berkeley Homes (Kent) Ltd* [1996] EGCS 75, HC*; *Shropshire County Council v Edwards* (1983) 46 P&CR 270, HC*

50   *Crest Nicholson Residential (South) Ltd v McAllister* [2004] 2 All ER 991, CA*; *Marquess of Zetland v Driver* [1939] Ch 1, CA*

51   *Roake v Chadha* [1984] 1 WLR 40, HC*

52   *P&A Swift Investments v Combined English Stores Group plc* [1989] AC 632, HL*

53   *Marten v Flight Refuelling* [1962] Ch 115, HC*

54   *Roake v Chadha* [1984] 1 WLR 40, HC*

55   *Re MCA East Ltd* [2003] 1 P&CR 9, HC*

56   *Miles v Easter* [1933] Ch 611*

57   *Wille v St John* [1910] 1 Ch 325

58   *Wrotham Park Estate Co v Parkside Homes* [1974] 1 WLR 798, HC*

59   *Newton Abbot Co-Operative Society Ltd v Williamson & Treadgold* [1952] Ch 286, HC*

60   *Chambers v Randall* [1923] 1 Ch 149*; *Miles v Easter* [1933] Ch 611*

61   *Miles v Easter* [1933] Ch 611*

62   *Brunner v Greenslade* [1971] Ch 993, HC*

63   *Application of Magney* (1981) 2 BPR 9358 (non-UK case); *Re Louis and the Conveyancing Act* [1971] 1 NSWLR 164 (non-UK case)

64   *Jamaica Mutual Life Assurance Society v Hillsborough Ltd* [1989] 1 WLR 1101, Privy Council*; *Williams & Anor v Kiley (t/a CK Supermarkets Ltd)* [2003] 1 P&CR D38, CA*

65   *Application of Caroline Chisholm Village Pty Ltd* (1980) 1 BPR 9707 (non-UK case); *Baxter v Four Oaks Properties Ltd* [1965] Ch 816, HC*; *Briggs v McCusker* [1996] 2 EGLR 197; *Emile Elias & Co Ltd v Pine Groves Ltd* [1993] 1 WLR 305, Privy Council (non-UK case)*; *Lund v Taylor* (1975) 31 P&CR 167, CA*; *Thompson v Potter* [1980] BCL 764 (non-UK case)

66   *Harlow v Hartog* (1977) 245 EG 140*

67   *Jamaica Mutual Life Assurance Society v Hillsborough Ltd* [1989] 1 WLR 1101, Privy Council*

68   *Lund v Taylor* (1975) 31 P&CR 167, CA*

69   *Lakhani and Weinstein* (1981) 118 DLR (3ed) 61 (non-UK case)

70   *Knight v Simmons* [1896] 2 Ch 294

Chapter 7

71   *Tulk v Moxhay* (1848) 2 Ph 774*

72   Mander v Falcke [1891] 2 Ch 554*; Oceanic Village Ltd v United
      Attractions Ltd [2000] Ch 234, HC*; Rogers v Hosegood [1900] 2 Ch
      388, CA*; Tulk v Moxhay (1848) 2 Ph 774*

73   Freer v Unwins Ltd [1976] Ch 288*

Chapter 9

74   Doherty v Allman (1878) LR 3 App Cas 709

75   Jaggard v Sawyer [1995] 1 WLR 269, CA*

76   Mathias v Davies (1970) 214 EG 1111

77   Wakeham v Wood (1982) 43 P&CR 40*

78   Shelfer v City of London Electric Lighting Co [1895] 1 Ch 287; Tamares
      (Vincent Square) Ltd v Fairpoint Properties (Vincent Square) Ltd [2007]
      1 WLR 2148, HC*; Wakeham v Wood (1982) 43 P&CR 40*

79   Amec Developments Ltd v Jury's Hotel Management (UK) Ltd (2001) 82
      P&CR 22, HC*

80   Wrotham Park Estate Co v Parkside Homes [1974] 1 WLR 798, HC*

81   Tamares (Vincent Square) Ltd v Fairpoint Properties (Vincent Square) Ltd
      [2007] 1 WLR 2148, HC*

82   Gafford v Graham (1999) 77 P&CR 73, CA*

83   Mortimer v Bailey & Anor [2005] 2 P&CR 9, CA*

84   Chatsworth Estates Co v Fewell [1931] 1 Ch 224

85   Gafford v Graham (1999) 77 P&CR 73, CA*; Shaw v Applegate [1997]
      1 WLR 970

86   Attorney General of Hong Kong v Fairfax Ltd [1997] 1 WLR 149;
      Hepworth v Pickles [1900] 1 Ch 108

87   Brown v Heathlands Mental Health NHS Trust [1996] 1 All ER 133, HC*;
      Cadogan v Royal Brompton Hospital NHS Trust [1996] 2 EGLR 115*

88   American Cyanamid Co v Ethicon Ltd [1975] AC 396

89   Mortimer v Bailey & Anor [2005] 2 P&CR 9, CA*

90   Richardson v Jackson [1954] 1 WLR 447

Chapter 11

91   Re (Practice Note) Jeffkins' Indentures [1965] 1 WLR 375

Chapter 12

92   Bedwell Park Quarry Co v Hertfordshire County Council [1993] JPL 349,
      CA*

93   Re Chatham Borough Council's Application (1970) 21 P&CR 661

94   Section 84(12) of the Law of Property Act 1925 (see appendix D)

95   Section 84(3) of the Law of Property Act 1925 (see appendix D)

96   Re Henderson [1940] Ch 835; Re Truman, Handbury, Buxton & Co's
      Application [1956] 1 QB 261, CA*

97   *Ridley v Taylor* [1965] 1 WLR 611

98   Section 84(1B) of the *Law of Property Act* 1925 (see appendix D)

99   *Re Snaith and Dolding's Application* (1996) 71 P&CR 104, LT*

100   *Re Ling's Application* (1957) 7 P&CR 233

101   *Re Ling's Application* (1957) 7 P&CR 233

102   *Re Truman, Handbury, Buxton & Co's Application* [1956] 1 QB 261, CA*

103   *Re Azfar's Application* [2002] 1 P&CR 17, LT*; *Re Lee's Application* (1996) 72 P&CR 439*

104   *Re Page's Application* (1996) 71 P&CR 440, LT*

105   *Re Page's Application* (1996) 71 P&CR 440, LT*

106   *Re Hunt's Application* (1997) 73 P&CR 126; *Re Hydeshire Ltd's Application* (1994) 67 P&CR 93, LT*

107   *Stockport Metropolitan Borough Council v Alwiyah Developments* [1983] 52 P & CR 278, CA*

108   *Re Beardsley & Co's Application* (1972) 25 P&CR 233; *Re New Ideal Homes Ltd's Application* (1978) 36 P&CR 476, LT*

109   *Lloyd's and Lloyd's Application* (1993) 66 P&CR 112, LT*

110   *McMorris v Brown* [1999] 1 AC 142; *Ridley v Taylor* [1965] 1 WLR 611

111   *SJC Construction Co v Sutton London Borough Council* (1975) 29 P&CR 322

112   *Re Bradley Clare Estates Application* (1988) 55 P&CR 126

113   *Stockport Metropolitan Borough Council v Alwiyah Developments* [1983] 52 P & CR 278, CA*

114   *SJC Construction Co v Sutton London Borough Council* (1975) 29 P&CR 322

Chapter 13

115   *Re Hopcraft's Application* (1993) 66 P&CR 475; *Re Jones' and White & Co's Application* (1989) 58 P&CR 512

Chapter 15

116   *Stuart v Jones and Nester* LP/53 & 62/2005

Index